*The Eloquence of*

FREDERICK JACKSON TURNER

*Frederick Jackson Turner at the time of his graduation from the University of Wisconsin in 1884*

*The Eloquence of*

# FREDERICK JACKSON TURNER

*by Ronald H. Carpenter*

**THE HUNTINGTON LIBRARY**
*San Marino, California*

Library of Congress Cataloguing in Publication Data
Carpenter, Ronald H., 1933-
    The eloquence of Frederick Jackson Turner.
    Includes bibliographical references and index.
    1. Turner, Frederick Jackson, 1861-1932.
2. Historiography—United States.   I. Title
E175.5.T83C37  1983   973'.072024   83-8370
ISBN 0-87328-078-4

*To*
*Ray A. Billington*

# Table of Contents

●

# *Preface*

●

IN JUNE OF 1959, I arrived in Madison to begin work on a doctorate at the University of Wisconsin. My major would be communication arts; anticipating a dissertation on some facet of recent American political oratory, my doctoral minors would be mass communications and modern American history. In the hectic days before classes started, an apartment could not be found. My eye was caught, however, by those enticing dormitories nestled among the trees along the scenic shores of Lake Mendota, and the University Housing Office informed me that some of those dormitories were set aside in the summer for graduate students. They accepted my check for eight weeks room and board, and I was assigned to Turner Hall.

The name Turner did not make an impression on me in June 1959. For all I knew then, Turner Hall might have been named after some wealthy donor to the university. But one cannot be at the Madison campus for long before becoming very much aware of the man after whom that residence hall was named—Frederick Jackson Turner.

The thesis on American political oratory never evolved (although I since have published several essays on the subject) as my academic interests became focused more and more on rhetorical theory generally and specifically upon the problem of the practical functions of style in discourse. The early doctoral minor in American history had been intellectually gratifying, and several years after gaining my degree I became involved with historians as persuaders and historical writing as rhetorical discourse. In one of the graduate seminars I taught in the late 1960s at Wayne State University, a subject for consideration was the rhetorical criticism of non-oratorical works. My students were asked to explore and analyze the functional presence of rhetorical elements (more typically employed in oratory) in other genres of discourse such as novels. One of those doctoral students, David Ling, had just completed a degree at the University of Minnesota; and he urged me to read David Noble's *Historians Against History: The Frontier Thesis and the National Covenant in American Historical Writing Since 1830*. Noble's analysis was intriguing, for he indeed was identifying mythic and hence persuasive elements in historical discourse. What caught my attention in particular, however, was learning of Frederick Jackson Turner's successes as a prize-winning orator while an undergraduate at the University of Wisconsin.

My hazy recollection of "The Significance of the Frontier in American History" was that it had a rhetorical tone. Then, after re-reading the frontier thesis, I concluded that the discourse had very much in common with an oration. My decision was to try to find out if there were any carryovers from Turner's prize-winning orations as an undergraduate to that statement which made him pre-eminent among American historians. After all, the frontier thesis as a document was originally developed for oral presentation to the Ninth Annual Convention of the American Historical Association.

The next step was a trip back to Madison to look in the University of Wisconsin Archives and the State Historical Society Library. Turner's prize-winning orations were there. Unmistakably, some rhetorical elements of style characterizing the frontier thesis address in 1893 were also present in his undergraduate oratorical successes in 1883 and 1884. As soon as possible thereafter, I arranged a short trip to the Huntington Library to examine Turner's memorabilia. A relatively brief examination of his scrapbook and correspondence prior to 1893 indicated that causal links could be established in the development of the historian's style in discourse. Although that rhetorical genesis of style was discussed in a brief 1971 essay, my intentions for the more complete study of Turner took another focus.

The crucial question about style in discourse deals with effect. What are the functional influences of a writer's unique syntax and lexicon upon the persuasiveness of his efforts? As a rhetorical critic, I typically have taken that orientation in examining discourse. But my underlying assumption always has been that the mere presence of certain rhetorical features in discourse is no conclusive evidence of persuasive impact upon readers or listeners. We know all too well that in many instances the statement which is a model of rhetorical usage can be a rhetorical failure. So often, circumstances of time, place, and situation prevent discourse from generating any of its intended effects among respondents. In other cases, the techniques typically known to produce certain rhetorical effects sometimes generate other, unanticipated reactions. And undergirding any critical endeavor must be the realization that only rarely can a rhetorical impact upon readers or listeners be attributed to their one exposure to a single discourse. It is more likely in rhetorical endeavors that resultant attitudes or actions evolve from exposure to a matrix of communications. Thus, any prudent, effect-oriented critic will try to discover documented evidence of people's reactions to the discourse being studied. For conclusions about the impacts of language become correspondingly credible as the critic demonstrates their presence with primary source materials provided by those people to whom the rhetorical efforts were directed.

I have applied this methodological orientation in the study of historians as persuaders. With a 1973 Social Sciences Institute grant from the University of Florida, I worked at the Library of Congress with the Alfred Thayer Mahan Papers and the Naval Historical Foundation Collection. My examination focused on all letters received by Mahan after the publication of *The Influence of Seapower Upon History,* as well as the correspondence of naval officers on active duty in the decade after publication of the book. The resultant essay (cited later) explained the effects of Mahan's writing which were attributed by readers to discrete stylistic features which they themselves identified. A 1976 award from the National Endowment for the Humanities enabled me to do similar research at Cornell University with the extensive correspondence from a mass readership received by a more noted historical stylist, Carl Becker.

I knew from my initial visit to the Huntington Library that the extensive Turner Collection would be particularly rich for a similar study. My application for financial assistance received positive response in the form of a 1973-74 fellowship award from the Huntington Library, and I was able to spend almost a month in

San Marino in an effort to identify and explain the effects of the eloquence of Frederick Jackson Turner. My focus was not upon the intellectual influence upon fellow historians over the years but rather upon the emotional impact of the frontier thesis upon a mass readership of Americans for several decades.

As is the case in many scholarly efforts, this work could reach fruition only because of assistance from many sources. I am grateful to my wife Suzanne for typing drafts of my essays and proofreading the text. My deeper gratitude is for her patience and empathy with the broad course which I am attempting to steer with my study of historians as persuaders.

In acknowledging the assistance of my wife, I undoubtedly conform to a precedent followed by many researchers with support from their families of one kind or another. In the case of my work with Frederick Jackson Turner, however, I must describe two other, invaluable sources of assistance. And these kinds of positive influences upon a research effort can be known only to a very few people. I am impelled to write in gratitude about a library and a man.

Research at the Huntington Library is an exhilarating experience. As a result of my two trips to San Marino, the work with Turner became truly a labor of love. This was not just because of the richness of the Turner Collection but also, if not more so, because of that library's scholarly aura. In every way, the staff promptly and enthusiastically serves the needs of those using the library's collections and facilities. Requests for help always are happily answered, in forms ranging from technical assistance by the photography and reproduction staff to bibliographical aid from the library's support people. And permeating that staff is that happy willingness to react to and help interpret any materials found in a collection.

The scholarly aura of the Huntington Library is derived from more than its staff. Research at the Huntington also is so exhilarating an experience because of the other researchers in residence at any given moment. During luncheons on the terrace, for example, one likely will be sharing a table with scholars from a diversity of disciplines, from this country and abroad. The resultant conversation and exchange of ideas are lively. That same vivacity extends to the interchanges during coffee breaks, either on the formal dining terrace or in the casual lounge. And if anyone would wish to ponder some thought arising from an interchange among scholars, what more fitting settings could be found than those afforded by a leisurely walk in any of the Huntington's gardens?

That personal element at the Huntington has had an even more specific and profound influence on me. In this case, I write of my contact with one of the library's Senior Research Associates, the late Ray A. Billington. He was a giant. Surely no one person was more knowledgeable about Frederick Jackson Turner than Professor Billington. His long work with Turner, and his Bancroft Prize biography, represented the very pinnacle of scholarly endeavor. Yet Professor Billington always encouraged and supported my own unique efforts with Turner. I shared my discoveries with him, whether in his office at the Huntington, in our correspondence over the past years, in occasional long-distance telephone conversations. Always, his enthusiasm for my work acted as an intellectual gauntlet placed down before me—not as a challenge to a duel of wits trying to outdo one another in finding new interpretations of old materials but instead as a friendly spur encouraging a mutual sharing of the pure joy and excitement of historical discovery. Professor Billington's enthusiastic encouragement of my efforts with Turner unquestionably helped inspire and sustain my attempts to explain how the eloquence of the frontier thesis evolved, and then to describe how that eloquent statement influenced our national psychology.

Perhaps the feeling described here can be known fully only by one who indeed has shared historical discoveries with the Huntington Library's Senior Research Associate. Still, I must try to express my gratitude. Surely my feeling is communicated more effectively simply by dedicating this volume to Ray A. Billington.

Ronald H. Carpenter
Gainesville, Florida

*The Eloquence of*

FREDERICK JACKSON TURNER

# On Eloquent Style
## and Rhetorical Impact

●

FREDERICK JACKSON TURNER was an eloquent man. And he himself identified a precise, pivotal factor which led to the persuasive style in his frontier thesis discourse having a profound rhetorical impact upon our national psychology.

On the evening of 24 May 1924, Turner attended a retirement dinner in his honor. Hosted by the Harvard History Club, the occasion called forth an after-dinner address by the guest of honor. The speech started with a carefully worded, lengthy prologue about listing "some of the forces that have influenced my career"; and Turner's stated objective was to explain "how far the little things as well as clearly obvious circumstances affect one's academic life."[1] The early discussion of family background was written in complete sentences but after four pages, the speech becomes simply a scrawled, phrase listing of topics to be covered. Among topics such as his graduate and undergraduate professors and courses at Johns Hopkins and the University of Wisconsin, the outline prominently lists "La Follette—Iago." So at the close of a distinguished career, Turner identified a dominant influence upon his life as an historian: the persuasive prowess of Robert M. La Follette in a prize-winning, senior oration which Turner heard in 1879 as a University of Wisconsin freshman.

Turner's historical career has been traced fully, eminently, and with obvious affection by Ray A. Billington.[2] But his rhetorical career is equally deserving of treatment. In classical Greece or Rome, Turner justifiably would have been called a *rhetor*, for he was an effective orator as well as a successful teacher of the art of discourse. Indeed, as a University of Wisconsin undergraduate, Turner achieved an outstanding record as a prize-winning orator on the strength of which his first university teaching responsibilities at Wisconsin were in rhetoric and oratory (while he worked

3

on a degree in history). Clearly, Turner had a range of experiences which could have influenced him as a creator of discourse, and thereby the vast readership he reached over so many years.

This essay traces the course of those rhetorical influences, with the intention of demonstrating their ultimate impact upon our national psychology and contributing to a fuller understanding of, and an appreciation for, the frontier thesis as the truly rhetorical discourse which it is. For Turner probably intended to shape attitudes with his address to the Ninth Annual Meeting of the American Historical Association in Chicago, in 1893—the original presentation of his celebrated statement articulating "The Significance of the Frontier in American History."

This introduction to Turner's orations and addresses is basically biographical, starting with Turner as a high school student in Portage, Wisconsin, and explaining his undergraduate experiences in oratory, as well as the dominant influence of La Follette. Then a critical perspective will suggest why and how the historian's rhetorical predilections were applied to help create the final form of that discourse now known as the frontier thesis. Most important perhaps, a broader sociological perspective will be utilized to explore the nature of the rhetorical impact of Turner's eloquence upon the American people over the course of several decades. For the purpose of ascertaining those effects upon our national psychology, this effort draws on valuable but heretofore relatively untapped primary source evidence in the Huntington Library's massive Frederick Jackson Turner Collection: numerous letters from students and readers among the general public, to Turner himself, or to the family upon his death. In these responses are the vivid examples of how Turner's eloquent statement about the past helped mold an attitudinal basis of action for the future. So explicating and illustrating the eloquence of Frederick Jackson Turner constitutes neither more nor less than studying the historian as persuader.

## I. The Oratorical Genesis of Style

GROWING UP IN Portage, Turner experienced much of what later helped him recognize the frontier's importance as a major but, until then, overlooked force in American history. During impressionable years of his youth, he learned about several facets of the frontier—a hunting party tracking down a vicious wolfpack, covered wagons moving through the streets of Portage bound for free lands, vigilantes recruited by the sheriff to capture a horsethief, a shootout on the main street of town, a lynching. In the period of his boyhood, "the frontier was near and meaningful to Fred Turner"; and the ultimate content of a document called "The Significance of the Frontier in American History" well might have some conceptual roots in observations which "placed an indelible stamp on him, and played a role in interesting him in the frontier as a molding force."[3] So too did the final form of the frontier thesis have compositional roots in an environment that helped encourage Turner to become skilled in the arts of language and rhetorical discourse.

Portage in the 1860s and 1870s was not a cultural or literary wasteland for Turner. True, some of his reading was of adventure, about Indian uprisings in the West and the massacre of Custer and his command at the Little Big Horn (and Indians were common enough on the streets of town). Nevertheless, more erudite endeavors were just as prevalent for many people in Portage. Although entertainment at that time was provided in large measure by traveling troupes of actors and musical artists, both local and itinerant, rhetoric also was a cornerstone of culture. In the latter part of the nineteenth century, the national environment fostered an appreciation for rhetorical artistry and the eloquent statement. Whether through formal Chautauqua lectures or more spontaneous debates in various meetings large and small, people heard and participated directly in discourse not only as a widespread means of spreading culture and education but as a viable mode for shaping and strengthening attitudes and exhorting others to action. Portage was no different. On the Fourth of July, for example, Turner would listen to readings of the Declaration of Independence as well as orations which were the culmination of parades ending at the courthouse. At fourteen, he was involved directly in regular debates and other oratorical activities in the Young Men's Lyceum. Furthermore, when Fred wanted to read examples of artistry in language, he could and did turn to the quite respectable library in his home; for the Turner household was a literate one.[4]

In that household, the dominant figure was the father, Andrew Jackson Turner. Development of the son's language prowess, however, was probably not one of explicit, parental directive as much as one of implicit, personal example since Turner's father practiced rhetoric and made his livelihood with language. In 1861, the year Fred was born, Jack Turner purchased a small newspaper, the *Portage Record*, for which he had worked initially as a typesetter. After combining with a rival newspaper, the emergent *Wisconsin State Register* became a weekly which the elder Turner continued to publish until Fred graduated from high school in 1878. Although Jack Turner speculated in several business ventures, which included investing in timber holdings and participating in the formation of a small railroad company, his prominence in Portage rested securely upon his position as editor and publisher of the *Wisconsin State Register*. With that role as a community opinion leader came a natural enough concomitant: political activity that was rhetorical.

Andrew Jackson Turner spoke regularly to a wide range of audiences, large and small, for various Republican candidates; he delighted in working on behalf of the Republican Party; in 1878 he was appointed by the Republican governor to the Wisconsin Railroad Commission; and in 1881 he was elected mayor of Portage and subsequently served four terms (two of them as the voters' unanimous choice). Throughout this period, the workings of politics became known to young Fred through countless dinner table conversations in the Turner home; and the son also had ample opportunities to observe his father as a practicing speaker in the world of everyday affairs.[5] In short, Frederick Jackson Turner learned in his youth that rhetoric worked.

As a youth, Turner also began to develop a personal sense of rhetorical style. Evidence of his emerging criteria for achieving eloquence can be seen in a scrapbook started in 1876 when Turner was fifteen. Items of interest were pasted therein, most notably excerpts from the discourse of Ralph Waldo Emerson as

6

well as from other orators and literary figures. Turner then had opportunities to select from his readings and have his conceptions of the best printed in a regular "Pencils and Scissors" column which he contributed to his father's newspaper. Although the excerpts chosen most frequently for publication are from Emerson, other authors and orators represented include Goethe, Disraeli, Harriet Beecher Stowe, Robert G. Ingersoll, Victor Hugo, Charles Lamb, Daniel Webster, Fielding, Rousseau, and Thomas Carlyle. Six issues of that column, from January and February 1878, appear in his scrapbook and suggest his early tastes for rhetorical style in discourse.[6]

In the shorter quotations that begin each column, antithesis is the prevailing feature of style, evincing itself in neatly turned epigrams such as "Art is long, life short"; "Love swells like Solway, but ebbs like its tide"; or "We should esteem virtue, though in a foe; and abhor vice, though in a friend." The longer passages rarely incorporate epigrammatic antitheses, but they almost always employ distinctly rhetorical parallelism by repeating the same word or phrase at beginnings of successive phrases or short sentences, often in groups of two as in "Every candid acknowledgement, every conquest..."; "Doubt springs from difficulty. Doubt is the recoil of the mind..."; or "It is a building of character. It is a building that must stand..." Thus, in what he chose to contribute for a newspaper column, Turner began to display distinct preferences for some discrete features of rhetorical style.

The future historian had more direct rhetorical opportunities in high school. He participated as one of a half dozen youths in Memorial Day declamations during his last two years of high school; but the most significant experience clearly was on 28 June 1878 with a commencement oration, "The Power of the Press," for which he won the first prize—a copy of Macaulay's *History of England*. Turner also received a favorable review in the *Wisconsin State Register:* "His thought was original, his style clear and forcible, and his manner self possessed and very earnest. He richly deserved the prize, which was afterward awarded him."[7]

Unlike a declamation, which calls upon a speaker to memorize and then deliver a speech written by someone else, an oration is an original composition. In it, the orator brings to bear his compositional prowess. In Turner's case, the ideational direction of that oration's content is a paean to the newspaper; in its stylistic form, the oration clearly shows the young man's efforts to produce *himself* the style of statements he preferred and contributed to his "Pencils and Scissors" column.

"The Power of the Press" displays a style that tends to rely upon parallel repetitions of a word or phrase to achieve rhetorical-like beginnings for successive clauses or sentences (*anaphora* or *epanaphora*), as in "*It* was conceived...*It* rose..." (in these quotations, and all subsequent excerpts from Turner's writing, stylistic features are italicized to aid in identification). Alliteration also appears easily in some instances, as in "*s*weetest *s*ongs" or "*w*ords of *w*isdom." He was capable as well of the stylistic inversion (*anastrophe*) of customary and idiomatic word orders, as in his very opening sentence: "About four centuries ago *was born* in the brain of John Guttenberg [*sic*], *an idea* destined to be the propagator of learning, of Christianity, and of civilization, and thus to sway the future of the world" (and note as well the alliteration, parallel repetition, and hint of climax order). Turner's major stylistic efforts, however, seem to be aimed at achieving the stylistic apposition and balance known as antithesis.[8]

In a few cases, young Turner's high school attempts at antitheses are relatively overt, placing opposing or contrasting meanings close together as in "*risen* and *decayed*" or "the *past* became the *present*." In the main, however, those high school efforts do not attain balance and apposition well. The constructions are less antonymous, as in "*of* the ignorant, *by* the ignorant," or "not only a *possibility*, but even a *probability*." Moreover, Turner's antithetical constructions are sometimes too diffuse and extended, undermining the desired epigrammatic quality, as illustrated by this passage: "The more *despotic* a monarch, the greater the *restrictions* does he place upon the utterances of the Newspaper; while on the other hand, as the *freedom* of the Press increases, so does the *freedom* of the people."

Although not yet a polished, artistic style, that high school composition reveals some discrete trends in language behavior. Furthermore, winning first prize for those efforts must have been deeply gratifying. After all, an oratorical contest is an emotional experience of considerable magnitude. In addition to the intense psychological involvement while creating and perfecting the oration as a finished product, the orator is on public display, with every nuance of voice and bodily movement part of the platform appearance. Furthermore, the orator has spent many hours memorizing and rehearsing. Emotion and expectations for success surely are heightened within; for even with prior experiences in declamation, Turner still had to feel some uncertainty, if not a degree of stage fright, in a contest observed by the community. Yet his emotion could be controlled; his expectations fulfilled. Turner learned he could be successful in public, oratorical endeavors.

One can only speculate now about his reaction to receiving that particular award, a copy of Macaulay's *History of England.* Of all historians who might have influenced Turner at this time in his life, Macaulay was among the most overtly antithetical in his own style in discourse. Sometimes criticized for excesses in stylistic virtuosity, Macaulay's use of antitheses did sharpen his historical portraiture, however, as in this characterization of King James II: "*To bend and break the spirits of men* gave him *pleasure;* and *to part with his money* gave him *pain.* What he had not the generosity to do at *his own expense* he determined to do at the *expense of others.*"[9] So at a relatively early age, Turner could perceive a place for rhetorical style in the writing of history, and that likelihood occurred to him at a high school graduation event which heightened his own awareness of personal rhetorical potentials.

When Turner entered the University of Wisconsin in the fall of 1878, one of the surest avenues to fame among college students was via forensic abilities generally and oratorical prowess specifically. At that time, a "big man on campus" at any university more than likely was the prize-winning orator. Turner engaged in the typical rhetorical activities of his day: freshmen and sophomores at the University of Wisconsin had a "Rhetoricals" program calling for six essays and six public declamations a year. They also were required to attend the rhetorical exercises in which juniors and seniors delivered chapel-stage orations and in which some underclassmen delivered declamations of special merit.[10] As might be expected, considering his previous successes, Turner

9

achieved percentage grades of 90 and 93 in his freshman and sophomore "Rhetoricals."[11] Moreover, his sophomore rendition of Marc Antony's "Address to the Romans" at the April 1881 College Rhetoricals was judged "the finest declamation and the best rendered that has been heard from the Assembly Hall stage."[12] (Turner was stricken with spinal meningitis in 1879 at the end of his freshman year and did not return to the University until 1881 shortly before the rhetoricals.)

To complement these experiences, Turner had still other opportunities to help perfect his sense of style and eloquence. As part of the curriculum in reading and composition of both Greek and Latin, freshmen studied, among others, Lysias and Cicero. From the latter, a student easily could acquire an appreciation for variety in styles of statement. Cicero's orations display changes in style appropriate to the particular rhetorical objectives: (1) proving or instructing through pure and correct language which is "arranged plainly and clearly" with a minimum of ornament— *genus tenue*; (2) pleasing or conciliating through "highly ornamented and copious" oratory in which "there is the greatest possible quantity of sweetness" evolving from the use of "every kind of ornament in speaking"—*genus medium*; (3) moving the passions through eloquence "which is borne along in an impetuous course, and with a mighty noise, which all men looked up to, and admired...to influence them in every imaginable way"—*genus grande*.[13] Lysias, however, offered a stylistic counterpoint. Of all Attic orators, Lysias more than others was acclaimed and studied for style characterized by "the avoidance of decidedly poetical ornament and the employment of sober prose"; and Lysian composition could be emulated as a model of simplicity, preeminently literal yet vivid in description, clear and yet concise.[14] From reading discourses such as theirs and Demosthenes in his sophomore year, Turner learned how classical orators used the very stylistic devices with which he had experimented as a high school senior. Moreover, examination of contrapuntal styles well could have led to an understanding on Turner's part that eloquence is derived not only from ability to use ornament and embellishment but also from the discretion which tells the orator when to refrain from their use. Surely that exposure to rhetorical discourse from the classics did contribute to the language prowess which Billington epitomizes only in passing as "a vigorous prose style."[15]

Still other experiences probably contributed indirectly to the evolution of Turner's eloquence, particularly during the 1881-82 school year. As indicated by a list in the back of his Commonplace Book, Turner attended several lectures and heard some prominent speakers who had included Madison and the University of Wisconsin in their itineraries. Among those speakers were Bayard Taylor, Henry Ward Beecher, Robert Ingersoll, John Fiske, Edwin Meade, and Matthew Arnold. Of these, Ingersoll was the person most likely to influence in some way Turner's concept of rhetoric.

As a result of his nominating speech for James G. Blaine in the Republican Convention of 1876, Ingersoll achieved national fame. For two decades thereafter, he was one of the most prominent platform orators in America. Effective delivery, engaging personality, and elegant style all combined to make Ingersoll one of the most listened-to lecturers in the country, and he was in constant demand for campaign oratory on behalf of Republican candidates and for occasional addresses in conjunction with national holidays such as Decoration Day. Listening to this man, Turner would have heard a superb platform orator and just might have had an impression similar to the one Hamlin Garland had when at the age of sixteen he heard Ingersoll.

> He came on the vast stage alone...addressing himself to us with unaffected directness....He appeared to be speaking to each one of us individually. His tone was confidential, friendly, and yet authoritative....I enjoyed the beauty of his phrasing and the almost unequaled magic of his voice....He bantered us, challenged us, electrified us. At times his eloquence held us silent as images and then some witty turn, some humorous phrase, brought roars of applause. At times we cheered almost every sentence like delegates at a political convention. At other moments we rose in our seats and yelled. There was something hypnotic in his rhythm as well as in his marvelous lines like a Saxon minstrel. His power over his auditors was absolute....His effect on his hearers was magical, but the magic lay in his choice of words, rather than in beautiful enunciation.[16]

11

In 1880, near the time Turner would have heard that lecture, Henry Ward Beecher introduced Ingersoll to a Brooklyn mass meeting as "a man who—and I say it not flatteringly—is the most brilliant speaker of the English tongue of all men on this globe."[17] Ingersoll too was a rhetorical model—and in the flesh.

Ingersoll provoked interest on Turner's part. One of the early pages of the 1881-82 Commonplace Book has this entry: "Read Plato, Emerson, Green, Ingersoll, Carlyle, More, Milton's Areopagetica." From the context, the tense is not clear. Turner was saying either that he had read Ingersoll during the early part of that academic year or that he had provided himself with a reminder to read him in the future. He probably was not referring to the famous "Plumed Knight" nomination speech of Blaine in 1876, however. Considering the staunch Republicanism of his father, Turner likely was familiar with his address already; and although Ingersoll's fame came initially from the nomination of Blaine, the orator's reputation at the time he appeared in Madison was based more securely upon his occasional addresses and lectures. Of the latter, one of the most popular was "The Liberty of Man, Woman, and Child," first delivered about 1877 but a mainstay of Ingersoll's lecture tours for many years thereafter. One of two quotations from Ingersoll in the "Pencils and Scissors" column was from this address; and the quoted passage ended with this basically antithetical statement: "Laughter should make dimples of joy enough in the cheeks of the world to catch and hold and glorify the tears of grief." Clearly, "The Liberty of Man, Woman, and Child" offers examples of Ingersoll's style in discourse at the time Turner was interested in him and had an opportunity to hear him.

Like many successful orators, Ingersoll utilized parallelism, and particularly the repetition of the same word or phrase at beginnings of successive clauses or short sentences, as in "*I believe in* the fireside. *I believe in* the democracy of home. *I believe in* the republicanism of the family. *I believe in* liberty, equality, and love."[18] Ingersoll also could combine such *anaphora* or *epanaphora* with a heaping of particulars about facets, qualities, or attributes of the item being discussed, a technique discussed in classical treatises on style as *frequentatio, symphoresis, synonimia*, or *sinathrismus.*[19]

> A little while ago I saw models of nearly everything that man has made. I saw models of all the water craft, from the rude dug-out in which floated a naked savage—one of our ancestors—a naked savage, with teeth two inches in length, with a spoonful of brains in the back of his head—I saw models of all the water craft of the world, from that dug-out up to a man-of-war, that carries a hundred guns and mile of canvas—from that dug-out to the steamship that turns its brave prow from the port of New York, with a compass like a conscience, crossing three thousand miles of billows without missing a throb or beat of its mighty iron heart....I saw at the same time the weapons....I saw, too, the armor....I saw at the same time their musical instruments....I saw....I saw....I saw their implements of agriculture, from a crooked stick that was attached to the horn of an ox by some twisted straw, to the agricultural implements of this generation....[20]

This speech utilizes some antitheses, too: Ingersoll made some from antonyms, as "I *hate* dictation. I *love* liberty"; others evolve from opposing meanings, as in "Our fathers worshipped the golden calf. The worst you can say of an American now is, he worships the gold of the calf."[21] Nevertheless, Turner would not have heard many balanced and epigrammatic antitheses in Ingersoll's platform lectures.

If Turner decided to seek out further examples of Ingersoll's skill with antithesis, he would have turned to a text for one of the occasional addresses. After all, a speech prepared in conjunction with a formal event lends itself easily to a more stylized statement. The platform lecture, however, reiterated on cross-country tours easily becomes an extemporaneous address, with sentences and paragraphs drawn from a wide variety of other addresses as the time, place, and audience dictate. One of Ingersoll's more noted Decoration Day addresses does evince somewhat greater polish and skill in antithesis, utilizing those between "a *brazen falsehood* and a *timid truth*," or "the *coffin* of honor and the *cradle* of war," or "*cheers* for the *living; tears* for the *dead*," or the long sequence in "Liberty and slavery—the right and wrong—the joy and grief—the day and night—the glory and the gloom of all the years."[22] An overall appraisal of style

13

would conclude, however, that Ingersoll did not rely to any significant extent on the elaborate and epigrammatic antitheses which seemed to fascinate Turner so much when he was a high school senior.

Therefore, although Ingersoll is mentioned in Turner's Commonplace Book, the brevity of that reference suggests that the foremost platform orator in America at that time did not have a particularly profound effect on the young man from Portage; and any inferences about Ingersoll's influence on Turner's rhetorical skill must be highly speculative. Furthermore, these early rhetorical experiences are relatively insignificant when contrasted with the direct, dominant influence of another orator and event during Turner's freshman year at the University of Wisconsin. Dramatic evidence of how Turner reacted appears on successive pages of his scrapbook at that time and in his retirement speech at Harvard, forty-five years later, in which the historian explained "how far the little things as well as clearly obvious circumstances affect one's academic life"—and then went on to list "La Follette—Iago" among "some of the forces that have influenced my career."

While Turner was a freshman, Robert M. La Follette was a senior, establishing a noteworthy oratorical career. With an oration entitled "Iago," La Follette won, successively, a contest at the University of Wisconsin in April 1879, a state championship on May 2, and an interstate contest in Iowa City a week later, defeating contestants from six states. "Iago" brought fame to La Follette. Upon his return to the campus after winning the interstate contest, La Follette received a hero's welcome at an extraordinary gathering in the assembly chamber of the state capitol, where he was congratulated formally by the University of Wisconsin regents as well as leading citizens of Madison.[23] In large measure because of the fame achieved through "Iago," La Follette was elected only eighteen months later as District Attorney of Dane County (wherein Madison and the University of Wisconsin are located).[24] His illustrious political career was founded in part upon a single oration.

Frederick Jackson Turner clearly was impressed. Indeed, on the evening of La Follette's triumphant return to Madison after

14

winning the state championship at Beloit, Wisconsin, Turner was part of a crowd waiting at the telegraph office for news of the contest result; and he marched in that group, with a band, to the station to await La Follette's 2:25 A.M. train. He also participated in the victory parade back to campus. Turner's scrapbook contains the newspaper story he wrote describing the event. The concluding paragraphs suggest the adulation therein and Turner's own *elan* about the event.

At half past one we fell in on the campus, with two drums—Loomis and Anderson—Capt. Cole presiding over the piccolo with his usual grace and dignity, and Curtis, a scientific "fresh" on the cornet. We whooped her right up all the way downtown, the police keeping out of sight in a most gentlemanly manner. Got down to the depot, and Captain Cole took command and dressed them into line. Then the train came in. There were about sixty boys on the train, and when the two crowds saw each other, maybe we didn't yell! We nabbed on to La Follette, and took him home to the inspiring strains of "The Brannigans' Band." When we got to the house, the band played "When Johnnie Comes Marching Home Again," in a touching manner. John Anderson, one of the defeated contestants at the home contest, made a handsome speech, welcoming La F. home. Bob then replied. His voice trembled a little when he thanked the boys for the splendid manner in which they greeted him. He then bade us good night, and we ended off by giving three rousing cheers for Bob, and three more for the Beloit boys who took a whipping like gentlemen. We then marched part way up to the University and disbanded, every one enthusiastic, and not a *drop* of liquor in the whole crowd.

Down at Beloit, the boys kept patting Bob on the back before he went on, and he went on and stood facing the audience for about ten seconds and began. He took the audience by storm. He held their attention all the time, and when he sat down there was a perfect roar of applause. His subject is Iago, one of the characters in Othello. His gestures are elegant, articulation simply wonderful, and his power of language is enormous. When the decision of the judges was read, every University boy jumped to his feet and went for Bob, got him on their shoulders and rushed into the street, cheered and cheered again, and sent us the news.

I haven't got over my enthuse yet—that's why I have so much to say about it. I didn't get in till long after 3 A.M., and not to sleep till 4. The boys have never shown any college feeling before, and when it did come out, it came. If Bob carries the interstate contest, how we will everlastingly make things hum.

Yours truly,

F.

And next to that newspaper account of La Follette's triumph, Turner's scrapbook contains a text of "Iago"—an exemplar of a rhetorical style in which the "power of language is enormous."[25]

In the thrust of its thematic content, La Follette's oration is portraiture with language as the medium of expression, exploring and identifying the facets and nuances of Iago's character. In the essence of its artistically stylized form, the composition of "Iago" clearly corraborates Turner's budding tastes in style. Parallel repetitions occur readily at beginnings of successive phrases or sentences, as in "*Whatever is most* mean, *whatever is most* hard, *whatever is* vilely atrocious" or "*All its* artful cunning, *all its* devilish cruelty" or "*He is* hardly human....*He is* wanting in ethical parts....*He is* a fraction....*He is* a paradox." The entire oration also is permeated with La Follette's affinity for alliteration, as in "*no*ble *n*ature," "*c*ursed *c*unning," "*h*ypocritical and *h*eartless," "*p*assionate, *p*owerful," "*c*ynical, *s*ly," and "*s*omber mingling of a *s*mile and a *s*neer."

The preeminent feature of style in "Iago" is antithesis. For the one hundred twenty sentences of La Follette's oration are founded stylistically on a total of sixty-five discrete antitheses! With neat balance and sharp apposition, La Follette achieves an epigrammatic style with references to "*poverty* of *sentiment* and *wealth* of *intellect*" or "a *twisted body* and a *majestic mind*." In developing its character portrayal of Iago as a "union of opposites," the oration shows off the writer's artistry in extending a theme antithetically:

> Richard III is more *humanly terrible*; Iago more *devilishly perfect*. Richard *loves nothing human*; Iago *hates everything good*....Richard is *fire*; Iago, *ice*. Richard III is more *objective*; Iago more *subjective*....Richard III *mounts* the *throne of England* on a score of dead bodies; Iago *wins* the *throne of Hell* in three strides. The *conscience* of Richard wakes from its swoon; Iago has *no conscience*.

16

Here is stylistic virtuosity predicated upon highly discrete and hence imitatable usages. Turner himself had shown a preference for these same language features in his "Pencils and Scissors" column; but when he tried to duplicate that style in his own high school oration, the final product was not artistic. La Follette provided Turner with a dazzling example of how it could be done, albeit carried to an utmost degree of compositional endeavor.

To the impressionable freshman from Portage, the rewards received by La Follette for his oratorical prowess must have exerted a compelling force. After all, Turner could perceive an initial basis of similarity between himself and La Follette. Both seemed to have an appreciation for the same stylistic tendencies, even if Turner had not yet perfected his. Such a perception of a common ground often is the cause of an orientation toward some person whose behavior will be imitated. Moreover, psychologists know that as the rewards to that model are esteemed, motivation to imitate the model's behavior is increased. This process of psychological identification likely accounts for what became Frederick Jackson Turner's goal: to emulate successfully the stylistic artistry and oratorical prowess of Robert M. La Follette.[26] For if he could imitate La Follette's eloquence, Turner would be successful in his own rhetorical endeavors, perhaps with equally impressive rewards.

Attempts to perfect that oratorical style are evident in Turner's 1881-82 Commonplace Book.[27] In addition to his required rhetorical text that year, Adams Sherman Hill's *Principles of Rhetoric*, Turner also read Herbert Spencer's "Philosophy of Style."[28] In several drafts of an oration called "The Imaginativeness of the Present," the pages of his Commonplace Book include efforts to create Spencerian inversions (*anastrophe*) of syntax such as *"Lament not....Weep not...."* Early drafts of that oration also suggest that Turner seems to achieve alliteration easily; and parallel repetitions for rhetorical effect are consistently at beginnings of successive phrases or sentences and noticeably in groups of two, as in *"He only* predicts...*he only* shows...." or *"Imagination* respects the cause....*Imagination* is a perception...." Moreover, an ability to achieve balanced antitheses now is evident in the sharp juxtaposition of opposites, as in that between "the *practical*" and "the

17

*ideal*" or "the *past dreamed*—the *present acts.*" Then, to amplify upon his assertions, Turner, like La Follette, lapses easily into a sequence of antitheses.

> The *useful arts* are gradually becoming merged with the *fine arts.* Instead of erecting a *monument to Vulcan* we build a *locomotive.* Our *shrine to Neptune* is found in an *ocean propeller.* In place of *dramatic poetry* we have now an *imaginative philosophy* which speculates and experiments with an end in view. The man who in the *past* would have written on the *parchment rolls* an *ode* to Liberty, *now* writes an *article* for the *daily press* and the multitude read it.

He is still learning, however, for some attempts at antithesis are poorly balanced. For example, as further amplification of his notion that "the past dreamed—the present acts," Turner disregarded the criterion for epigrammatic quality whereby one element offsets another in contextual meaning as well as number of words, as in this statement: "Plato wrote his Atlantis, Moore (*sic*) his Utopia—But the Americans erected a republic based on the great progressive possibilities of a free people and our faith in humanity." But the rhetorical critic of style has no difficulty discerning a dominant trend in the development of a style in the Commonplace Book. Turner is trying to master the technique of antithesis.

Surely no other effort on Turner's part would be more indicative of his decision to be eloquent. After all, the compositional process leading to the creation of antithesis is one of the most difficult to manage from the standpoint of overcoming psychological constraints upon a writer. Native users of English are subject to the influence of certain psycholinguistic pressures as they write. In essence, the strongest of these pressures upon a writer are those to produce statements which conform in syntax and lexicon to the norms of the common idiom. One such constraint takes the form of a preference for affirmative rather than negative information, and therefore writers typically do not produce statements articulating *both* a positive and a negative in proximity, as in "to be not a curse but a blessing." Furthermore, idiomatic arrangement favors the contiguous placement of words associated by similarity of meaning. For instance, as the phrasing of a sentence might include the words "devil," "fearful," and "sinister," its writer would be constrained to respond next, almost automatically, with an associative word such as "dark" or "evil" rather than an antithetical term such as "light" or "blessed"; and because the last word written in a sequence tends to produce the greatest influence upon which other word is chosen next, the likelihood is extremely small that people will put antonyms close together in a sentence or in direct juxtapositions such as La Follette's "sublimely hideous" or "devilishly perfect."[29] Thus, by writing antitheses in his Commonplace Book, Turner provided further evidence of his developing sense of style; for his efforts to place opposites in close proximity represents a determined and conscious effort to be eloquent.

Admittedly, the sense of style being perfected in Turner's Commonplace Book is consonant with several trends in the teaching of rhetoric and oratory during the latter part of the nineteenth century. Foremost among these was a belief that persuasiveness was derived in large measure from stylistic skill. Moreover, the study of rhetoric was being viewed as a vehicle for the development of techniques for written discourse rather than oratory. One of the teachers in America who helped set these trends in motion was Adams Sherman Hill—the author of Turner's required text in rhetoric and oratory.

> Adams Sherman Hill, Boylston Professor of Rhetoric at Harvard, published his *Principles of Rhetoric* in 1878. It is perhaps of interest chiefly because it indicates the extent to which the Boylston Professorship had come to deal with the written rather than the spoken word. Hill defined rhetoric as "the art of efficient communication by language," and although he does include the speaker as well as the writer in his concept, the book is addressed to the writer....[30]

Students reading Hill's textbook might come to believe, too, that form was more a contributor to persuasiveness than content. The "principles of rhetoric" virtually excluded the classical canons of *inventio* and *dispositio*, respectively the faculties for finding appropriate arguments and motivational appeals and then arranging them in a suitable order. As Hill argues in the text's "Introduction," rhetoric as an art "does not undertake to furnish a person with something to say; but it does undertake to tell him how best to say that with which he has provided himself."[31] Thus, Turner read a text in which principles of rhetoric were reduced to considerations of grammatical purity through avoidance of barbarisms, solecisms, and improprieties as well as choice and use of words whereby the writer achieved desired qualities of "clearness, force, and elegance." Although that text introduced relatively short chapters on argumentative composition, including some suggestions about propositions and proof, the pragmatic subject of "persuasion" was reduced essentially to considerations of style.[32] Turner, however, did not become preoccupied with an impulse to subordinate content to form.

Of all that Turner read in Hill's text about style and persuasion, one dictum in particular obviously had an effect on the young man's emerging outlook toward eloquence. A practical wisdom pervades *The Principles of Rhetoric*. While eloquence in language is advocated as an advantage for the persuader, stylistic prowess is not viewed as an end in itself. According to Hill, an audience which is very much aware of communicator's skill with style is a group of people who also are on their guard and therefore less likely to be persuaded.

> A reputation for eloquence, on the contrary, is an obstacle to success in Persuasion. It procures clients, but it puts juries on their guard. It attracts large audiences, but it deepens the hostility of those who disagree with the speaker. So long as the audience are thinking about an orator's eloquence or his reputation for eloquence, so long he is not eloquent, so far as they are concerned. Until his eloquence makes them forget his reputation for eloquence, he is unsuccessful.[33]

Then, to illustrate such stylistic "excesses," Hill takes two historians—Gibbon and Macaulay—to task about the use of antitheses as they became "clauses which add little or nothing to the sense, and which have been compared to the false handles and keyholes with which furniture is decorated, that serve no other purpose than to *correspond to the real ones*."[34] Similarly, Hill also argued that sometimes the fault of the writer "consists in so frequent a use of

Antitheses as to give the composition an artificial air," often forcing the stylist who strives for symmetry in the use of opposites to "exaggeration" rather than desired "*real* antitheses, corresponding to a real opposition between ideas."[35] Clearly, Hill's textbook also taught a restraint in style, particularly as that discretion was pertinent in the writing of history.

Turner's Commonplace Book indicates that he was learning that restraint in style. While he was impressed very favorably by La Follette's "enormous" power of language, Turner nowhere approaches that degree of preoccupation with antitheses, alliteration, and parallel repetition. Furthermore, some examples of Turner's writing suggest that the young man was coming to view antitheses not as "artificial" but as "*real*...corresponding to a real opposition between ideas." Several pages have Turner's directives to himself as a writer, saying "Show that the *practical* is needed now in raising the masses toward the *Ideal*"; or in planning a passage about an age in which Americans perceive aesthetic value in what is practical, Turner reminds himself to "show that it is filled with all...the...*beauty* and *grandeur* of ancient art but to us looking at it from the near position...it cannot be appreciated, seems *rough* and *harsh*."[36] Antitheses, then, were not studied artifices, imposed *afterward* upon some statement. Rather, Turner seemed on occasion to think antithetically, to conceptualize in terms of dichotomies between real enough opposites. The composition of an oration then became for those passages the fulfillment of those directives to himself to "show" the dichotomy. Thus, in Turner's evolving predilections for eloquence, style was congruent with substance.

The 1881-82 Commonplace Book offers still another index of the young man's attitude toward style. Passages for speech drafts are not characterized by extensive revision. Rarely are phrases crossed out, rewritten, and polished further. The style certainly is not devoid of ornament in the Lysian mode, nor does Turner strive for a Ciceronian model of writing which abounds with "every kind of ornament in speaking." His style during the 1881-82 school year displays a sense of restraint, a discretion which allows him to know when not to cross that line whereby attempts at eloquence become so blatant as to be obtrusive, putting audiences on guard and creating suspicions about the speaker's having designs upon them. A "golden mean" for style seems to prevail in Turner's early attempt to be eloquent.

The Commonplace Book also demonstrates what will become another of Turner's rhetorical predispositions—the tendency to use statements from previously written speeches in discourse developed in response to subsequent exigencies. Such "cannibalization" became a characteristic behavior on Turner's part as a student orator at the University of Wisconsin. For instance, many segments of "The Imaginativeness of the Present" are basically reworked and reworded ideas from Turner's high school oration, "The Power of the Press." In turn, 1881-82 drafts of "The Imaginativeness of the Present" furnish ideas, if not almost word for word paraphrases of passages, that will be the bases of the next rhetorical milestone in the historian's life: his Burrows Prize oration of 1883.

At the Junior Exhibition of 18 May 1883, Turner won the University of Wisconsin Burrows Prize with an oration entitled "The Poet of the Future." Portions of that speech were rehearsed earlier in his Commonplace Book, but he still worked hard in anticipation of the event. In a letter from home dated a full month before the contest, Turner's father says he is "Glad that you have your oration completed. Now that you have got it in form you will be able to reconstruct sentences and add some ideas that will suggest themselves without giving you much labor."[37] Thus, even for last minute revisions of the composition, the father expected diligence and attention to style from the young man. That effort also could coincide with Turner's appraisal of the contest, for the Junior Burrows Prize might be more important psychologically, to bring ego satisfaction, than the Senior Lewis Prize for Oratory at commencement. After all, a winner of the Lewis Prize left the campus and environs soon after graduation exercises. Any accolades thereafter would be offered probably only on the rare occasions when former faculty or classmates would be encountered. The Burrows Prize winner at the Junior Exhibition, however, had a full year remaining on campus in which to bask in the glow of that oratorical triumph. Efforts to produce a winning oration were worth it. Success in such an oratorical contest represented a personal triumph of the greatest magnitude.

And "The Poet of the Future" reflects efforts at perfecting an artistic style in emulation of La Follette. Turner's own compositional prowess is subtle but nevertheless discernible in such alliteration as "*l*isping *l*ines," or "*c*old *c*ritical," or "*p*roclaims the *p*rogress"; and parallel repetition for rhetorical effect occurs easily and idiosyncratically by now in groups of two at the beginnings of successive phrases or short sentences, as in "*Beneath every* literature there is a philosophy. *Beneath every* work of art there is an idea of nature and life." Prophetically, that utterance founded upon parallelism almost anticipates the essence of the frontier thesis as discourse. But if "The Poet of the Future" is a self-fulfilling prophecy on the part of its author, that prediction of his own life's work appears in more ways than one in Turner's virtually autobiographical antitheses: "He will unite the *logic* of the *present* and the *dream* of the *past*" as well as "He will *reflect* all the *past* and *prophesy* the *future*."

In general, "The Poet of the Future" relies on La Follettesque appositions for essential thematic statements: "The reign of *aristocracy* is *passing*; that of *humanity begins*." Nowhere, however, does Turner approach the studied artifice of La Follette's strings of antitheses in succession. The audience is not overwhelmed by prowess too apparent; the style is subtle. And in its total effect, the oration clearly was a superior effort. The Madison newspaper put it this way:

> The verdict of the audience was in perfect accord with the judges. There was no possibility of doubt regarding the justice of the award. To the audience Mr. Turner's oration was the superior one of the evening in all the essential points of thought, composition and delivery.[38]

Recognizing the already established stature of the orator, the campus newspaper observed that "Mr. Turner, as predicted, had an excellent production"; and after comparing the strengths of the oration to others in content and delivery, the article concluded succinctly: "As was expected, the judges decided in favor of Mr. Turner of Adelphia."[39]

Rhetorically, the young man had arrived; and for the coming

23

year, he could enjoy the accolades for his efforts. One major oratorical effort remained, the competition for the Senior Lewis
Prize at commencement, 18 June 1884. For that event, Turner
wrote a neat, professional oration entitled "Architecture through
Oppression." With antitheses drawn from his 1881-82 commonplace book oration, Turner amplified his theme that "the history
of humanity has been a *romance* and a *tragedy*."

> *Millions groaned* that *one* might *laugh*, servile tillers of the soil,
> *sweating* that others might *dream; drinking the logwood of life* while
> their masters *quaffed its nectar*. Many are the historians who have
> painted the *glories of the past;* few there are that tell the *lamentation
> and the ancient tale of wrong*.

In addition to its now almost inevitable alliteration and parallel
repetitions at beginnings of successive phrases or short sentences,
Turner's style in "Architecture Through Oppression" suggests
he could be La Follette's equal in developing a theme of the oration antithetically; and several other antitheses appear, apposing
*"peasantry"* with *"noblemen"* and the *"squalor of the hovel"* with the
*"cathedral's beauty."* But this oration, too, is characterized by
stylistic restraint. Turner could copy La Follette's style—but
artistically, without the style's calling attention to itself. As anti-
climax to his winning orations, the young man's junior and senior
"Rhetoricals" grades were 96 percent and 98 percent. No wonder
that with the addition of the Senior Lewis Prize to his Junior
Burrows Prize, Turner graduated to become known later as
Wisconsin's "remarkable boy orator."[40]

Looking in retrospect at Turner's career as orator, the trend is
unmistakable. In an age when rhetorical prowess was prized,
young Turner seemed to set a goal for himself: he would be eloquent. High school experiences suggested he had the potential;
university performances showed his poise and polish. Turner's
Commonplace Book, the items pasted in his scrapbook, and the
final drafts of his orations all support but one interpretation
about who was the precise, prime mover in the development of
his skill in rhetoric. Turner himself identified that person explic-
itly when he retired from Harvard in 1924; for in listing "the
forces that have influenced my career," the historian singled out

24

that speaker and speech which he heard in 1879 as a University of Wisconsin freshman: "La Follette—Iago." From his observation and analysis of that single rhetorical event, and with the accompanying *elan* he experienced, Turner undoubtedly came to a conclusion about style and impact. Paraphrased succinctly, an influential factor contributing to persuasiveness is stylized portraiture or characterization. That facet of eloquence on Turner's part would become a pivotal factor in his life thereafter.

## II. The Rhetorical Predilection in Writing History

AFTER EARNING his baccalaureate, Turner worked a year as a newspaper reporter; but he then returned to the University of Wisconsin as a graduate student to earn a master's degree in history. The attractiveness of a career as an historian may have evolved in large measure from his feelings of satisfaction as a result of an undergraduate class project. Professor William F. Allen had received a request from Herbert Baxter Adams at Johns Hopkins for information on early land holdings in Wisconsin (actually, to be incorporated in a book Adams was doing on the origins of New England institutions). As a junior, Turner was one of six students who were allowed to participate in the project. Working through friends of his father and examining records and diaries of early Wisconsin settlers, he developed a monograph on "The History of the 'Grignon Tract' on the Portage of the Fox and Wisconsin Rivers." Early that summer of 1883, the monograph was published in his father's newspaper.[41] Thus as an undergraduate, Turner learned that his prose could appear in print and therefore be just as much in the public eye—even if it was in the mode of historical writing instead of orations.

But the life of a graduate student without income might be distasteful to a person who had acquired even by then somewhat of a "champagne-taste" life style. Fortunately, on the strength of his fame as an orator, Turner was employed by the University of Wisconsin to teach rhetorical skills to underclassmen. In the 1885-86 and 1886-87 issues of the *Catalogue of the University*, he is listed among "Instructors and Assistants" in rhetoric and oratory; in 1887-88, he is designated as an "Instructor in History and Oratory." Although by this latter date committed to a career as a historian, Turner still taught freshmen rhetorical skills in the program headed by the esteemed David B. Frankenburger.[42]

Turner's admiration for Frankenburger never ceased (nor for the study of rhetoric either). This is revealed most clearly perhaps in the historian's 1906 eulogy of Wisconsin's beloved teacher. After praising Frankenburger's "unselfish devotion to his students," the eulogy delineated the ideal for which that teacher "gave unstinted of his time and his energy." Turner epitomized his mentor's role antithetically, *"Others* might teach *classes; he* taught the *individual."*[43] In its brief characterization of Frankenburger, that eulogy also inadvertently suggests the depth of positive feeling that Turner himself felt toward his own rhetorical experiences as an undergraduate. For the oratorical prowess attained by the young man from Portage undoubtedly was in part derived from Frankenburger's personalized attention. As a teacher, he likely encouraged Turner's perfection of the La Follottesque skills with which the undergraduate Burrows and Lewis prizes were won. In the total emotional experience of that eulogy, Turner did seem to acknowledge his debt to Frankenburger for helping him attain oratorical prowess. But the more dominant early influence had to be that of La Follette's artistry in a stylistic characterization of Iago.

During his graduate work at the University of Wisconsin, Turner tried some characterization in an 1887 review of *Franklin in France.* Answering the question "Who was the first great American?" his attempt previewed a frontier thesis portrayal:

> If we accept as necessary conditions of this title that the recipient must be preeminently the representative of the leading tendencies of the nation, original as it is original, and that he must have won and held the admiration of the world, whom can we find to fulfill the requirements before Benjamin Franklin, and who has better satisfied them? His greatness lay in his ability to apply to the world a shrewd understanding that disclosed in the ordinary things about him potent forces for helpfulness. His life is the story of American common sense in its highest form, applied to business, to politics, to science, to diplomacy, to religion, to philanthropy. Surely this self-made man, the apostle of the practical and

the useful, is by the verdict of his own country and of Europe entitled to the distinction of being the first great American.[44]

Actually, Turner pursued that theme of character in a still later address: "The question has sometimes been asked 'who was the first great American?' I suppose that this means 'great' in the sense of having achieved recognition beyond the confines of one's own nation—great in the recognition of the world; and to be the great American, one must be representatively great—great in the qualities which characterize Americans at their best."[45] While the theme is virtually the same as that praising Franklin, Turner went on to laud Lincoln! So the possibility of characterization, as a vehicle in some historical writing, was on Turner's mind very early in his professional life.

The next rhetorical milestone in his life was reached during the 1888 American Historical Association Convention. Attendance at that meeting led Turner to conclude decisively that skill in persuasion did have a place in compositional efforts of historians. In a letter to Professor Allen after the convention, Turner observed that "the papers were good, but many of them, especially those of the younger men…were too much in the nature of detailed research—facts not *illuminated*—not of the most interesting character for a spoken address."[46] Thus, even in 1888, the young historian virtually predicted his own performance in 1893, for his reaction to papers at that convention led Turner to perceive the value of some rhetorical elements in historical writing, at least at that point for papers presented orally by historians.

That perception was given a sharper focus in 1889. The possible applications of character portrayal in historical publications came to Turner's mind again after reading Theodore Roosevelt's *The Winning of the West* in that year and heavily underlining passages about "*individual initiative*" and the hunters who became the "*peculiar heroes of the frontier*"; for Turner then began an 1890 file folder on "The Hunter Type," paraphrasing Roosevelt's portrayal of men who "found too little elbowroom in town life" and "loved to hear the crack of their long rifles, and the blows of the ax in the forest."[47] Turner's appreciation actually was reinforced by correspondence from Roosevelt emphasizing that "my aim is

27

especially to show who the frontiersmen were and what they did, as they gradually conquered the west....I have always been more interested in the men themselves than in the institutions through and under which they worked."[48] Indeed, in the retirement speech to the Harvard History Club in 1924, the outline suggests that Turner also extemporized about "Roosevelt's writings" and the extent of "my admiration for him."

So Turner came to have an early facility for characterization as it might be used rhetorically in historical writing. And that facility was conspicuous throughout the historian's life. Deeply impressed by the lines in Dante's *Inferno* (xxxvi. 112), depicting those "who through a hundred thousand perils have come unto the West," Turner himself translated the episode into English from a Latin typescript in his possession and amassed still other translations in a file folder.[49] That same folder includes a similar literary characterization, a heavily marked copy of Rudyard Kipling's "The Foreloper" (also variously titled "The Pioneer" or "The Explorer"):

> His neighbors' smoke shall vex his eyes, their
>     voices break his rest;
> He shall go forth till south is north, sullen and
>     dispossessed;
> He shall desire loneliness, and his desire
>     shall bring
> Hard on his heels, a thousand wheels, a people
>     and a king.
> He shall come back on his own track, and
>     by his scarce cool camp,
> There shall he meet the roaring street, the
>     derrick and the stamp;
> For he must blaze a nation's way, with
>     hatchet and with brand,
> Till on his last won wildernesss an empire's
>     bulwarks stand.

Upon the death of the historian, his daughter recalled how this particular verse has "always been father to me."[50]

The importance of characterization or portraiture simply cannot be ignored or dismissed in Turner's concept of historical writing when he composed the frontier thesis. In the mid 1890s, for example, the vivid portrayal of a character was very much on Turner's mind. He praised Woodrow Wilson's *Division and Reunion* as the "wedding of a good literary form to historical writing" to achieve "flesh and blood" vitality, while editors pressed him to continue writing "real, definite, human pictures of pioneer life" as well as "vivid character sketches of the men, mingling biography, interpretation of achievement and dramatic presentation of important episodes in their lives."[51] Turner also praised characterization in his eulogy of fellow historian Reuben Gold Thwaites, superintendent of the State Historical Society of Wisconsin for twenty-seven years. Thwaites "saw his characters, not as lay figures, but vividly and dramatically as real people. He had...a knack for keen but kindly characterization....He never read or penned a note that he did not see the picturesque, the human scene behind the bare record....The history of institutions, or industrial development of laws and governments, appealed to him less than the history of individual achievement."[52]

Those students who worked with Turner also came to know of his appreciation for rhetorical facets of composition generally and characterization specifically. From one student finishing a thesis, Turner as advisor asked for illustration to relieve "the dryness of the subject, as well as to give it its element of personality and human interest"; from another he demanded description and portraiture to "make your leaders *live*, by clothing them in reality" to create "a picture that can be seen and appreciated."[53] In their later years, students consistently recalled how Turner's "was never an abstract frontier, never an abstract section that he was describing—it was toiling, thinking, loving, hating human beings of whom he was thinking"; and the effect was clearly the product of Turner's "rich prose."[54]

By incorporating characterization in his concept of historical writing, Turner was relying upon a pervasive and influential factor in the process of motivation. Although he undoubtedly had an instinctive appreciation for the value of such portraiture, Turner himself would not have been cognizant of the persuasive implications of that technique. For the state of the art in rhetoric was founded then largely upon time-honored, classical dicta. Contemporary persuasion theory of the twentieth century had yet to isolate and explain the motivational role of characterization. Still, its potential as a source of persuasiveness could have existed in the latter part of the nineteenth century as Turner was perfecting his sense of portraiture and beginning to apply that technique in his own writing.

Essentially, portraiture is a vehicle by which a persuader achieves one of the basic objectives of discourse: identification. Several critics have written at length about the persuasive dimensions of identification as it functions across a wide spectrum of discourse. In a comprehensive overview of human, symbolic activity, Kenneth Burke has argued that all rhetorical effectiveness in essence is a function of identification which produces an ultimately desired "consubstantiality" or "*acting together*"; for "you persuade a man only insofar as you can talk his language by speech, gesture, tonality, order, image, attitude, idea, *identifying* your ways with his."[55] As persuasion theorists now write about the process of identification, however, modeled behavior is viewed as the final outcome. For an identification effect is one in which "some of the characteristics of a model belonged to the individual and the individual behaved as if some of the characteristics and affective states of the model belonged to him"; and in coming to act as if "the goal states of the model belonged to him, a person strives to imitate aspects of the model's behavior."[56] Furthermore, that imitated behavior can become a pattern which extends over a relatively long period of time.[57]

In discourse, successful persuaders are often those who present portraits of models worthy of emulation, personae whose behaviors are rewarded and thereby worthy of imitation. In assessing this mode of rhetorical influence, Weiss has concluded that "sentiment toward a character is at the root of identification"; and if that character is portrayed as successful, he becomes a model for others who desire achieving the same rewarding or satisfying state.

> If a person perceives that his own behavior and personality are exhibited by an identificand who is successful, the "match" can serve as confirmation or reinforcement....One incentive for

identification is the perception that the model commands or attains a rewarding or satisfying state. Psycho-logic may lead the identifier to conclude that, if he possessed the characteristics of the identificand, he too would achieve desired goals.[58]

Turner would not have appreciated the jargon-ridden terminology in that explanation of the "psycho-logic" of identification, but he certainly sensed the value of a portrayal which epitomized the "attractiveness" of some person after whom others might model their own behavior.[59] Turner's entire career attests to his affinity for characterization in writing history.

Turner also made it quite clear that characterization as content would be articulated in a form relying upon rhetorical style. After reflecting upon his reactions to the papers at the American Historical Association convention of 1888, Turner finally had an opportunity to set forth formally his broad concept of rhetoric in historical writing. In 1891, Turner's essay on "The Significance of History" offered evidence of his belief that eloquent style had a role in historical writing. Admitting that attempts to "force dull facts into vivacity" could result in distortion, the young historian would "gladly admit that in itself an interesting style, even a picturesque manner of presentation, is not to be condemned, provided that truthfulness of substance rather than vivacity of style be the end sought."[60]

By acknowledging the value of vivacity in writing history, Turner was restating precepts of style learned during his undergraduate education and oratorical training at the University of Wisconsin. According to Hill's *Principles of Rhetoric*, a writer's first obligation is to use language which "his readers understand, and understand as he understands it." Furthermore, "it is not enough to use language that *may be* understood; he would use language that *must be* understood." This quality of "clearness" is the cornerstone of eloquence which is *"the power to translate a truth into language perfectly intelligible to the person to whom you speak."* Beyond the prerequisite of articulating *"truth"* with clarity, however, discourse may have additional objectives, when writing is to do far more than "convey information or impart instruction." At these times, the writer will try to attain a quality of style known to Hill as "force" but which is similar to that quality discussed in other treatises as "vivacity." And attaining both clarity *and* force (or vivacity) often will result from the use of stylistic techniques such as antitheses and parallel repetitions as well as other schemes and tropes. According to Hill's textbook, these aspects of style in discourse would help direct the attention and interest of an audience to the advantage of the persuader.[61] Thus, at the advent of his career as he looked forward to the writing of history, Turner looked backward for advice and found it in rhetorical precepts studied and mastered as an undergraduate at the University of Wisconsin. And an oratorical genesis of a distinct style in discourse evolved into habitual applications of eloquence in the actual writing of history.

That rhetorical predilection may have exerted one of its most subtle and yet profound influences upon Turner's historical writing early in 1891. For in rhetorically adapting a paper on "American Colonization" for presentation in a speech to the Madison Literary Club, on the evening of 9 February 1891, the historian's stylistic revisions—crossed out words and phrases and their substitutions—show him moving closer conceptually to the essence of the frontier thesis.[62]

Ray A. Billington attempted to trace the conceptual origins of Turner's monumental contribution to American historical thought; and in *The Genesis of the Frontier Thesis* he decided that Turner "had arrived at most of his conclusions by January 1891."[63] But Billington's "hypothetical timetable" describing the conceptualization of the frontier thesis is predicated upon a psychological model of creative thinking; and among stages of intellectual activity to be ascertained is what psychologists call "the leap forward" or "the moment of illumination, when the significant idea, the defined hypothesis, the brilliant solution suddenly presents itself."[64] *The Genesis of the Frontier Thesis*, however, was based primarily upon studying what Turner read from 1885 to 1893 and then examining his correspondence, his lectures, his published essays, and his celebrated mass of 3x5 note cards— only *indirect* evidence from which Billington could infer the long-term workings of Turner's mind. And to retrace an intellectual progress through these materials does not reveal Turner's thought processes at a specific, crucial time so much as it demonstrates Billington's eminent historical inquiry and insight about a period of several years! A more direct index of Turner's "leap forward" and "moment of illumination" is attained by close stylistic analysis of language in the draft, with Turner's longhand revisions and marginal notes, of his address on "American Colonization" to the Madison Literary Club. This analysis suggests that Turner's pivotal moment of historical creativity occurred in late January and early February of 1891, at the time he stylistically polished this particular address for public presentation and rhetorical effect.

The rationale for close stylistic analysis of Turner's language in this speech is implicit in Buffon's celebrated epigram, "the style is the man himself" ("*le style est l'homme même*").[65] Originally, Buffon's 1753 statement was about man in the abstract. As a zoologist primarily interested in biological more than aesthetic ideas (and the phrase occurs in his great *Natural History*), Buffon meant that the essential variety inherent in the notion of style distinguished the language of man from the far more limited if not monotonous communication patterns of other species. In its more current paraphrase as "the style is the man" ("*le style c'est l'homme*"), Buffon's concept has come to advance a somewhat different but nevertheless provocative assumption about one's unique syntax and lexicon: that a person's style in discourse reflects his essence as an individual.[66] And if one's style in discourse does evince important aspects of his individuality, it also may be an index of his intellectual processes, particularly when the longhand, lexical, and syntactical revisions on a manuscript reveal the workings of a mind *during* the creative endeavor. For as Turner rhetorically adapted his syntax and lexicon toward the persuasion of his audience, the stylistic revision of "American Colonization" also altered the essential substance of its content and emphasized certain concepts in his own mind, thereby moving the historian inexorably closer to his ultimate frontier thesis.

Billington agrees that the address on "American Colonization" brought Turner "well along the road" and "anticipated most of the concepts made famous by his 1893 essay on the significance of the frontier."[67] That assessment, though, seems to be founded on those statements in "American Colonization" which in their *final* form were articulated later in the frontier thesis.[68] The overlooked but important factor is the *initial* form of those statements and what happened psychologically as Turner polished them stylistically for a persuasive presentation to the Madison Literary Club. Clearly, Turner's marginal notes and longhand revisions—crossed-out words and phrases as well as their linguistic substitutions—are direct evidence of his important intellectual progress toward the frontier thesis *at the very moments he was engaged in creative efforts.* Viewed chronologically, from the first sentences of the "American Colonization" manuscript to its ultimate conclusions, these stylistic indices of historical creativity may suggest more precisely that a period in late January and early February 1891 was the time of the "leap forward" or "moment of illumination" which Billington tried to ascertain.

The first page of "American Colonization" is highly stylized, reflecting Turner's rhetorical predilection for achieving a strong introductory impact upon his audience. As he initially developed a broad perspective on ancient impulses to colonize, Turner relied, for instance, on two antitheses: "The völkerwanderung had hardly resulted in the *downfall of Rome* and the *rise of the feudal system,* when the crusades followed, and the *last scene* in the crusades was the *first scene* in the exploration of the New World" (this latter antithesis was moved to the first page from the fourth page of an earlier but incomplete draft which is contained in the same file folder). He also relied on the other features of his characteristic rhetorical style by using alliteration and parallel repetition: "*From island to island,* and *from cape to cape,* these traders *p*lanted their *p*osts in the Mediterranean, bringing *a*rts and the *a*lphabet to Greece and *s*owing the *s*eeds of *c*ivilization in Carthage and in Spain." What is crucial to a consideration of Turner's historical creativity, however, is what also happened stylistically in some subtle but important changes preceding these statements. In the very first sentence, "The colonizing spirit is one form of the nomadic instinct," Turner had crossed out his original and perhaps more generic word "migratory," which might apply to all animal life, and substituted instead the more specific word "nomadic," which applied more clearly only to human activity. Indeed, in the above-mentioned fragments of an earlier draft of the address,

Turner had even appended to that first sentence a reference to "the instinct that sends the bird to the new skies." The point is that as Turner began the address, his deletion of a reference to birds' instincts and his stylistic substitution of "nomadic" for "migratory" probably helped focus his own attention upon an essentially human and highly personal activity as opposed to more generically animal or even broad racial impulses (as suggested by an even later deletion on the seventh page of the word "stocks" in favor of "tribes"). And however subtle, those changes are consonant with a rhetorical predilection for characterization.

The same focus upon the activities of humans, specifically, was implied on that first page in still another, subtle way. After the sentence "Phoenicia was the first great colonizing power," Turner deleted the following sentence, "Her ships and caravans were the shuttles that wove together the fabric of Oriental civilization, and into her ports came the riches of the East." He proceeded instead directly to the sentence referring to the "traders" who brought arts and the alphabet to Greece and sowed the seeds of civilization. By deleting those references to inanimate ships and impersonal caravans, Turner may have been adapting rhetorically to a feeling that for an audience one can maintain interest most effectively when talking about other humans as specific types. In so doing, however, he brought himself ever closer conceptually to a position articulated on the fifth and sixth pages of his draft: "American history is the account of how this environment was occupied by a new organization. It is the history of the application of men and ideas to these physical conditions." Even after a broad discussion of several diverse examples of ancient colonization and then, briefly, of the geographical features of North America, Turner seemed to arrive intellectually at what is clearly a synthesis—that as a historian he was interested in how a specific group of people reacted to a specific environment. Although subtle, the stylistic adaptations preceding this statement appear to sharpen that focus on human and personal factors in response to local conditons.

In effect, Turner's manuscript at that point begins his repudiation of the then widely accepted belief that each of our nation's institutions had evolved from an English institution, and beyond that from its "germ" in the forests of medieval Germany (and to historians of Turner's generation, this was logically true because their comparisons revealed unmistakable similarities with ancient Teutonic practices that were certain proof of common origins).[69] Turner's repudiation of that "germ" theory was established more firmly, though, still later in the "American Colonization" manuscript. Over the next eleven pages, he had ranged widely over several aspects of his subject, discussing the geographical features of North America, the geology of the continent and its influence upon prehistoric inhabitants, Indian settlements, maritime activites of the English, trade routes, the defeat of the Spanish Armada, and the settlement of Virginia and subsequently the middle colonies. Then, on the nineteenth page of his manuscript, Turner seemed to arrive at another synthesizing statement:

> The colonization of the central region resulted in the formation of middle colonies in every respect. As mixed in its nationality as any of the existing states; with a variety of social divisions, the middle class preponderating; varied in its industries, being agricultural like the South, and commercial like New England, possessing the mixed town and county form of local government, heterogeneous in its religious sects; characteristically western in the west and in the east a typically eastern colony; it was, in a word, a mediating region—a region which interpreted New England to the South and the East to the West. It was also a pivotal region, a fighting ground for ideas and social forms.

To a certain extent, this passage reflects Turner's tendency to achieve his typical antithetical style with the balance between the South and the New England as well as his apposition of "western in the west and in the east a typically eastern colony." The passage seems to be one in which Turner exercised some stylistic effort. And in the margin to this particular passage, there is a sharp vertical line drawn next to the notion of a "mediating region" and a "fighting ground for ideas and social forms." That marginal signpost also is accompanied by Turner's underlined, longhand conclusion: "typical of U.S." As a result of his striving for a more rhetorical style, the historian apparently emphasized in his own mind a concept that brought him still closer to a rejection of the germ theory of transplanted institutions and a realiza-

tion that local, typically American factors were major determinants in the development of this nation's history.

Admittedly, the repudiation of the germ theory was not complete as of this point in the address. Turner still equivocated to
some extent. On the very next page he asserted that the New
England towns were the "products of three forces: the congregational polity, the revival of the old English town organization, and
the peculiar local conditions." Thus, although he now acknowledged specifically the "peculiar local conditions," Turner still
could not discount completely what he chose to call "the revival
of the old English town organization." That equivocation also
was present on the very next page (p. 21) when he said "There are
too many analogies between the New England town and the 'tun'
of our German forefathers to be overlooked. Placed again in the
wilderness environment, the descendants of the Anglo-Saxons
reproduced many of the characteristics of the early towns." Still,
Turner could follow that sentence with a reiteration of his developing notion that "we must not neglect the local conditions as
factors in producing the New England town."

Other evidence of equivocation is present in this speech.
Turner was still using the terminology reflecting the then popular neo-Lamarckian conception of biological environmentalism in
the realm of human society.[70] In following the trend to describe
social conditions in essentially biological terms, Turner said of
the congregational form of church organization, for instance,
"being a self governed body it was sufficient unto itself, and like
some forms of animal life it was capable of subdivision without
destroying the life of the parts" (p. 21). While still using this
metaphorical theme rather consistently in "American Colonization," Turner nevertheless had crossed out the word "organism"
very early in the address (p. 2) and substituted "institution," an
indication that he was breaking away intellectually from another
of his earlier conceptual patterns.

What happened stylistically on the immediately succeeding
page (p. 22) may have been still another subtle but important
element in leading Turner away from his equivocation to a more
distinct conception of the frontier's influence. The passage in its
final form is this:

The first period of New England history has been characterized as the period of settlement, when Plymouth and Salem were planted. The second is that of budding, when these parent towns sent colonies to other places. Thus little groups of towns grew up around Plymouth and around Boston; in the same ways the Connecticut River towns were settled; New Haven with a group of neighboring towns, and Rhode Island followed a like process. Had the New England town been like the Greek city this dispersion might have gone on indefinitely. But the capacity of the town for representation saved us from this result. Shortly before the middle of the seventeenth century a movement of combination began. The various towns of Plymouth sent representatives to a general court. The towns of Massachusetts Bay, of Connecticut, of New Haven, and of Rhode Island did the same.

After referring to the little groups of towns around Plymouth and Boston, Turner originally had said "thus the Connecticut river towns were settled." By crossing out "thus" and substituting in longhand "in the same ways," Turner seemed to begin the development of an inductively based historical analogy. To have left the sentence in its original form with "thus" as the copula, the historian might have regarded the Connecticut River towns more exclusively as the result of what happened around Plymouth and Boston. Instead, he apparently perceived more clearly that those towns were essentially only additional examples of a pattern identified earlier in the address as "peculiar local conditions." This pattern of repeated rather than derivative phenomena probably became even sharper to Turner at the conclusion of this passage, when he crossed out his original but relatively accurate phrase "followed a like process" and substituted in longhand "did the same." In this case of minor stylistic option, the very repetition of the specific word "same" suggests that Turner was becoming more aware of still another piece of evidence for constructing an inductive, historical analogy.

And Turner clearly decided in February 1891 to develop such an analogy more fully. The most dramatic evidence occurs as he neared the conclusion of the "American Colonization" address. After three more pages describing the Puritan colonies in contrast to the French and Spanish concepts of colonization, Turner said, "In the period of settlement were produced many of the

38

germs of our national institutions and characteristics." Although he still used the word "germ" (perhaps by force of habit), he had come to grips with "our" national institutions and characteristics. Then, on the twenty-sixth page of his manuscript, Turner came to *the* crucial, synthesizing statement:

> Indeed, it is only in the present that the colonizing era is coming to a close. I do not hesitate to say that this fact is the key to American history. As the occupation of the New World transformed Europe so the occupation of the Great West has determined the flow of American energies, been the underlying explanation of political history, and has had profound reactive effects upon the social and economic life of the East. What first the Mediterranean Sea, and later the New World, were to the Aryan peoples, breaking the bond of custom, and creating new activities to meet new conditions, that the undeveloped West has been to the American descendants of these Aryans.

In finally focusing on the influence of "the Great West," Turner had found "the key to American history." Admittedly, there are similar statements earlier in the address (recall his saying on the fifth and sixth pages, "American history is the account of how this environment was occupied by a new organization. It is the history of the application of men and ideas to these physical conditions"). But this later, more rhetorical passage is unquestionably the most crucial. For in the margin next to it, Turner wrote in longhand, "need of studying this."

By deciding there was a "need of studying this," Turner had in effect emphatically isolated the thrust of his frontier thesis; and the remainder of the address on "American Colonization" bears this out in still another way. In the seven remaining pages after the above passage, Turner's manuscript reveals a distinct tendency to identify specific facets of the American experience which should be studied:

> We can never understand our country properly until we know the materials out of which our Western States have been constructed. We need students who shall neglect Pocahontas and the question of the first white child in Brown County, in order that they may study where and by what means the characteristics and population of western states like Kansas, California and Wisconsin were

produced. What was contributed by New England? by the Middle States? by Spain? When State and county history shall be studied in the light of the world history, we shall begin to know our country better and this is the goal of history—to know the present by the study of its development from the past.

Turner went on with his conclusion that "the story of the peopling of America has not yet been written. We do not understand ourselves." He had set the tone that was to predominate in 1893's "The Significance of the Frontier in American History," wherein he identified fourteen specific facets of the American frontier that should be studied for major insights into our history.

Perhaps the final indication of the importance of the passage on the "key to American history" and "breaking the bond of custom" is in the frontier thesis itself. Just as Turner was concerned and knowledgeable (by practice and training) about the rhetorical impact of the introductory remarks in the discourse, so was he cognizant of the need to have a peroration which stated his concept in compelling terms for an audience. Admittedly, his address to the Madison Literary Club does not have a particularly strong concluding statement. Turner ended merely by asking a tangential question about whether or not the United States should follow the trend of German colonial policy and try "to secure at least substitutes for colonization by attaching South American economic life to its own." The audience is left hanging. Considering Turner's propensities when writing, however, it is entirely possible that the concluding pages of his address simply were removed from that file and utilized in another speech. Of course 1893's address to the American Historical Association concludes with a much stronger rhetorical tone with these final two sentences:

> What the Mediterranean Sea was to the Greeks, breaking the bond of custom, offering new experiences, calling out new institutions and activities, that, and more, the ever retreating frontier has been to the United States directly, and to the nations of Europe more remotely. And now, four centuries from the discovery of America, at the end of a hundred years of life under the Constitution, the frontier has gone, and with its going has closed the first period of American history.[71]

So to achieve the ultimate, persuasive statement to articulate his frontier thesis of 1893, Turner chose as its basis that particular synthesizing statement of 1891 that led him to conclude "need of studying this." And when considered critically as a total compositional effort, all those rhetorical adaptations in the text of the address on "American Colonization" *do* suggest that stylistic revisions themselves, *during* the artistic effort, contributed to Turner's celebrated historical creativity.[72]

Admittedly, a version of that concept of the frontier's significance was published by Turner before the 1893 paper. His "Problems in American History" appeared in a November 1892 issue of *Aegis*, a University of Wisconsin undergraduate newspaper. Actually, Turner had been invited to prepare a paper on some aspect of Wisconsin's early history; but as Billington puts it, the young historian "delayed preparing his essay until the last moment, as was his custom."[73] Perhaps an opportunity to publish in a student newspaper was not attractive enough, and fulfilling the request was easy to put off. As a deadline approached, however, the request for copy could be met with a paper about "the key to American history" which the historian had isolated in his "American Colonization" address. And reacting to his own directive about a "need to studying this," Turner likely had been thinking about a statement much along the lines of 1892's "Problems in American History," which advocated the study of local or "frontier" factors as a dominant influence upon the course of events constituting the settlement and development of this country.[74]

In its broad outline, this 1892 article presents almost the same points in the same sequence as 1893's "The Significance of the Frontier in American History." What is missing in 1892 for Wisconsin undergraduates, however, is the considerable illustrative amplification and the refined and extensive rhetorical language behavior. Admittedly, the first footnote of the frontier thesis acknowledges its "foundation" in 1892's *Aegis* publication.[75] But Turner likely sensed the professional appropriateness of citing a published paper rather than an earlier public lecture as the conceptual antecedent of the frontier thesis.

"Problems in American History" proved to be important to

Turner for another reason. As was his custom, the young historian sent reprints of this essay to professional peers around the country. There was some favorable response. Albion Small at the University of Chicago wrote back to Turner and expressed his delight, suggesting as well that the publication deserved "a more prominent place than the columns of a college newspaper."[76] Far more important for the professional development of Turner, Herbert Baxter Adams at John Hopkins read the article and invited the young historian to present its point of view in longer form at an American Historical Association meeting scheduled for Chicago on 12 July 1893. Turner accepted.

And Turner procrastinated. Writing to Woodrow Wilson on 16 July 1893, he apologized for not responding earlier to a letter from the former because he had been in the "final agonies of getting out a belated paper for the American Historical Association."[77] As he usually did in preparing any speech, lecture, or article, Turner waited until the last minute, even for as professionally important an event as this for a young historian. After all, while nominally a paper for historian peers, the Chicago presentation had the added aura of being part of a "World's Congress of Historians and Historical Students," held in conjunction with the "World's Columbian Exposition" commemorating the four-hundredth anniversary of America's discovery. While some sophisticates deplored an AHA role amid the whoopla and amusements of a world's fair, an ambitious historian from a midwestern college or university easily might perceive an opportunity to prove that prairies produced more than corn and Populists.[78] Still, as Billington argues, little if any of the frontier thesis address was prepared by the end of April 1893, and the essay as delivered likely was written "in the few weeks—or days, or hours—before it was due."[79] So probably on the train from Madison and perhaps even in his room at the University of Chicago, Turner prepared under pressure.

Last minute preparation invariably exerts some influence upon the style of discourse. In Turner's case, preparing under the pressures of time—and his sense of the importance of the event professionally—probably led to a heightened drive state. In other words, Turner likely was experiencing increasing motivation to write and perform well at his Chicago presentation. Therefore, he would have been subject to what psychologists explain as a "tuning-up" function leading to a *"stereotyped"* style in language whereby a writer relies upon word choices and word arrangements which for him are "the most familiar, the most often practiced, the most expected."

> Following certain notions expressed by Hebb, the generalized, energizing effects of drive may be identified with arousal of a neural system in the brainstem from which there is diffuse, nonspecific projection into the cortex, these impulses having a facilitative, "tuning-up" function. Assuming, with Hull and Spence, a multiplicative relation between habit strength and drive in producing reaction potential, the effect of increased drive, including encoding behavior, should become more *stereotyped*— the alternatives selected at all choice points should tend to be the most familiar, the most often practiced, the most expected.[80]

For oral presentations, Turner clearly had established his stereotyped style, and certain techniques for eloquence *were* thoroughly familiar to him and the most predictable language responses in an event calling for rhetorical discourse.

Just as Turner's style was the product of constraints operative upon him so too was the substance of the frontier thesis. To understand better the constraints influencing the content of the statement which evolved during those last minute compositional efforts on the train and very likely in his Chicago room, consider the opportunity to present that paper in the context of a what can be called a "rhetorical situation."[81] In this case, an important facet of the event is an *"exigence"* or "an imperfection marked by urgency; it is a defect, an obstacle, something waiting to be done, a thing which is other than it should be....An exigence is rhetorical when it is capable of positive modification and when positive modification requires discourse or can be assisted by discourse."[82] In the summer of 1893, the discourse created by the young historian from Wisconsin was intended to modify attitudes in a rather specific way.

In terms of those who heard Turner on the evening of 12 July 1893 as well as those who would later read his treatise, the American Historical Association was an audience described by

43

Billington as having a widespread preconceived "Germanic germ" notion of the essential movement of American history.

> Historians of that generation stood almost solidly behind the "germ" theory to explain the genesis of their nation's institutions. Each had evolved from an English institution, and beyond that from its "germ" in the forests of medieval Germany; this was demonstrably true because comparisons revealed unmistakable similarities with ancient Teutonic practices that were sure proof of common origins. To suggest, as Turner did, that this was untrue, and that American customs were shaped by contact with the wilderness no less than by inheritance from a medieval brotherhood flew in the face of tradition, logic, and common sense.[83]

The exigency created by Turner's different philosophical basis led him to seek a well delineated response from the 200 or so members of the immediate audience and the profession at large: more study and research into the distinctly American frontier factors that influenced national history and development. After a brief reference to the census of 1890, that theme is stated emphatically in the introductory remarks, and it is repeated fourteen times in references to specific facets of the frontier that should be studied. In an autobiographical statement twenty-nine years later, Turner could still say in retrospect that his 1893 paper was in some degree "a protest against eastern neglect, at the time, of institutional study of the West.[84] And perhaps thinking about the repetitiveness in that discourse, the historian also admitted around the same time, "the truth is that I found it necessary to hammer pretty hard and pretty steadily in the frontier idea to 'get it in'."[85]

Ample reason existed to acknowledge his working so hard rhetorically in 1893. Overcoming the "germ theory" conception of American history was a rhetorical exigence of prodigious scope. For along with the "slavery" thesis of Hermann Von Holst and James Ford Rhodes, the Germanic "germ" concept of transplanted medieval institutions dominated historical thought and research among historians at the more prestigious eastern universities. No wonder Turner received little acclaim from his immediate audience that evening. After listening to five lengthy addresses on the program that hot night in July, the 200 or so historians in attendance at Chicago responded only with "the bored indifference normally shown a young instructor from a backwater college reading his first professional paper"; and according to the memory of one person in the audience, the paper provoked no discussion whatsoever.[86]

Turner must have experienced a feeling of deep disappointment. After all, he was accustomed to success in rhetorical endeavors—and resultant praise. He found neither in Chicago. Admittedly, we do not know for certain what, specifically, Turner read to his audience on the evening of 12 July 1893. Fifth on the program, Turner's presentation followed George Kriehn on "English Popular Uprisings of the Middle Ages," George P. Fisher on "The Social Compact and Mr. Jefferson's Adoption of It," Jesse Macy on "The Relation of History to Politics," and Reuben Gold Thwaites on "Early Lead Mining in Illinois and Wisconsin."[87] Surely Turner did not read the entire thirty-eight page paper which we now know as the frontier thesis. Considering the heat, the hour, and the length of the program already, he most likely only summarized the statement with excerpts from it. Whatever he did choose to say, however, had no impact. For although the *Chicago Tribune* described the papers in this session as "interesting," the reporter covering the event decided that only George Kriehn's presentation was worthy of being summarized in two paragraphs. Other speakers and topics were mentioned just by name and title. Thus, the man accustomed to rave reviews for his rhetorical efforts had to be content with this newspaper reaction: "Prof. J. F. Turner concluded the evening's program with a paper entitled 'The Significance of the Frontier in American History'."[88]

During the next days, weeks, and months, Turner could find no solace in any other reactions to his efforts that night. The official report of the Congress for *The Dial* and *The Independent* did not mention "The Significance of the Frontier in American History" (although Thwaites' discussion of lead mining in Wisconsin was praised). University of Wisconsin President Charles Kendell Adams most likely was in the audience that night but was not motivated to mention the paper five days later when writing a letter about Turner's qualifications as an historian. In a newspaper account of the trip to Chicago two days after the event, Turner's father described how his son was an admirable guide to the fair—but did not mention the paper. And even back at the University of Wisconsin, three months later, the student newspaper analyzed the effects of the Columbian Exposition on historical writing. Turner's paper was not mentioned.[89] Surely Turner was disheartened.

After the paper's first publication in 1894, reactions still must have been disappointing to Turner. He had presented the paper in December 1893 to the annual meeting of the State Historical Society of Wisconsin, and the Society published the essay early in 1894 in its proceedings. In 1894, the American Historical Association also published the essay, and Turner purchased reprints which he sent far and wide among the profession. After assessing the trends in the letters which Turner received in response, Billington epitomizes those reactions in the main as "less-than-enthusiastic."[90] The primary reason is self-evident. In its substance, Turner's essay advanced an interpretation of American history counter to the two most-widely held views at that time. As Billington rightly observes, "new ideas displace old ideas only slowly; man is a conservative creature and changes his mind as reluctantly as he changes his living patterns."[91]

All of this changed, however. And initial negative response in and after Chicago contrasted sharply with the ultimate positive reaction nationally. After those first publications in 1894, "The Significance of the Frontier in American History" appeared over the years in several anthologies and then as Chapter One of Turner's 1920 book, *The Frontier in American History*.[92] By 1921, Charles A. Beard lauded its "immense and salutary" influence: "In the literature of American History there is perhaps no essay or article more often cited or quoted than Professor Turner's."[93] While some historians achieved prominence during the 1930s and 1940s with anti-Turner critiques, most scholars again accepted his basic premise by the 1950s; and Turner's influence upon American historical thought is now generally admitted.[94] Certainly some degree of the early acceptance of Turner's outlook coincided with a then-developing science of evolutionary human geography which viewed social organisms adapting biologically to environment.[95] But as the conceptual integrity of the 1893 statement became more and more apparent, an ever-increasing number of Turnerian disciples did devote themselves to "respectable" research in areas identified by the frontier thesis.[96] Indeed, during the period between 1910 and the Great Depression of the 1930s, that statement of outlook about the course of research "dominated the profession so completely that the American Historical Association was branded one great Turner-verein."[97] So Frederick Jackson Turner ultimately achieved his intended impact upon historiography and historians.

But other people read the frontier thesis. In its many reprintings, and particularly as chapter one of his 1920 book, Turner's statement came before college students and people in public life, businessmen and housewives—in short, all the elements of a mass public readership whose attitudes are the bases of a national psychology. What were the effects of Turner's rhetorical prowess upon them? And to what discrete facets of his eloquence can that impact be attributed?

## III. The Influence of Turner's Eloquence upon the Public Mind

THINK OF THE frontier thesis as an oration. For "The Significance of the Frontier in American History" *is* replete with language behaviors which are not nearly the scientific or epistemological usages that might be expected to predominate in scholarly, historical writing but rather more the hortatory or evocative elements typical of discourse with persuasive design.[98] And that rhetorical tone in the frontier thesis has caused consternation among historians to this day. Hofstadter, for instance, writes admonishingly of Turner's "vagueness," "imprecision," "overstatement," "obsessive grandeur," and "disposition to illustrate but not define."[99] Billington also finds fault with Turner's rhetorical tone. As a statement to academicians, the frontier thesis was sparse in its evidence but full of exaggeration and inexact terminology. Reacting with suspicion to Turner's "lack of caution in defining terms or stating principles," professional peers finally did accept the content but remained steadfast in rejecting the form of the statement; for in Billington's assessment, Turner's "assertions were too positive, his generalizations too sweeping, to convince historians who regarded themselves as exact scientists."[100] In short, historians have perceived the form of the frontier thesis as more appropriate for oratory.

Considering Turner's background, however, that oratorical tone might be expected. After all, he had concluded as early as 1888 that rhetorical elements *were* appropriate in papers presented before the American Historical Association.[101] So when he wrote under pressure at the last minute, to complete his paper for presentation at Chicago in 1893, Turner had a personal justification for incorporating rhetorical formats for his language which he learned from Robert M. La Follette. Thus, the frontier thesis came to have a style, verbal behaviors more reflective of a writer's individualistic syntax and lexicon rather than the customary and familiar idiom for that person's language system.[102] As departures from idiomatic norms, those language options reflect the unique, individual imprint of the creator of that discourse—even if that writer indeed was only emulating the style in language of some other person.

A close reading of the frontier thesis discloses a La Follettesque style. Reflecting rhetorical predispositions, Turner lapses easily into alliterative sequences such as "*t*raders and *t*rappers," "*f*locks or *f*urs," "*i*deas and *i*nstitutions," and "*d*ecade to *d*ecade *d*istinct a*d*vances." The discourse also tends to rely on a repeated alliterative pairing of *s*avagery and *c*ivilization, perhaps reflecting his father's continued editorial condemnation in the *Wisconsin State Register* of "savages" who massacred innocent settlers as well as drunken, "worthless savages" who alarmed women and generally menaced life and property in Portage (as an impressionable twelve year old, Turner would see troops arrive in Portage in early 1873 to remove forcibly the nearby "savages" to a Nebraska reservation).[103]

Parallel repetitions are prominent, too, usually repeating the same word or words uncommonly at the beginnings of successive phrases or short sentences (and often in twos). Turner characteristically develops rhetorical parallelism: "*to the changes* of an expanding people...*to the changes* involved in crossing a con-

tinent"; "*Stand at* Cumberland Gap....*Stand at* South Pass...";
"*The exploitation of* the beasts...*the exploitation of* the grasses...*the
exploitation of* the virgin soil..."; and "*It was western* New York...*it
was western* Virginia....*" Several instances of such parallel repetition are discernible in "Problems in American History" which
Turner published in 1892; and almost as further evidence of his
tendency to utilize extracts from previously written manuscripts,
these particular passages tend to be carried over virtually intact
to the 1893 address.[104]

By far, a salient source of style in the frontier thesis is antithesis. Consistently, Turner seems to use antitheses to phrase his
main theme or application for the audience initially and, then, to
amplify his ideas for readers or listeners.[105] To a certain extent,
what Turner wrote in 1892 as "Problems in American History" is
somewhat antithetical in the relatively longer passage which sets
forth the essay's theme:

> The true point of view in the history of this nation *is not the Atlan-
> tic Coast; it is the Mississippi Valley.* The struggle over slavery is a
> most important incident in our history, but it will be seen, as the
> meaning of events unfolds, that the real lines of American devel-
> opment, the forces dominating our character, are to be studied in
> the history of westward expansion.
>
> In a sense, American history up to our own day has been colo-
> nial history, the colonization of the Great West. This ever retreat-
> ing frontier of free land is the key to American development. The
> work of the historian of the United States is to account for the
> predominant characteristics of the United States of today, by
> comparative and genetic study; *to enable the present age to understand
> itself by understanding its development from the past.* To state this is to
> show the inadequacy of our histories. American history needs a
> connected and unified account of the progress of civilization
> across this continent, with the attendant results. Until such a
> work is furnished we shall have no real national self-conscious-
> ness; when it is done, the significance of the discovery made by
> Columbus will begin to appear.[106]

In the frontier thesis, however, that theme is articulated far more
succinctly and antithetically: "Our early history is the study of
*European germs* developing in an *American environment. Too exclusive*

attention has been paid by institutional students to the *Germanic origins, too little* to the *American factors.*" The influence of the frontier upon the arriving European is immediately illustrated with two antitheses: "It takes him from the *railroad car* and puts him in the *birch canoe.* It strips off *the garments of civilization* and arrays him in *the hunting shirt and the moccasin.*"

Much of the amplification in the address is developed similarly. For instance, "the West was not content with bringing the *farm to the factory*...tariffs were passed, with the cry of bringing the *factory to the farm.*" Forty-seven antitheses develop within single or successive sentences such juxtapositions as those between "*slender paths of aboriginal intercourse*" and "*complex mazes of modern commercial lines*"; "*good*" and "*evil*"; "*dangers*" and "*benefits*"; "*primitive*" and "*developed*"; "*bonds of custom*" and "*unrestraint*"; as well as a repeated antithesis between "*savagery*" and "*civilization.*"[107] Even while quoting others for amplification, Turner favors the well-turned antithetical phrase. He relied on Lamar: "In 1789 *the states were the creators of the federal government*; in 1861 *the federal government was the creator of a large majority of the states.*" There is the familiar line from Lincoln that "this government cannot endure permanently half *slave* and half *free.* It will become *all of one thing, or all of the other.*" There is also an extended illustration about the difference "between a *talking* and a *working* politician."

So the La Follettesque style which Turner emulated as an undergraduate in 1879 is evident in 1893 as he addressed the American Historical Association. And that eloquent style was unchanged throughout the many reprintings of the essay, including its incorporation as Chapter One of Turner's 1920 book, *The Frontier in American History.* No wonder, perhaps that Charles Beard's review of the book concluded this way about the frontier thesis chapter: "of its thirty-eight pages fully one-half are narrative and descriptive, and bear on the main theme only by way of illustration."[108] An evocative or hortatory tone did prevail in the discourse. And that rhetorical style complements Turner's persuasive introduction and conclusion. For the address begins by establishing a sense of timeliness (if not urgency) by delineating an epochal moment.

In a recent bulletin of the superintendent of the census for 1890 appear these significant words: "Up to and including 1880 the country had a frontier of settlement, but at present the unsettled area has been so broken into by isolated bodies of settlement that there can hardly be said to be a frontier line. In the discussion of its extent, its westward movement, etc., it cannot, therefore, any longer have a place in the census reports." This brief official statement marks the closing of a great historic movement.

Similarly, the final sentence of Turner's peroration re-emphasizes the arrival at that same pivotal point in our development: "And now, four centuries from the discovery of America, at the end of a hundred years of life under the Constitution, the frontier has gone, and with its going has closed the first period of American history."

Reacting in retrospect to those rhetorical elements, Daniel Boorstin acknowledged Turner's "historical skill and poetic imagination" and pessimistically pronounced the frontier thesis "more an autopsy than an anatomy of our institutions." For while the 1893 statement was "a declaration of the uniqueness of the American past," it "was equally a prophecy of a lack of uniqueness in the American future." After all, the critical factor which made the history of the United States different from that of Europe was "disappearing," was "ceasing to exist." And as if to clarify this pessimistic reading of the frontier thesis, Boorstin quotes that last sentence of Turner's oratorical peroration: "And now, four centuries from the discovery of America, at the end of a hundred years of life under the Constitution, the frontier has gone, and with its going has closed the first period of American history."[109] Also reacting in retrospect to that hortatory or evocative tone, David Noble called the frontier thesis a Jeremiad; and Turner (along with some other American historians since 1830) was a Jeremiah. Like Puritan theologians of the second half of the seventeenth century, Turner "accepted the burden of warning the people" who would stray from the "purity and simplicity" of the New World and thereby return this society to the tragic vicissitudes of life characterizing Europe of the Old World.[110] To Noble, any historian in this context was a "political theorist" who warned his readers of those "alien forces" which jeopardized their

51

well being and then attempted to rally them in support of those "real" values by which they might preserve their presumed progress toward a better life.[111] In essence, therefore, some historians like Noble and Boorstin have read into (or out of) the frontier thesis a meaning quite in addition to Turner's argument about a desired new direction in historical research; and in reactions such as these, our later intellectual historians perceive an essential pessimism in what was originally that address to the American Historical Association in 1893.

Of course other historians, and most notably Ray A. Billington, have perceived an essential optimism prevailing in Turner's composition. After all, the people emerging triumphant from Promethean struggles against an untamed wilderness could be capable of coping with any other problems—even if bred in the crowded tensions of an industrialized, urban sprawl rather than a dark, impenetrable forest. As Billington epitomizes this reading of Turner, "the outstanding feature of the frontier thesis was the optimism" which "satisfied the need of Americans for a rose-tinted view of the future."[112] Clearly, Turner's discourse was more than a statement about historiography! So for all of the historian's efforts to repeat this motif, and even to delineate specific areas for research, another thematic element was present in the frontier thesis, one which in its ultimate effect became the rhetorical source of a mythic, national self-image among a mass readership.

Turner himself had alluded to such a possible rhetorical role of historical writing *before* he articulated his 1893 conception. Recall that while advocating a "connected and unified account of the progress of civilization across this continent, with the attendant results," his 1892 essay on "Problems in American History" also suggested that "until such a work is finished we shall have no real national self-consciousness." An end product of such scope, if achieved, would be essentially a persuasive myth created by discourse. Rarely is historical writing considered in this rhetorical context. But historians *are* potential persuaders. Like their counterparts in politics, for instance, many historians also adapt language rhetorically to achieve impact. After all, historians often have interpretations of events in which they would have their readers believe. And when, as Cushing Strout suggests, the public responds to such historical discourse "not only as a mode of understanding but also as a final destiny," we have a strong impetus to explore a rhetorical vehicle by which many Americans arrive at their "acceptance of the concrete world of human history as the source of ultimate values and fulfillment."[113]

And the conclusive, most compelling evidence about the popular myth created by the frontier thesis is not found in later, scholarly interpretations by historians (although some of Turner's professional peers do provide valuable insights and perspectives about public reactions to the concept's publications). The vividly meaningful indices of a national public's focus are in the multitude of letters written to Turner by typical readers and students in his own time, in the extensive newspaper reviews and editorials about Turner's conception as it was being published, and in the obituaries and letters to the family after the historian's death, wherein people gave their interpretations of what the frontier thesis meant to them personally and on an emotional level.[114]

A trend in those responses is unmistakable. Over and over, people responded to one specific thematic element in the frontier thesis. Indeed, they often pinpointed the precise two-sentence passage in which that theme was articulated. In the public reaction to Turner's discourse, the most persuasive statement was a characterization founded rhetorically upon a heaping of particulars about the attributes of the frontiersman (in more traditional rhetorical theory this technique was known as *Frequentatio, Symphoresis, Synonimia,* or *Sinathrismus*).[115] In one reviewer's interpretation of *The Frontier in American History,* for instance, that crucial passage was singled out this way: "The author's thesis is set forth in the following extract, which also shows something of the quality of his writing."[116] The single passage from Chapter One, which was Turner's original frontier thesis address, reads as follows:

> To the frontier the American intellect owes its striking characteristics. That coarseness and strength combined with acuteness and inquisitiveness; that practical, inventive turn of mind, quick to find expedients; that masterful grasp of material things, lacking in the artistic but powerful to effect great ends; that restless, ner-

vous energy, that dominant individualism, working for good and for evil, and withal that buoyancy and exuberance which comes with freedom—these are traits of the frontier, or traits called out elsewhere because of the existence of the frontier.

Other reviewers also quoted these lines as embodying the essence of the frontier thesis for Americans; and even for overtly commercial objectives, a five-page promotional statement from the National Book Buyers' Service had as one of two direct quotations from the book this exact same passage.[117]

Stylistically, this particular passage incorporates several variables of language which reflect Turner's concept of eloquence. To be sure, better balanced antitheses appear in other parts of the frontier thesis. Still, this portrayal has those between "good" and "evil," "lacking" but "powerful," as well as "coarseness and strength combined with acuteness and inquisitiveness." Far more prominent is stylistic parallelism evolving from rhetorical, like beginnings (*anaphora, epanaphora*): "*That* coarseness and strength...*that* practical inventive turn of mind...*that* masterful grasp...*that* dominant individualism...and withal *that* buoyancy and exuberance...." To complement that heaping of particulars about the character of the pioneer, several facets of Turner's sense of eloquence came into play in this one passage. Moreover, indices of the attention focused on this one statement suggest that for the general public these eighty-six words—in themselves and more than any others—epitomized the essence of the frontier thesis. A portrait of the pioneer came to be (in psychological terminology) a differentiated figure standing out from an undifferentiated ground.[118] Thus, what many people perceived as the central content of the paper had been influenced by "something of the quality of his writing."

Current critics of style recognize the "foregrounding" capability of uncommon, conformational devices rather than the more "automized" language of the common idiom.[119] But that basic concept of function has been with us since the earliest efforts of classical rhetoricians in the fourth century B.C. The original, Aristotelian rationale for utilizing "deviations from ordinary usage" was that people are "struck" by language which is "out of the way."

Words are like men; as we feel a difference between people from afar and our fellow townsmen, so it is with our feeling for language. And hence it is well to give the ordinary idiom an air of remoteness; the hearers are struck by what is out of the way, and like what strikes them.[120]

As Cope's well-known commentary has clarified this Aristotelian concept of stylistic effectiveness, the orator should create discourse in which language is divested of "its mean everyday commonplace character" so as to be "unusual, not familiar, novel, out of the common way."

> To alter or vary language, ἐξαλλάξαι, in this way invests it with a higher dignity; for we feel towards language just as we feel towards men; "familiarity breeds contempt" for the words we are constantly meeting in everyday intercourse, whilst "strangers" assume a higher importance and interest and dignity in our eyes. Hence we are to aim at a "strange" *i.e.* unusual, not familiar, novel, out of the common way, diction, ξένην ποιεῖν τήν διάλεκτον; people *admire* strangers whom they don't see every day, and "admiration" ( τό θαυμαδτον, "the marvelous," anything that excites our curiosity) is agreeable.[121]

Then, as a functional effect of an "uncommon" style which "strikes one as singular and unusual," the orator achieves the "novel" which forces itself "upon the attention."[122] As a prominent, classical dictum about style in discourse, this notion of functionalism easily might have been familiar to Turner during his undergraduate education at Wisconsin.

Contemporary terminology might clarify further the possible functional effect of Turner's style in the passage singled out by those reviewers. Perceptual psychologists know that attentional advantage is attained from novelty. As a stimulus attribute, novelty evolves from the interaction between expectations of a perceiver as reader or listener and the appearance of an unusual element which deviates from that expectancy. In short, the novel stimulus is one that "is not completely new; it consists of unfamiliar elements in a familiar context."[123] The pivotal element is identified by Dember as "*discrepancy*."

Novelty must be thought of in terms of an interaction between stimulus and perceiver. In particular, it is instructive to think of novelty as involving a *discrepancy* between the individual's expectancy about the stimulus and his present perception of that stimulus.[124]

Moreover, it is axiomatic that novelty is a factor of attention which is operative in man's perception of communication.[125] In the very processes of choosing and arranging words in discourse, a writer can create novel statements which are prepotent for being noticed and remembered.[126]

Within this frame of reference, reconsider those two sentences singled out by a popular reviewer as *the* eighty-six words in which Turner's "thesis is set forth." Recall that the passage contains antitheses. This stylistic conformation is not in the common idiom; people customarily do not write or speak in antitheses. For to do so, they must overcome psycholinguistic constraints favoring close placement of words associated by similarity in meanings.[127] In his desire to emulate La Follette and be eloquent himself, Turner mastered the technique of putting opposites instead in close proximity. When other people heard or read his words in that conformation, they were presented with a stimulus discrepant with their expectations—based upon their own, familiar usage—about how words are ordered in discourse. And if anyone should doubt the efficacy of antithesis as a novel conformation capable of influencing attention, this observation might be contemplated: literally millions of Americans did notice and *do* remember antitheses such as John F. Kennedy's "Ask not what your country can do for you—ask what you can do for your country" or Neil Armstrong's "One small step for man; one giant leap for mankind"—even though years have passed since many of those people last heard or read the statements. Admittedly, Turner's antitheses in that oft-quoted passage are subtle. Nowhere in these two sentences does he approach the balance and epigrammatic quality of a Kennedy, an Armstrong, or his own personal model, La Follette. So some other facet of style must have been responsible for the attention drawn to this passage.

Repetition is the more influential element. Yes, people do repeat in the common idiom. As a statistical probability, native users of the English language likely cannot utter a statement of ten to fifteen words in length without repeating one of them.[128] In terms of different words (types) appearing in a total number of words (tokens), a type-token-ratio of .90 to .93 describes the average and familiar—and hence expected—proximity of repetition in segments of the common idiom that are ten to fifteen words in length. As a numerical index of the syntactical proximity of repeated words, a type-token-ratio is derived by dividing the number of different words in a statement by the total number of words in that utterance. Thus, when one word is repeated out of a total of ten, as is likely in the common idiom, the nine types divided by ten tokens have a TTR of .90.[129] Of course a writer can manipulate arrangement for closer arrangement of repeated words, and the resultant TTR is lower than that of the common idiom. For instance, in Churchill's "so much owed by so many to so few," the nine tokens and seven types have a TTR of .78; in Lincoln's "government of the people, by the people, for the people," the ten tokens and six types have a TTR of .60.

Surely little evidence is required to substantiate the efficacy of such rhetorical repetitions for influencing attention. One example might serve to clarify the point, however. In its meaning, Franklin Roosevelt's First Inaugural conception was not unusual, nor were the specific words uncommon or discrepant with expectations—"but," "fear," "have," "itself," "nothing," "to," and "we." But he repeated one of those words in closer proximity than expected in the common idiom (*diaphora, epanodus,* or *traductio*); the result was a statement noticeable and memorable for millions of people: "We have nothing to fear but fear itself." So an orator—or a writer, for that matter—can influence attention through repetition when the very proximity of repeated words departs from the common idiom to be novel.[130]

Turner had such repetition in those two sentences singled out by reviewers as embodying the essence of his thesis. To complement whatever degree of attentional effect was attained by his subtle antitheses, Turner began successive phrases with "that" as he listed the positive attributes of the frontiersman. That *anaphora* or *epanaphora* in turn is complemented by the *traductio* of "...traits of the frontier, or traits called out elsewhere...."

This passage of eighty-six words embodies still another element of eloquence which utilizes novelty to influence attention. In the common idiom, speakers and writers tend to rely on sentence conformations that are relatively easy to construct. Formats which postpone utterance elements for a later than customary appearance impose a strain on memory; and rather than exert that additional effort, people are apt to avoid such suspensions.[131] One of the specific ways to achieve uncommon suspension is that of withholding a word or phrase with the greatest semantic signification until the end of a sentence; and as this conformation is recommended in traditional rhetorical theory, the speaker or writer precedes the withheld item with a step by step progression of words or phrases suggesting increasing importance (*auxesis* or *incrementum*).[132] This type of progression is evinced in Turner's ordering of attributes as he lists first those which are passive ("acuteness and inquisitiveness") or practical ("inventive...quick to find expedients") and then moves on to list those suggesting activity ("restless, nervous energy") and power ("masterful grasp," "powerful to effect great ends," and "dominant individualism"). The passage ends with an attribute suggestive of the greatest importance in this context, as heightened by Turner with an introductory modifier: "and withal that buoyancy and exuberance which comes from freedom" (notice too the alliterative quality of this segment with the repetition of *fr* and the initial and medial *b*). The more common way of ordering these character traits would reflect the axiom of syntax about "nearer the heart nearer the mouth," putting the most important first and adding the others subsequently. Turner was willing to exert the psychological effort necessary to postpone the most important to be the conclusion of a sequence. The result for Turner's writing is still another facet of eloquence.

So one particular passage of the frontier thesis incorporated several rhetorical techniques of style. These uncommon conformations of language are prominent among the recommendations by rhetoricians over the centuries; in the frontier thesis, these novel usages are the direct outgrowth of Turner's rhetorical education at the University of Wisconsin as well as his emulation of La Follette. And that eloquence did influence the attention of readers. According to reactions among and for the general public, these two stylized sentences, singled out as evincing "the quality of his writing," managed to achieve for Turner an effect known among contemporary theorists as the *"emphasis"* which conduces to a "significant influence upon the learning and remembering process."

> A general principle is that the stronger or more potent the stimulus, the greater impress it will make upon the responding person. The best omnibus word to describe this principle in operation is *emphasis*, the special stress or weight given to particular stimuli. In the communicative situation this means the emphasis given to particular stimulus units (whole arguments, propositional sentences, key words) by presenting them with special potency.[133]

What must be noted about these two sentences, however, is that they were *not* about historiography! For all of Turner's efforts to advocate a new direction for historical research, and even to specify fourteen types of studies which should be done, the public noticed another motif in the frontier thesis; and their attention to the characterization of the frontiersman was the cornerstone of the mass persuasion which ensued.

When contemporary persuasion theorists look at the process of influence through discourse, a sequence of reactions typically is delineated. In the paradigm offered by Hovland, Janis, and Kelley, persuasion is the sum product of "at least three different aspects of audience responsiveness which might be differentially affected" through discourse: attention to the verbal content of the communication; comprehension of the message of the communication; acceptance of the conclusions advocated by the communication.[134]

What remains here is to move as a critic beyond those reviewers' responses which suggest a focus of attention among the general public, for a fuller understanding of Turner's persuasive impact must consider as well what his readers then understood and accepted. Stated another way, from the perspective of communication theory, this examination of eloquence in the frontier thesis must answer questions about "the semantic problem" of what meanings indeed were evoked in readers as well as "the effectiveness problem" or how those meanings "affect conduct in the desired way."[135] In the case of Frederick Jackson Turner, however, the critical posture must be one of forsaking an appraisal of what people *should* have understood and accepted if they were epitomes of objectivity. By ignoring the chain of Turner's discursive argument about the desired direction of historical research, the general public tended to have a more intuitive, subjective response. And the vectors of those reactions demonstrate convincingly the nature of the mass persuasion achieved by the historian.

Turner's portrayal of the frontiersman struck the responsive chords in readers that can lead to the creation of a persuasive myth. Moreover, that myth seemed to imply a universality of application lending itself to the foundation of a national self-consciousness; for the rhetorically favorable reactions spanned two generations (at the least) as well as an ocean. As salient examples of the way in which their reactions resulted from this compositional element of portrayal, some people said the characterization made Turner's topic "a human sort of thing, rather than just a chronicle of events which happened on certain remote dates, hazy even in the imagination"; and by infusing "real life into the dead bones of a good deal of evidence which is coming to be heard," the paper "touched not merely on the historical, is not merely scientific in treatment and value, but has its element of romance as well."[136] Another critic saw the characterization as part of "an admirable account of the types of settlers in the various districts at various periods" in which "no incident seems to be too small to escape his scrutiny."[137] And some responses to Turner's portrayal of the frontiersman were as glowing as one which said that the "able discussions of men...had the flavor of Attic Salt and the grace of English from the well undefiled."[138]

Consistently, most readers responded positively to several attributes of the pioneer character delineated by Turner, such as cooperativeness, optimism, individualism, self-reliance, resiliency, steadfastness, neighborliness, confidence, wholesomeness, enthusiasm, calmness of purpose, or spirit of adventure.[139] A unique reaction even projected the virility of Turner's frontiersman:

> Far from the tumult of the elder world,
> Long hidden in the mists of untried seas,

Waited the western lady untamed and fair.

Then came each European breed to woo her.
Smiling she reached her open arms;
But like a beast, with tooth and claw
She rent and tore and gnashed, and laughed
To see her weakling lovers falter and recoil.
Rose then the elemental man,
Stripped of his European rags,
Naked and stark. And with bare hands
He seized her, spread over her broad bosom,
clutched mountain, plain, and valley, wood
    and stream.[140]

Still another character trait which impressed readers was initiative, as it flowed from the frontiersman's "unbounded confidence in his ability to make his dream come true."[141] One person so impressed was another historian, Carl Becker, whose review of Turner's book also quoted in its entirety the same two-sentence passage about pioneer character traits. In a brief paragraph interpreting that quotation, Becker himself repeated "initiative" in a positive context seven times![142] Clearly, Turner's portrayal called to mind personal attributes to which most people could react favorably.

Admittedly, not every response was positive. Some people altered Turner's characterization to reflect peculiar biases. For instance, when a Milwaukee reviewer restated Turner's crucial characterizing passage, he subtly omitted just one word, "coarseness."[143] While midwesterners might identify with all other attributes, some did not see themselves as coarse. A Bostonian saw the frontiersman as one who took "civilized ways with him into the wilds" and then "relapsed toward barbarianism."[144] Some other negative interpretations occurred among Turner's students at Harvard. After grading final examinations for Turner's History of the West, the graduate assistant for the course quoted from answers about how pioneer life produced "virtually anarchic individualism" and how "the dangers of Indian warfare brought the frontiersman to the verge of communism—and a little beyond it"; and in another student's notebook for that course, Turner's frontiersman was interpreted as one who "goes to his end without scruples leaving out more and more the moral phase and with a certain increasing element of coarseness."[145] As is so often the case in human responses to discourse, people perceived what they expected to perceive. In these instances, prior attitudes helped shape the meanings which were evoked in some of Turner's readers or listeners; and for those respondents, the resultant closures did not have a positive impact.

Despite these variant interpretations, however, Turner's portrayal of the pioneer more consistently *was* persuasive to most of his readers or listeners over the years. Think again of the frontier thesis as an oration which now can be analyzed critically (and profitably) through its projection of what Edwin Black has called a "second persona." This perspective assumes that "rhetorical discourses, either singly or cumulatively in a persuasive movement, will imply an auditor, and in most cases the implication will be sufficiently suggestive as to enable the critic to link this implied auditor to an ideology"; for we also can believe that respondents do "look to the discourse they are attending for cues that tell them how they are to view the world, even beyond the expressed concerns, the overt propositional sense, of the discourse."[146] So Turner's readership and audiences over the years likely would have responded to more than the discursive logic of his argument about historiography. Black avers that "what the critic can find projected by the discourse is the image of a man, and though that man may never find actual embodiment, it is still a man that the image is of"; and this second persona implied by a discourse in effect becomes "a model of what the rhetor would have his real auditor become."[147]

Surely the salient cue about the essence of that model was the character portrayal singled out by so many respondents to the frontier thesis. But that characterization was developed throughout a broader context of discourse incorporating an underlying hortatory or evocative tone created by Turner's rhetorical style. What remains is to move from the posture of a critic examining the manifest evidence of Turner's style and characterization to a consideration of how the human personality portrayed therein became what Black has called a "beckoning archetype."[148] For as Turner's readers and listeners over the years projected pioneer attributes into their own personal lives, they eschewed merely a general rose-tinted optimism and drew instead pragmatic conclusions about specific, practical applications. From a sociological perspective, then, the frontier thesis contributed to the creation of that kind of national self-consciousness which *is* a public's attitudinal basis of action for the future.

Whether it was in the 1890s or the 1930s or in between, those Americans who read the frontier thesis or heard Turner in class came to see pioneer attributes as applicable in a variety of real situations in their lives. In short, the frontier thesis projected a myth which came to be regarded by Turner's readers or listeners as *their* social reality. Recognizing a distinction between *"discursive logic"* and *"creative imagination,"* Ernest Bormann argues that *"language*, man's prime instrument of reason reflects his mythmaking tendency more than his rationalizing tendency." As if explaining how the general public overlooked Turner's argument about historiography, Bormann suggests that the more potent elements of discourse are those which contribute to fantasies and dramatizations which catch on and chain out in small groups to become, ultimately, the symbolic reality or "rhetorical vision" of a larger public. For in turn, those myths may "serve to sustain the members' sense of community, to impel them strongly to action (which raises the question of motivation), and to provide them with a social reality filled with heroes, villains, emotions, and attitudes."[149] As vividly portrayed by Turner, a national hero was delineated, one whose mythic character attributes were such that no difficulty was too great to overcome. For virtually any problem facing Americans, at any time, the best solution was emulation of the pioneer's way, as described by Turner. Of course that portrayal occurred initially at an opportune time. The depression of 1893-97 created a general mood of pessimism.[150] People sought images to emulate during that depression, specifically, but the attractiveness of the pioneer model behavior extended well beyond the 1890s.

Admittedly, some readers neither synthesized in their own minds nor verbalized the precise problems for which frontier ideals were so appropriate. Theodore Roosevelt, for instance, thought that Turner had "put into definite shape a good deal of

63

thought which has been floating around rather loosely," but he did not state the possible implications of pioneer attributes.[151] Other readers only could sense generally that the frontier thesis was "uplifting and timely," providing a "clearer view" of "the ideals of the true American"; and for 1896, Turner had "done the country a great service in publishing it at this time."[152] Reacting much later to a broadening notion that the pioneer's personal attributes were pertinent at any time of "stress and strain," another reader saw Turner's portrayal not only as having "meaning for the life of his own time" but for the "present and future life of America."[153]

Americans first applied Turner's frontier ideals to economic issues, reflecting the "stress and strain" of the depression during which the frontier thesis first appeared. Reacting to the "agitation and ferment of the silver problem before us," one 1890s commentator saw frontier ideals as "a constructive force of the highest significance in our life"; and subsequent 1920s reviewers perceived value in the pioneers' "cooperation in economic enterprises" as those principles might "deal effectively with the economic issues that have come forth in the last few years."[154] Indeed, as people perceived practical implications of the frontier thesis, the pioneer spirit of cooperation and "group consciousness" might be applied by a "new frontiersman" for "concerted political and economic action" in necessary "legislation against monopolies."[155] By the time of the Great Depression and the 1930s, such a frontier spirit of cooperation might counteract our "individualistic way of thinking" which made it so "difficult to secure social regulation of business enterprises that are essentially public."[156]

But the Turnerian ideal was used to argue either side of economic issues! For in the long run, Turner's readers came to reconcile "massive corporate organizations" with the "individual entrepreneur" as well as "Big Government" with the "cult of the log cabin."[157] They were able to do so, perhaps, because of growing realization, as expressed in a western newspaper, that many prominent captains of industry and corporate moguls were self-made men from frontier environments:

We hear a great deal about the man who comes West to make his fortune, but we do not hear so much about the man who has made his fortune or his career in the west going east to become a great figure in the world of affairs. One movement is as real and vital as the other. Harriman left the Illinois Central to go to New York; Hill went from St. Paul, Rockefeller from Ohio. The four biggest traffic men in Chicago are from the Pacific coast. The railroad world is run by men from the west. Ride along Fifth Avenue and listen to the guide as he tells off the names of the owners of the great palaces that line the richest residence street in the world. Take out a dozen old New York families, and what have you got left? Men who come from western oil fields or copper mines or steel plants or harvester works....They grew up in the west, they made their pile, and now they are laying down the law to Wall Street.[158]

One of Turner's students at Harvard may provide the most vivid example of such a closure on the part of someone among the general public reacting to the frontier thesis concept. After listening to Turner's portrayal of the individual drive and opportunism among frontiersmen, George Bell concluded that in the twentieth century, Daniel Boone would have been a "great captain of industry."[159] With the closing of the frontier as a geographical entity, there was relatively less and less opportunity to conquer the wilderness and carve out an empire as a spatial entity. In the twentieth century, however, as some of Turner's general public saw it, the same pioneer attributes could result in a different direction to people's energies: carving out an economic empire. The world of business might have its own unmapped elements of the unknown and risk. And to some interpreters of Turner, anyone overcoming those perils to become economically successful was a latter-day Daniel Boone.

Thus the frontier thesis seemed to offer people an arsenal of arguments for any side of the economic issues facing the country. The portrayal of the frontiersman could be on one hand a compelling argument justifying group or cooperative efforts against monopolies, for concerted political action was consonant in the minds of Turner's respondents with the pioneer spirit. And on the other hand, the initiative and power of the frontiersman "to effect great ends" was a natural channel for the accumulation of wealth through individual enterprise. In either case, however, the conclusions drawn by Turner's readers and listeners were pragmatic applications of the ideal portrayed in the frontier thesis.

Because economic issues are interwoven with politics, Turner's readers found other applications for frontier attributes of character. For the "present political unrest" in the 1890s, western ideals as "new forces" were clearly the desirable "trend of the times"; in the 1920s, people saw Turnerian models as alternatives to those "essentially communistic in their intent"; and pioneer attributes were even applicable in the spring of 1933 to the "great national emergencies, such as we have been going through during the past few weeks."[160] The interweaving of political and economic issues also was perceived by Turner's students, many of whom later taught history themselves and found "his treatment of the fundamentally social and economic nature of our politics to be clarifying and stimulating" for their own students.[161] And even after going on to occupy "responsible offices in government, business, and other affairs," many of Turner's former students still "dropped in on him for advice on their problems."[162] So the impact of Turner's conception upon his readers and students came as well from subsequent personal contacts which undoubtedly helped reinforce attitudes—if only by the growing stature of the historian.

Another important application of the frontier thesis occurred during World War I. As part of American propaganda and public information activities, a National Board for Historical Service had as one of its functions the indoctrination of those troops training to fight in France.[163] Turner had been involved at the outset with the National Board for Historical Service. Writing to Max Farrand under the Board's letterhead, Turner explained his view of this rhetorical role of history: "The underlying idea is that both in the matter of public opinion and national policy in respect to the war, and in regard to the American interests and principles respecting conditions on which peace may be made, American historians ought to have useful contributions to make...there is, in American habitual ideals much that needs enlightenment from men with the historical temper and historical point of view."[164] As this outlook was implemented by other historians in the actual indoctrination of troops, slide lectures often were utilized. In these, Turner's influence apparently came to be felt. For example, Edgar Robinson of Stanford deplored the fact that the presentations all too often focused primarily upon European factors; and recognizing that many of the troops had little formal education, he wrote of giving these men instead "the torch of the American frontiersman."

> It might be possible to tell them of the way in which this continent was peopled; of the work of the national government in the west; of the opportunities for individual development; to narrate to them how it has been that this government has come to stand for the things that it does; to show that American ideals have meant something in our life—say, in the period since 1900. Why not give these men the torch of the American frontiersman, instead of at this late date attempting to make a mass of Americans, citizens of the world in the European sense.[165]

So a portrayal of the pioneer and his ideal attributes could be viewed as well by Robinson as the foundation for "presenting adequate and accurate information to the masses" about the "meaning of the struggle." And if Turner's own assessment is accurate, applications of frontier ideals were pertinent not only in the armed forces but on the home-front as well; for the historian concluded that the pioneer's "ideals and deeds" were evident in the enthusiasm for the war, and its ensuing liberty bond purchases, which "flared up even more brightly in the West than in the East where it had its earliest manifestation."[166]

A wartime application of Turner's conception also was sensed in Europe. Recalling his own frontline experiences, the French High Commissioner to the United States, Louis Aubert, saw direct parallels between the trenches of France and the pioneer west:

> I will remember, when I was in the trenches over there how in order to find an analogy to the strange existence I was thrown into, I who had always lived in cities and whom war had surprised in a study, had to go back to a chapter of your historian F. J.

Turner in "The Significance of the Frontier in American History." Those trenches marked the farthest line of our civilizations—trails—paths—wagon roads—RRs—so in our turn we passed through the different stages of your frontier life.[167]

For some people actually in combat, then, the trenches of France were perceived as a latter generation's wilderness. And Aubert could foresee as well the direct relationship of pioneer ideals to the combat soldier's role: "Likewise I can safely predict that the qualities of your frontiersmen will come out in the sons of Illinois who are to fight in France."[168]

After the war, people even saw the frontier thesis as a source of their arguments about internationalism and the League of Nations. Faced with the problem of building an equitable and enduring peace, some Americans were alarmed about selling "our frontier ideals, all for a mess of pottage, in order to follow in the path marked by men who cannot really understand America"; and for them, the "conquest of a continent was certainly a healthier occupation for Americans than the social struggles and international entanglements of the present."[169] Just as on economic matters, though, Turner's thesis was applied to argue both sides of the internationalism issue. A New York City bank vice-president, for instance, implied that the national character shaped by our westward movement might counteract "the gentlemen who are trying to convince us that present day Americanism calls for a foresaking of all international cooperation and that it is almost un-American to favor the League of Nations."[170] As that banker epitomized his application of Turner's characterization of the frontiersman, "the American type and American ideal" were the rallying points behind which "we can muster a united nation in these days of international problems."[171]

Thus, for a wide range of concerns, Turner's portrayal of the pioneer came to represent a mythic ideal for most Americans. The frontier thesis provided a ubiquitous model for emulation by any reader who sensed a need to "apply the old spirit to modern life"; for as another of Turner's respondents put it, almost anyone could utilize pioneer attributes in "much of his contacts with people all his life."[172] The ubiquity of the frontiersman model was evident in another way, too. Turner was asked repeatedly to

68

make the frontier thesis easily available to a wider audience than that of his students and peers in the historical profession. Many people thought that the concept should be published in more popular vehicles reaching a wider readership than that of "technical journals," for example.[173]

Clearly Turner's mass readership for the most part perceived frontier attributes as ones they themselves possessed or certainly wanted to possess, particularly in times of need or stress and strain. By emulating the pioneer, Turner's readers might succeed in their endeavors as did the frontiersman in conquering the wilderness. In this way, the frontier thesis helped Americans to become what Michael McGee has called a "people"; for in contributing to the creation of a "social unity and collective identity," Turner's discourse was the vehicle for a rhetorical transaction in which "the audience, essentially a group of individuals, reacts with a desire to participate in that dramatic vision, to *become* 'the people' described by the advocate."[174] That participation of "the people" took a unique form, however. In more likely instances of providing "not a description of *reality*, but rather a political *myth*," McGee avers that the creator of discourse "warrants his argument with abundant examples."[175] This was not the case in the frontier thesis, though. Turner did not specify what his readers or listeners in the general public could do or should do in their own lives. Rather, the abundant, tempting examples of personal applications were created in the minds of Turner's respondents! And surely this form of participation is the more conclusive evidence demonstrating the rhetorical impact of the frontier thesis.

What remains is only to suggest the compelling quality of Turner's characterization. To what extent did that portrayal become a "beckoning archetype" in the national self-consciousness of the American people? As the most vivid example of this compelling quality, consider one person's feeling, as expressed to Turner, that the nation's children should have a "thorough appreciation of the great strength of the Americans of the past."

> Our boys and girls are growing up possessing wealth which their fathers and mothers did not. With this wealth has come false ideals. Your great work, it seems to me, has been to impress upon

our young people here the great work which their fathers accomplished. You gave them an insight into the true greatness of America and the true greatness of the West, which I believe no other man can do.[176]

Surely there can be no more beckoning an archetype than that which a people would hold up for emulation by their children.

## IV. Toward America's "Rhetorical Vision" of Itself

The frontier. Of all impelling forces determining the course of American history, perhaps none is regarded as so pervasively important as the westward movement and settlement of this continent. A dominant factor in our national heritage, the frontier is omnipresent in this country's popular culture. And so is our imaginative conception of this pioneer. Almost atavistically, our national self-consciousness responds favorably across a vast spectrum of activities ranging from children's playtime emulation of frontiersmen to their parents' political receptivity to John F. Kennedy's "New Frontier" catchwords.

Of course the mythic stereotype of the pioneer has been reinforced in the public mind over the decades by popular literature, so many motion pictures, and that almost steady diet of television programming incorporating western and pioneer motifs. Still, the potency of Turner's rhetorical role in that evolution of myth must be assessed, for his essay of 1892, "Problems in American History," in effect prophesied his intention as historian to provide Americans with a "real national self-consciousness."[177] Surely an intellectual awareness of the frontier's historical importance was a pivotal factor in that cultural development, and such understanding *was* created by a document which was the product of the mind and pen of one man: Frederick Jackson Turner and an 1893 address entitled "The Significance of the Frontier in American History." Therefore, final assessment here must be directed toward evaluating this historian's degree of *long-term* influence not upon historiography but rather upon our country's national psychology. From perspectives offered by theories of persuasion and the mass media, consider now Turner and the persuasiveness of his image or *ethos* as a person and the effectiveness emanating from his hierarchical position within a process known as the two-step flow of communication. For any final analysis of Turner's impact must acknowledge the fact that his eloquent discourse was not the only statement being made about the frontier and frontiersman attributes. Why, then, were his words particularly influential over the longer span of time?

While delineating the sources of rhetorical effectiveness, Aristotle extolled the functional role of *ethos* or the perceived, favorable image of the persuader's character. In the Aristotelian paradigm, "the character of the speaker is a cause of persuasion when the speech is so uttered as to make him worthy of belief"; and Aristotle went on to categorize this factor of *ethos* as "the most potent of all the means to persuasion."[178] Specifically, his *Rhetoric* identified three dimensions of an image conducing to belief, for *ethos* is operative when an audience perceives a persuader as possessing knowledge or sagacity, high moral character, and good will (in that the persuader has no ulterior motive or personal gain but only the best interests of readers or listeners at heart).[179] In contemporary studies, the word *ethos* is used interchangeably with credibility or source credibility; and the potency of this factor is still acknowledged as being just as important in the process of persuasion. Now, however, the three Aristotelian dimensions of *ethos* tend to be subsumed under two headings as competence and trustworthiness, and recent research has isolated other factors contributing to credibility (albeit their function in persuasion is subject to far more variance, depending on the situation). Among the latter are similarity and dynamism; for in some contexts, a persuader's message may be more credible simply because that person is perceived by an audience as being similar in values and attitudes as well as being moderately active and dynamic. Finally, persuasion theory typically makes a distinction between intrinsic *ethos*, or the image created during an event by interaction of the persuader and message content, and extrinsic *ethos*, or the prior image brought to an event because of the persuader's credibility before readers or listeners react to the message (and prior *ethos* may be the more influential of the two).[180]

In a rhetorical analysis accounting for sources of persuasiveness in the frontier thesis, Turner's *ethos* undoubtedly was a factor. For example, several readers reacting positively to Turner admitted that they were familiar with similar statements being made by other people. The observation of Theodore Roosevelt in 1894 surely suggests this likelihood:

> I have been greatly interested in your pamphlet, "On the Frontier." It comes at *the* right time for me, for I intend to make use of it in writing the third volume of my "Winning of the West," of course making full acknowledgment. I think you have struck some first class ideas, and have put into definite shape a good deal of thought which has been floating around rather loosely.[181]

A similar reaction in 1894 held that Turner's statement was "not merely valuable but it is interesting" in contrast to "a good deal of the evidence which is coming to be heard."[182]

Those people responding to Turner in the latter 1890s could have been reading as well among a wide range of "evidence" or "thought which has been floating around rather loosely." One such work might have been Josiah Strong's *Our Country: Its Possible Future and Its Present Crisis*. Published in 1885, the Reverend Strong's book began (as did the frontier thesis) by identifying an epochal moment.

> There are certain great focal points of history toward which the lines of past progress have converged, and from which have radiated the molding influences of the future. Such was the Incarnation, such was the German Reformation of the sixteenth century, and such are the *closing years of the nineteenth century*, second in importance to that only which must always remain first; viz., the birth of Christ.
>
> Many are not aware that we are living in extraordinary times. Few suppose that these years of peaceful prosperity, in which we are quietly developing a continent, are the pivot on which is turning the nation's future. And fewer still imagine that the destinies of mankind, for centuries to come, can be seriously affected, much less determined, by the men of this generation in the United States....It is proposed in the following pages to show that such dependence of the world's future on this generation of America is not only credible, but in the highest degree probable.[183]

Strong then went on to expound upon the resources of the West and its people, but his treatise takes on the tone of a diatribe—against immigration, Roman Catholicism, Mormanism, intemperance, socialism, mammonism, and the city as a "menace to our civilization."[184] Praise of the pioneer is in the book, particularly as the early settlers were Anglo-Saxons, for "there can be no reasonable doubt that North America is to be the great home of the Anglo-Saxon, the principal seat of his power, the center of his life and influence."[185] But there is no mistaking the final, persuasive thrust of Strong's appeal: the readers of the book should "be persuaded to make the principle of Christian giving regnant in their lives."[186] Thus, the persuader's goal, as such, is known to the readership.

This was not the case for Turner's readership among the general public. His praise of the pioneer could not be linked to some ulterior motive or personal gain. Indeed, the passage so persuasive to many readers even might be viewed as incidental to an argument about a desired direction of historical research in this country; they need not be on their guard; and Turner might project to some small degree that dimension of *ethos* known as good will. Turner's title in those early years might have been conducive to projecting as well a minute measure of the competence dimension of *ethos*. Surely some of his readers could have attributed knowledge or sagacity to a writer who was a "professor" at the University of Wisconsin. Nevertheless, Turner likely was not able to capitalize in the late 1890s upon a prior image or extrinsic *ethos* evolving from his title and position at the University of Wisconsin. The school did not have the stature yet—nor did Turner himself. Within the frontier thesis, however, Turner's portrayal of the pioneer well could have worked in another, specific way to his advantage in creating the *ethos* so instrumental in persuasion.

In those two sentences synthesizing frontiersman attributes, Turner was praising pioneer dynamism. In his use of stylistically derived climax (*auxesis* or *incrementum*), the historian successively heightened the importance of the words "quick," "masterful," "powerful," "energy," "dominant," and "withal that bouyancy and exuberance which comes with freedom." In so doing, he helped build his *ethos* by praising attributes which his readers held in high regard. Thus, Turner was saying, in effect, "I am similar to you because I share your values." More important than projecting similarity, perhaps, praise of those attributes projected for Turner himself an image of dynamism. Writing in overview of studies dealing with dynamism and credibility, Bettinghaus has argued that this dimension of *ethos* is "a meaningful factor that receivers use in judging message sources."

> The majority of receivers...seem to judge the credibility of a communicator, in part, by the appearance he makes as either a dynamic or undynamic person. A source rated high on the dynamism factor would be described as aggressive, emphatic, frank, forceful, bold, active, energetic, and fast.[187]

Although he undoubtedly evinced dynamism in his voice and body during delivery of his speeches and lectures, Turner also projected this dimension of *ethos* through his writing.

Reacting to the frontier thesis over the years, reviewers and popular readers often indicated that Turner himself personified the dynamic pioneer about whom he wrote; and those respondents leave no doubt that such an impression of Turner's character came from the words of his which they read. One reviewer thought *The Frontier in American History* "breathes the spirit of adventure"; and another reviewer suggested that the "commanding and charming style" of that book led directly to this impression about Turner as an individual: "No reader of the book can doubt that the author himself typifies 'the courageous creative American spirit' which is necessarily the main theme."[188] During his career, people perceived Turner as personifying "the highest ideals of American manhood"; and at his death, the historian was remembered as "the very spirit of the manifest destiny which so intrigued him."[189] And reacting to both the classroom teacher and the writer, fellow historian Samuel Eliot Morison recalled Turner as a man of "vigor and forthrightness."[190] So Frederick Jackson Turner did project dynamism, and this factor of *ethos* could have been operative during the early stages of his career when credibility was not being derived in large measure from professional stature as an historian.

As the years went by, however, the frontier thesis could be more credible and persuasive to Americans because its author was recognized more and more as highly competent to interpret accurately the importance of pioneer attributes. The knowledge and sagacity attributed to Turner constituted a dimension of *ethos* held in common by all historians—legitimacy. Almost sacrosanct in their public image, many prominent historians do have a credibility by which their writing is accepted, as Strout suggested, "not only as a mode of understanding but as a final destiny." Surely Turner was in this category. For with each successive year after initial publication of "The Significance of the Frontier in American History," Turner in his profession became more and more prominent in just that way. In turn, Turner became correspondingly more credible with his national readership. Certainly that credibility contributed to the ever increasing receptivity among a national readership to that historian's conception of the sources of our successes as a people.

This *ethos* or credibility has another subtle but pervasive implication for the historian as persuader. What college or high school readers of history would assume that the creator of that discourse has persuasive intentions? Who would suspect the historian's veracity? Of all modes of discourse, one most widely (and naively) thought to be free of bias is history. The general public reacts to historical discourse with an anticipatory set: concepts articulated therein constitute "truth" *because* they are in a history book. More sophisticated analysts know this is rarely the case. Historians interpret; they offer views about past events in which they would have their readers believe. Sometimes, those efforts to interpret the past are undertaken with deliberate intentions to persuade a readership, as might be the case when a textbook about our history is developed in ways to shape the attitudes among the young deemed desirable by a school board, or teacher, or state department of education. Still, these more blatant uses (or abuses) of history are not germane to the crucial point here. Essentially, *all* history shares a unique rhetorical advantage, even that written as the epitome of scholarly objectivity and detachment. In historical writing, the very medium is part of the message (to paraphrase Marshall McLuhan). Even to those who would eschew any hint of naivety on their parts, history is potentially persuasive simply because it is history.

Any prominent historian derives still another functional advantage from the very persuasiveness of the medium itself— that of hierarchical position amidst an entire mainstream of popular culture at a given point in time. In its portrayal of the pioneer, the frontier thesis did not provide Americans with any new description. Indeed, our popular culture for decades previous to 1893 had been replete with stories about frontiersmen (and women) and their positive attributes. As a nation, we were widely read about people such as Leatherstocking, "Old Hicks" the guide, various trappers and mountain men in David H. Coyner's *The Lost Trappers* (1847) and Emerson Bennett's *The Prairie Flower* (1849), as well as numerous heroes and heroines in countless dime novels—Seth Jones, Kirk Waltermyer, Pete Shafer, "Old Avalanche," Rowdy Kate, Nathan Todd, Henry Denton, Deadwood Dick, "Dove-Eye" Kate Robinette, Hurricane Nell, and Calamity Jane. In a comprehensive overview and analysis of such literary characterizations, Henry Nash Smith has noted that the numbers of these publications in circulation extend well into the hundreds of thousands and "almost baffle enumeration"; and equally important here is his conclusion that these fictional characters became "fixtures of American mythology."[191] And to complement all those stories about fictional, frontier characters, Americans also read countless fictionalized narratives about real frontiersmen; for prior to and after Turner's statement in 1893 this nation was reading widely about the exploits and presumed character traits of Daniel Boone, Davy Crockett, Kit Carson, and Buffalo Bill Cody, for example.

So in effect Turner was a corroborator. Actually, Smith argues that Turner was so influential primarily because his writing had "found an echo in ideas and attitudes already current" among the general public at the time the frontier thesis was being published.

> Brilliant and persuasive as Turner was, his contention that the frontier and the West had dominated American development could hardly have attained such universal acceptance if it had not found an echo in ideas and attitudes already current. Since the

enormous currency of the theory proves that it voices a massive and deeply-held conviction, the recent debate over what Turner actually meant and over the truth or falsity of his hypothesis is much more than a mere academic quibble. It concerns the image of themselves which many—perhaps most—Americans of the present day cherish, an image that defines what Americans think of their past, and therefore what they propose to make of themselves in the future.[192]

Obviously, the "universal acceptance" to which Smith refers is not one of Turner's views about historiography. That "massive and deeply held conviction" *is* about the high regard for frontier or pioneer attributes which we as a nation acquired from decades of mass communication through print media—and Frederick Jackson Turner held an unique advantage within that milieu.

Contemporary research has identified several causes of influence as masses of people react to discourse, whether presented via print or electronic media. One of these is a phenomenon of process known as "the two-step flow of communication." As synthesized by Klapper, this concept of persuasiveness suggests that people are "more crucially influenced in many matters by 'opinion leaders' than they are by mass communications"; and "although most studies of opinion leadership have to date focused on the leaders' role in producing change, there is good reason to postulate that they frequently exercise their influence in favor of constancy and reinforcement."[193] This process was delineated originally during the presidential campaigns of 1940 and 1948 by Lazarsfeld, Berelson, and Gaudet, who observed that "ideas often flow *from* radio and print *to* the opinion leaders and *from* them to the less active sections of the population."[194] An essential criterion for whether or not an individual does become a group's opinion leader, however, is that of similarity, for "opinion leaders and the people whom they influence are very much alike and typically belong to the same primary groups."[195] Because a group's opinion leader also is regarded as better informed about the matter at hand, another important criterion is pertinent knowledge.[196] Admittedly, in most cases of their influence, opinion leaders function through face-to-face personal contact.[197] But for the analysis of Turner's long-range persuasion, an assessment of influence must move beyond those relatively few people who read or heard the historian directly and consider as well those millions of Americans who were exposed only indirectly to his praise of the westering pioneer.

Frederick Jackson Turner easily fits within the paradigm of functions and effects summarized in Klapper's discussion of the "two-step flow of communication."[198] "To begin with, the opinion leader has been found, in many studies, to be a kind of super-representative of his group. Comparison of influentials in most of the areas thus far studied reveals that the leader is characteristically more competent, within his specialty, than are his fellows, and that he characteristically has access to wider sources of pertinent information." As an historian, with ever-increasing stature among his profession, Turner *was* capable of being regarded as more competent, with access to pertinent information. Furthermore, an opinion leader "is also typically found to be 'like everyone else, only slightly moreso' in reference to group norms"; and his "influence is related…to the *personification of certain values* of the group to which leader and follower belong." In his praise of pioneer attributes, Turner *was* like everyone else and more so because of the eloquence with which he could express himself; and responses to Turner suggest that he *was* perceived as personifying those ideals himself. And an opinion leader's "guidance seems to be sought or accepted in specific areas partly—or perhaps largely—because it provides his followers with the sort of satisfactions they seek in those areas." In their letters to Turner over the years, people suggest that he *was* providing guidance in areas where Americans could apply his thoughts directly. Finally, "regardless of the role they play in processes of *individual* opinion change, the influence of opinion leaders in reference to group norms is, theoretically at least, quite likely to be expended often in favor of reinforcement"; and this leadership "would seem to be reinforcing not only for the group, but for a considerable number of individuals as well." Clearly, Turner's characterization of frontiersmen *was* an authoritative, highly credible corroboration, or reinforcement, of what Americans had been reading for decades in their popular culture.

Of course this assessment of Turner's influence must acknowledge the fact that millions of Americans have never read the frontier thesis, nor have millions of people in this country ever heard of Frederick Jackson Turner. Writing in 1932, shortly after the historian's death, Joseph W. Schaefer lamented the fact that the "smaller newspapers of the country did not mention him."[199] "Undoubtedly this neglect can be justified," as Schaefer wrote, because "his name was unknown and meaningless to the average reader." So within the span of a generation after publication of *The Frontier in American History,* an observer could offer the reaction that "the man who contributed more...than any other thinker of his generation died last March at his home in California and the American public did not even know his name." An equally dismal fact is that now, two generations after Turner's death, even far fewer people have read the frontier thesis or know its author's name! But the concept as articulated by Turner still has power to persuade.

Discourse need not have been heard or read to exert influence. That is the clear understanding evolving from several studies in communication. For example, relatively few people heard Turner in person on 6 June 1900, when he delivered a Phi Beta Kappa address at the University of Minnesota. But more people who did not hear the statement nevertheless found out what he said. The next day, the *Minnesota Daily* carried a story about the event and summarized the essence of the address. Indeed, at one point the story quotes Turner in a virtually exact repetition of that two sentence passage which so captivated those readers of the frontier thesis itself:

> Western conditions have fostered individualism in American thought. The West is a field of opportunity where advantages are equal, where the man of keenest insight, quickest action and steadiest endeavor wins the prize. This free competition had a remarkable effect upon the intellectual character of the people in that it developed originality and rapidity of thought. It produced "coarseness and strength, combined with acuteness and inquisitiveness, a practical, inventive turn of mind, quick to find expedients, a masterful grasp of the material conditions of social well being, lacking in the artistic, but powerful to effect great ends, a strenuous will power, that compels his dreams to come

true—these are western intellectual qualities that have deeply influenced our national traits."[200]

The reporter covering the event apparently was not completely accurate in the summary, for the account has Turner saying that the pioneer was characterized by "calmness of purpose"—and dynamic Turner put a question mark next to that phrase in his copy of the story.[201] Nevertheless, the portrait of the frontiersman was passed on to people who did not attend the event. Surely some of those readers were opinion leaders in their own right who could disseminate further the essential idea. Such a "chaining out" of Turner's conception in this event and subsequent ones is quite likely, considering his own ever-increasing stature in the field.

The actual pervasiveness of messages which chain out in this way can be quite remarkable. In a classic instance during a sustained persuasion campaign in Taiwan about birth control, "three out of four acceptors of the advocated method...had had no contact with the official communicators (or field workers) and, by the end of the year in which the campaign occurred, a fourth of the acceptors came from areas not even reached directly by the formal campaign."[202] A more dramatic case of wide diffusion—with singular speed—is that of people learning about the death of John F. Kennedy. He was shot at 12:30 P.M. (C.S.T.) on 22 November 1963. Doctors announced his death 30 minutes later; and by that time, two out of every three adults in the United States knew of the shooting. Within five and one-half hours of the shooting, 99.8 per-cent of the people in this country knew about the tragedy—*but less than one-half of those people got their initial information from the news media.*[203] It is true that President Kennedy's assassination was a particularly unusual and tragic event, which certainly contributes to the extent and speed of diffusion. But any message with significance for people has some degree of potential for similar chaining out. Turner's statement as an opinion leader falls into this category.

Another point is pertinent now about the diffusion of Turner's eloquent statement to people who never heard or read him directly: some messages do chain out and retain *in actual wording* a close approximation of what was written originally. Admittedly, communication can be a highly fallible process in some situations, and we are familiar with a parlor game in which one person whispers a story to someone else who in turn whispers it to another person and so on. Then, we are amused at how the story has been distorted in transmission by the time it returns to the original sender. But in cases of important communication from prominent figures, the message can be passed on with a high degree of accuracy by readers or listeners, some of whom are opinion leaders in their own rights, to still wider audiences. In a case study of such "language-in-use," particular words used in President Lyndon Johnson's address of August 1964 (on the Gulf of Tonkin crisis) were found afterwards to recur frequently not only in media diffusion but in congressional speeches shortly thereafter and in institutional correspondence of union leaders and officials in veterans' groups. While demonstrating how "the density of key words found in institutional mail corresponds closely to Johnson's language," Cherwitz suggests that a public can take on someone's "biases through the acquisition of his vocabulary—a process analogous to the manner in which children learn attitudes and beliefs via their internalization of language"; and a "nation's internalization" of the "vocabulary and thesis" of discourse can play "a key role in guaranteeing" that kind of rhetorical success by which specific words can give wide publics "a set of prescribed roles and acceptable behaviors."[204] Turner's eloquence contributed to his potential for such effectiveness.

The preceding pages have presented perspectives from which Turner's long-term influence can be assessed. Within the framework of an aura of *ethos* or credibility—derived partly from the medium itself and partly from Turner's hierarchical position as an opinion leader in a two-step flow of communication—a pivotal element in the frontier thesis likely chained out to affect our national psychology, for a portrayal of the pioneer became salient in the public's mind after encountering "The Significance of the Frontier in American History"—whether directly or indirectly. People concluded that imitating the frontiersman could bring success in a wide range of endeavors from individual economic enterprise to governmental control of big business, from the waging of war to the making of peace. This is what our popular culture had been saying in effect for decades, and Turner provided an authoritative corroboration of that myth for Americans. But those people were not responding to Turner's explicit directives! Rather, the effect evolved intuitively from the compelling characterization in the frontier thesis. In this more subtle way, our past became prologue. People acquired a reinforcement of their viewpoint about the past after reading the historical writing of Frederick Jackson Turner, or reinforcement for them came through other opinion leaders who articulated Turner's words. The resultant strengthening of attitudes in turn became the basis for many of their subsequent behaviors, as individuals or collectively as a nation.

Looking in retrospect at these applications of Turner's theme, the people persuaded by the frontier thesis found in its implicit moral their solutions for solving not only personal problems but for approaching clearly defined national crises—like that of developing Americans' will to fight in World War I. Moreover, people applied frontier ideals as bases of stock arguments (commonplaces or *topoi*) to support various if not vastly differing points of view about other national issues such as our debate over entering the League of Nations or the appropriate means to counteract economic crises like the Great Depression. Almost invariably those Americans could reminisce afterward and be reinforced in their attitudes, for we as a nation ultimately seemed to meet successfully so many of those challenges during the early decades of the twentieth century. Thus, no matter what factors in actuality *were* the sources of our successes, people could conclude that those frontier virtues had played a part. In this way a myth was molded: the pioneers' way worked.

Emulation of the frontiersman, then, *was* a rhetorical effect of Turner's eloquence. Dramatic proof of that impact is in the form of primary source evidence supplied by frontier thesis readers themselves: reactions articulated in those many letters from students as well as the general public, to Turner directly or to the family upon his death. Complemented in those years by other responses in newspaper and periodical reviews of Turner's statement, that composite wealth of commentary reflects a public's attitude as it was molded and directed by the historian during his lifetime. The clear evidence is in the extensive Turner Collection at the Huntington Library. But what was the subsequent, longer-term rhetorical impact of Turner's eloquence? Recall the frontier thesis reader who concluded that the statement should be read by the next generation, "our boys and girls" growing up with "false ideals," who should return to and adopt the pioneers' guiding principles. Has the frontiersman indeed become a beckoning archetype? The Huntington's Turner Collection cannot answer that question conclusively, for the chain of evidence in it ends with Turner's death. The question nevertheless is pertinent for an understanding of the historian as persuader who would create what Turner called a "real national self-consciousness."

An answer to that question here must be anecdotal and hence suggestive, serving only to provoke further consideration on the part of others. Still, a trend is discernible. After the Great Depression, the next overwhelming crisis confronting this nation was World War II. Massive mobilization was needed—of material, men, and minds. Public sentiment at home, outraged initially by the attack on Pearl Harbor, had to be endowed with sufficient force and direction to sustain the sacrifices necessary to win the war. Servicemen needed to be persuaded about the righteousness of their cause and the evil of our enemies. In this broad propaganda campaign, motion pictures had an important function; and in Hollywood's treatment of World War II, the enduring quality of Turner's portrayal of the frontiersman becomes more evident.

Believing "the films of a nation reflect its mentality in a more direct way than other artistic media," Julian Smith has concluded that "the treatment of *war* in a nation's films provides a crucial index to popular concepts of patriotism, national purpose, and relationships with the rest of the world." After studying thirty years of American war films since *Sergeant York* in 1941, Smith argues convincingly that Hollywood's fighting man often is an allegorical portrayal of archetypal cowboys or westerners, wherein "strong, silent, lonely men ride in from the prairie, conquer their aversion to the use of weapons and, without profit to themselves, defend freedom-loving farmers against gangs bent on grabbing land and power...." Certainly this was true for John Wayne, one of Hollywood's most enduring stars, a "folk hero" and "the midwesterner who became frontiersman by dint of repetition"; for after starring in *Stagecoach*, Wayne played an archetypal role repeatedly in frontier epics, wearing U.S. cavalry blue in *Fort Apache*, *Rio Grande*, or *She Wore a Yellow Ribbon*, or civilian garb in *Chisum*, *True Grit*, or *The Searchers* (for examples). During World War II, though, he easily donned twentieth-century combat apparel—whether for land, sea, or air—in numerous films such as *Back to Bataan*, *Sands of Iwo Jima*, *They Were Expendable*, and *Flying Tigers*. Wayne's own company later made the *only* film directly about the Vietnam War *during* the conflict, and *The Green Berets* does have a frontier motif in presenting one view of our national purpose in Southeast Asia. A major episode depicted Viet Cong attacking a fortified hamlet whose defense perimeter and watchtowers resembled a frontier stockade fort with blockhouses. Arriving "air cavalry" repulsed the assault; and the film's dominant theme thereafter has star John Wayne converting a cynical newsman to the proper attitude about Vietnam. That basic if not simplistic outlook is epitomized by this quotation from John Wayne's son Michael, producer of *The Green Berets:* "...we're making a picture about a bunch of right guys...Cowboys and Indians....The Americans are the good guys and the Viet Cong are the bad guys...."[205] Hindsight says America did not accept so universally the pertinence of frontier ideals in the Vietnam War, but that this did happen for many people among the generation for whom World War II was the central if not cataclysmic event in their lives—even if they did not serve in the armed forces![206] As Henry Nash Smith traces the evolution of frontier myths after the demise of the dime novel, "the movies...have tidied up the morals, or at least the manners, of the genre, but plot construction and characterization follow an apparently unbreakable pattern."[207]

A generation later, sons and daughters of those Americans also responded favorably to a frontier theme. Although much of John F. Kennedy's political success was derived from the interplay of several factors, including an image of dynamism (particularly in the first and most influential of the televised debates with Richard M. Nixon), the "New Frontier" was a viable political catchphrase. As Kennedy's inaugural address articulated the notion, Americans could live up to the heritage of their "forebears" in so many military, social, and political endeavors, including those atavistically appealing to any 1960s pioneer who might "meet any hardship...explore the stars, conquer the deserts...." Many young people in particular responded eagerly to service abroad in the Peace Corps, leading a life as arduous as that of any frontiersman, albeit wielding textbooks or stethoscopes in lieu of axes or muskets.

As America moved on into the 1970s, the frontiersman image became implanted even more firmly in our national consciousness. Examining the societal predispositions so ubiquitous in our mass media, Larson reminds us that "every culture has its own myths and set of heroes who do things valued by that culture." In the latter half of the twentieth century, one of these cultural myths is what Larson calls the "wisdom of the rustic."

> One of the most pervasive images or legends in American literature, and one with great persuasive impact, is the belief in the common sense of the plain and uneducated but sincere and clever rustic, who because of his simplicity will win out in the end. No matter how devious or sophisticated the opposition, let the simple wisdom of the backwoods emerge, and truth will become clear. Numerous folk tales rely on this image—all of the Daniel Boone tales, the stories about the inventiveness of Paul Bunyan, and the incredible number of sage Lincoln stories. Even today, we have faith in the humble beginnings of persons when we look for leaders....As Americans we have a belief that humble beginnings and the world of obstacles and difficulty can teach even the most uneducated of us to be wise in a worldly way.
>
> Persuaders have repeatedly used the image, portraying themselves as rustics who have wisdom. There are obvious examples— Lincoln, George Wallace, the advertisements focusing on the cleverness of rustics (*e. g.*, Mrs. Olson, the Folger's lady; or Josephine, the lady plumber). Inculcated in these images are several cultural values and predispositions: a faith in common sense; a belief in the spontaneous and instinctive act (think of maxims like "trust your initial judgment"); and reliance on physical and mental prowess.[208]

85

Three generations after Turner's initial, synthesizing statement in 1893, a commentator on the American scene could articulate a characterization which comes so close to the historian's original praise of our "...strength combined with acuteness and inquisitiveness; that practical, inventive turn of mind, quick to find expedients; that masterful grasp of material things, lacking in the artistic but powerful to effect great ends...."

In this context, consider the presidential campaign of 1976. Jimmy Carter and his advisors could resurrect with confidence an image appealing to a fundamental value we seem to place upon the integrity and common-sense wisdom of the rugged individuals of our frontier heritage. For in the aftermath of Watergate, and our search for candor and credibility in the Presidency, simple honesty was *the* paramount dimension of an image to project to be elected in 1976. Although his background as businessman and naval engineer could have evinced aspects of what Turner called that "practical, inventive turn of mind," Carter relied on our attraction to the rustic presumably on an agrarian frontier. Furthermore, he did so in a way which no one could misinterpret, with television commercials showing the candidate dressed in denim jeans and work shirt, standing Lincolnesque next to a fence in a rural setting.[209]

As America ended the decade of the 1970s, some indicators suggested movement away from a faith in the frontiersman as a beckoning archetype. For as Turner depicted that person for us, the pioneer was an optimist with "buoyancy and exuberance." More than one observer at this time, however, has sensed some degree of pessimism creeping into our national consciousness. In more and more public commentary, the essence of the message is simply this: the American dream is ended. Some Americans feel that in this period, the perseverance of the pioneer no longer will pay off. Nor will the frontiersman's industry and initiative. Strained economically, many people no longer think in terms of added advantages for themselves and their children. Disappearing are dreams of another car, or a summer home at the shore, or sending sons and daughters away to expensive educations at private universities. A husband now works harder, and very likely so does his wife, to achieve the necessities of life.

The clear concomitant was a decreasing mobility in America of the latter 1970s. Among the most mobile people in the world, Americans heretofore tore up roots and moved readily at the prospect of gaining some advantage for a better life—whether across town or across the country. The average American family used to move every five or six years, but now the national impulse to change homes or locales is slowing down to the lowest rate in a generation. We certainly no longer live up to that frontier phenomenon observed by de Tocqueville in 1831, whereby typically the pioneer "settles in a place, which he soon afterwards leaves to carry his changeable belongings elsewhere." Rejecting a mobile lifestyle, Americans now are reluctant to move. The working wife might have to give up a vital source of income for the family (offsetting any raise attained by the husband's moving to a better job). Our families no longer are so eager to give up the recreational advantages of an area in which they live, reflecting a more introspective but appreciative view of quality of life *per se* rather than simply "getting ahead." And, unfortunately, the cost of finding comparable or better housing at the location of a new job is rarely possible—without wiping out any advantage gained by a raise in pay. The present inflationary trends in housing, also influence people to curb their impulses to move. They cannot afford it. We were a people ever looking optimistically toward the next move at the slightest prospect of a better life. Now, we are a more static society, seemingly a pessimistic antithesis of the pioneer portrayed eloquently by Frederick Jackson Turner.

Some still move, though, including college professors. In the halcyon days of higher education, university teachers moved easily and frequently. College enrollments were high because of the jump in the birth rate after World War II; federal monies were furnished lavishly to support higher education; and teaching jobs were plentiful. By the end of the 1970s, all that had changed. A university rarely filled a slot vacated by retirement with some relatively senior candidate when another fresh out of graduate school was less expensive to employ. Even the senior professor who did have an invitation to move weighed the alternative carefully, thinking about the tremendous increase in his cost for housing elsewhere. No wonder that any professor who did accept

another position might view the move as fraught with as much
difficulty as a frontier move. And a likelihood that just such a
feeling might have been present, at some level, is suggested by
this fact: to notify the *Chronicle of Higher Education* of a new
address to which his subscription should be sent, the professor
filled out and mailed in a form on which was a line drawing at the
top—of a pioneer's covered wagon.

Other indications suggest that the universality of Turner's
beckoning archetype is as viable as we begin the 1980s as before.
Some of these signs are subtle. For example, consider that in 1978
America's automobile manufacturers adapted to a clearly developing preference nationally for trucks rather than cars as personal
vehicles.

> In many sections of the nation today lightweight trucks are
> outselling passenger cars by a country mile. The popularity of
> vans, compact pickups, car-trucks, utility vehicles and conven-
> tional pickups has surged to the point that the two dominant truck
> makers, General Motor's Chevrolet Division and Ford Motor's
> Ford Division, are now selling more trucks than automobiles in
> numerous regions where car sales traditionally outpaced truck
> sales.[210]

As television commercials depict those trucks in action, American drivers will go off the road into the wilds with vehicles capable of fording streams, crossing barren deserts, and climbing
untracked, steep hills—all with a feeling of tough, dynamic go-
anywhere ruggedness. But, in actuality, for many of the buyers
at whom the commercials are aimed, the most awesome treks will
be those of only several miles on paved streets and highways to a
shopping center or country club! With the advent of the energy
crisis and soaring gasoline prices, television commercials changed
to emphasize the fuel economy of some of these trucks; and
Americans now have the option of buying small, subcompact
trucks to fill their needs. The preference remains patent, and a
national buying trend seems to suggest a latent readiness to pick
up and go with all the spirit of our frontier forebears—if only the
right opportunity should present itself.

Perhaps Americans of the late 1970s and early 1980s are no
different from their counterparts several decades earlier who

were observed by a *Washington Star* reviewer of Turner's book:

> The great popularity of summer camping—real roughing it, I mean, not the deluxe kind—is an indication that many people would be glad to drop out of the super civilized conditions in which we live and would like to have a part in the taming of the wilderness, much as our forefathers and our western near contemporaries of yesterday experienced.[211]

This was the same reviewer who thought that Turner's two-sentence portrayal of the pioneer set forth the "thesis" of *The Frontier in American History.* Certainly camping and several outdoor sports so popular reflect the present appeal of the "real roughing it" perceived in 1923 as evidence of our national longing for former, frontier experiences. Even the most perilous of those experiences still might be appealing, too, considering the empathic response many people had to a recent film called *Deliverance,* in which some urban, highly civilized men of the late 1970s attempted a camping-canoe trip down a wild Georgia river and met with dangers and death akin to any of the most fearful of experiences by our pioneer forefathers.

A more tangible (and pertinent) index of our latent pioneer outlook is in the responses to the 1978 publication of Frederick Merk's *History of the Westward Movement.* A student of Turner's at Wisconsin, Merk followed his mentor to Harvard, ultimately succeeding Turner as Harvard's premier lecturer on the history of the west ("Wagon Wheels" was the affectionate name given by students to Merk's course on the Western Movement). In one review of *History of the Westward Movement,* fellow historian Gordon Wood singled out for praise that book's emphasis on portrayal and characterization; for "people—particularly individuals doing concrete things—are everywhere in Merk's story."[212] Surely a tendency toward character portrayal could be expected in the historical writing of any of Turner's students. Remember how Turner not only praised that quality in the discourse of others but also required it of his students. What is far more important here, however, is the way in which that frontier characterization still is seen as the basis of a national model we can and should emulate.

Moving on into the decade of the 1980s, America is beset with problems of national magnitude, crises touching *directly* upon all our lives (unlike the Vietnam War). Environmental problems of one kind or another affect all parts of the country; other concerns are about energy and the economy, drugs and crime, overpopulation and mass transportation, adequate financing of education and deteriorating quality of living in the cities—any or all of which might be attributed to something called the modernization of our former way of life. In looking at these factors so salient in the day-to-day experiences of Americans, Wood argues that "our heightened sense of limits and depleted resources" provides the "context that makes Merk's book on the Westward Movement so timely." And Wood ventures another statement about pertinence: "this book based on a course that comes out of another time is in no way out of date....its publication now is more fitting to our times and our concerns than it would have been to those of two or three decades ago."[213]

The historical perspective contributing to that observation about timeliness surely was given some focus by Merk's explicit directive. In a final segment titled "Afterward," Merk reminds his present day readers that some people in the past "misread" Turner's frontier thesis, thinking the essay was saying that "the frontier in all its aspects had ended." No, counters Merk, our frontier still persists but in different domains. The very last three sentences of Merk's book state his own thesis about the pertinence of pioneer ideals in the here and now "to make things better for the future."

> Increasingly, however, the open frontier has become one in the realms of science and technology, of man's control over the environment, and of the relations of man to his fellow man. This is the frontier now challenging the national energies. The hope of the future is that all the optimism, all the indomitable will to overcome obstacles, all the love of freedom and of democratic process, and all the determination to make things better for the future, which the old frontier nourished and symbolized, will remain part of American thought and aspirations.[214]

Compare Merk's statement with that one passage from Turner which was singled out so often and so favorably:

90

> To the frontier the American intellect owes its striking charac-
> teristics. That coarseness and strength combined with acuteness
> and inquisitiveness; that practical, inventive turn of mind, quick
> to find expedients; that masterful grasp of material things, lacking
> in the artistic but powerful to effect great ends; that restless, ner-
> vous energy, that dominant individualism, working for good and
> for evil, and withal that buoyancy and exuberance which comes
> with freedom—these are traits of the frontier, or traits called out
> elsewhere because of the existence of the frontier.

The master's influence is evident.

In essence, Merk's concluding sentences are his version of a
rhetorical peroration, approximating in specific form and content
the eloquence of the frontier thesis itself. How fitting it is that to
help achieve a final, emphatic impression upon his readers Merk
relied upon the Turneresque mode of stylistic parallelism by repeating the same word at the beginnings of successive clauses, as
in "*of* man's control over the environment, and *of* the relations of
man to his fellow man." How like Turner as well to utilize for
emphasis that very same rhetorical heaping of particulars to
achieve a characterization (also relying upon a stylized, parallel
repetition): "The hope of the future is that *all the* optimism, *all the*
indomitable will to overcome obstacles, *all the* love of freedom
and of democratic process, and *all the* determination to make
things better for the future...." And how appropriate, too, that
the History Book Club's promotional statement about the book
should end with a quotation from that very passage. After all, the
very same pioneer portrayal was used successfully to promote
Turner's book, *The Frontier in American History,* fifty-eight years
earlier! The notion as phrased now by Merk must be as appealing
in 1978, for many people who requested the July 1978 History
Book Club selection of Merk's volume received instead an apol-
ogy. The organization was "doing everything possible to expedite
delivery" of *History of the Westward Movement,* but the shipments
would be delayed "*because of exceptional demand.*"[215]

This response is one more link in a chain of anecdote and evidence leading to an inescapable conclusion that Frederick Jackson
Turner's rhetorical prowess contributed to his goal of creating for
us a national self-consciousness. Only one more link might be

added with profit to this analytical chain. In effect, this present essay has traced Turner's impact upon our national attitudes and actions over several decades. To do so, people's responses to an eloquent statement were examined, and the progression of reaction since 1893 clearly is akin to an evolution of that earlier mentioned social reality which Bormann calls a "rhetorical vision." The frontier thesis portrayal did chain out persuasively among successively larger groups—ranging from statements in correspondence intended for one other person, to journal and newspaper interpretations aimed at wider audiences, and then to mass media dramatizations directed toward millions of Americans. And what happens now in the public speeches of Americans as they address their efforts to solving the problems of the everyday world of affairs? According to Bormann, a people's rhetorical vision of itself has "dramatic personae and typical plot lines that can be alluded to in all communication contexts and spark a response reminiscent of the original emotional chain"; and when a rhetorical situation does call for the generation of an emotional response, a speaker should be able to resurrect the dramatization, perhaps adapt it slightly for the different occasion, but nevertheless give voice however briefly "to what the listener already knows or feels and accepts."[216] A public speech cannot help but be persuasive, in a reinforcing way, when it in essence repeats what an audience wants to hear. Effective speakers know this; and to attain their objectives, they often incorporate and appeal to those rhetorical visions of their audiences—whether in terms of "a recollection of something that happened to the group in the *past* or a dream of what the group might do in the *future*."[217] Thus, current references in public discourse to applying frontier ideals could be regarded as a mode of rhetorical shorthand—intended to capitalize on the *already established*, mythic and still persuasive appeal of the pioneer as portrayed by Turner.

One poignant instance should be sufficient. Surely New York City and its people are beset with most of the serious problems stemming from our modernized life. Hardly a week went by in the late 1970s without some newspaper story or television coverage of a New York City event which epitomized our difficulties in "control over the environment, and of the relations of man to his fellow man," or as Merk also phrased it, "the frontier now challenging national energies." If Turner's original characterization still is as persuasive as before, the archetype should be a basis of rhetorical appeal in the discourse of New Yorkers as they seek ways, in Merk's words, "to make things better for the future." The archetype does appear.

In April of 1978, Princess Beatrix and Prince Claus of the Netherlands visited New York City. A reception for them was held at the Netherland Club of New York, a business and social organization for Dutch-Americans (celebrating its seventy-fifth anniversary). Mayor Edward Koch appeared on the program, and in his speech he took the opportunity afforded by the occasion to draw a meaningful analogy for his audience. Reminding those listeners of the city's financial problems, Koch predicted a return to the determined, pioneering spirit of the first Dutch settlers as they conquered the wilderness in 1625. Specifically, as a way of solving the problems of today, "we are going to bring back the same feeling we had in New Amsterdam."[218] The archetype still beckons.

Attributing this long chain of impact to one statement—perhaps even a single paragraph—by Turner may seem rash. After all, we know that on the one hand a people's attitudes and actions are molded by a matrix of message inputs, many of which are "scattered and unorganized" and in effect "overlayed" to form the large and complex communication world or "mosaic" in which each of us exists.

> This mosaic consists of an immense number of fragments or bits of information on an immense number of topics...scattered over time and space and modes of communication. Each individual must grasp from this mosaic those bits which serve his needs, must group them into message sets which are relevant for him at any given time, and within each message set must organize the bits and close the gaps between them in order to arrive at a coherent picture of the world to which he can respond.[219]

And every critic ought acknowledge the practical wisdom existing in the corallary observation that "any one communication encounter, or even a series of encounters by a single speaker or writer, accounts for only a small portion of the variance in human behavior."[220] Yet, consider this final interpretation of the rich, primary source evidence in the Huntington Library's Turner Collection. *He was indeed instrumental in the development of America's rhetorical vision of itself as a nation and as a people.* The many responses to Turner or reactions about his discourse demonstrate the extent to which people were persuaded directly by that compelling characterization of a pioneer in "The Significance of the Frontier in American History." To those Americans, that synthesis of attributes stood forth prominently as a well-defined, ideal concept of ourselves amid a mosaic of hazy recollections, literary allusions, and fragments of popular culture. To extend this interpretation with the terminology of perceptual psychology, the frontiersman became for the first time in our national consciousness a differentiated figure distinct against an undifferentiated ground.[221] That concept was credible, for it appeared in a mode of discourse widely respected for credibility, and it was articulated by an historian of ever-increasing stature. Moreover, the characterization undoubtedly was endowed with some additional measure of emphasis and ensuing memorability because of the rhetorical style with which Turner wrote.[222] Turner's was an eloquent statement with the greatest potential for chaining out to become a basis for America's rhetorical vision of itself now and for the future.

The origins of that rhetorically compelling characterization can be traced back through the historian's experiences to his days as an undergraduate at the University of Wisconsin. But Turner's predilection for portraiture was not a product of his coursework in history. For his undergraduate class notebooks essentially are impersonal lists only of dates, places, or treaties.[223] An affinity for characterization in discourse, expressed stylistically, had another, rhetorical genesis. Indeed, all of Turner's persuasive skill and stylistic prowess had a clearly defined model: the rhetorical artistry of Robert M. La Follette. Certainly the conclusive evidence is provided by Turner himself in his 1924 retirement speech to the Harvard History Club. For in summing up all the major influences upon his life, Frederick Jackson Turner prominently identified a speaker and an oration which he heard as a University of Wisconsin freshman in 1879: "La Follette—Iago."

Looking back at Turner's undergraduate experiences as an orator and persuader, this critic of his eloquence and impact must acknowledge an essential restraint in the historian's discourse. To be sure, "Iago" was a dazzling example of stylistic prowess, and Turner unquestionably decided to master those techniques of style in emulation of La Follette. Never, though, did Turner later subordinate content to form, substance to style. His sense of a golden mean always was operative. Tucked away in his undergraduate Commonplace Book is one of those lines epitomizing a thought which was impressive to young Turner: "He is the true Orpheus who writes his ode not with syllables but men." An older Turner did just that. In the frontier thesis, eloquence was handmaiden to an idea.

Clearly, Frederick Jackson Turner is an exemplar of the historian as persuader. His frontiersman was and is and likely will continue to be a beckoning archetype for Americans. To appreciate more fully this impact of the frontier thesis, we can look to the evolution of Turner's rhetorical artistry—through his winning high school and college orations, his eulogies and other occasional addresses, as well as his more academically oriented statements—and always mindful of Turner's personal, motivational model, La Follette's "Iago." In their sum total, these rhetorical efforts evince the eloquence of Frederick Jackson Turner.

# NOTES

●

1. Turner's longhand draft is in Box 56 of the Huntington Library's Frederick Jackson Turner Collection, typically cited as HEH, TU. Unless stipulated otherwise, all citations herein are to materials at the Huntington Library.

2. Ray A. Billington, *Frederick Jackson Turner: Historian, Scholar, Teacher* (New York: Oxford University Press, 1973). This book received the Bancroft Prize in History.

3. *Ibid.*, pp. 15-16. See also Ray A. Billington, *The Genesis of the Frontier Thesis* (San Marino: The Huntington Library, 1971), pp. 4-5.

4. See Billington, *Frederick Jackson Turner, pp. 9-10.*

5. *Ibid.*, pp. 6-7, 12-14.

6. Turner's scrapbook is initially dated 1876, in Box 62. I first utilized this scrapbook and other memorabilia to explain "The Rhetorical Genesis of Style in the 'Frontier Hypothesis' of Frederick Jackson Turner," *Southern Speech Communication Journal* 36 (Spring 1972), 233-48. Billington has used the "Pencils and Scissors" column to suggest the "unusual talent and catholicity of reading interest of a scholar." See *Frederick Jackson Turner*, p. 10.

7. *Wisconsin State Register*, 26 May 1877 and 1 June 1878, as well as 22 June and 6 July 1878. Turner's scrapbook also contains his text of the oration as well as the newspaper account of the event.

8. For discussion of the various species and functions of antitheses, see Ronald H. Carpenter, "The Ubiquitous Antithesis: A Functional Source of Style in Political Discourse," *Style*, 10 (Fall 1976), 426-41; or "The Essential Schemes of Syntax: An Analysis of Rhetorical Theory's Recommendations for Uncommon Word Orders," *Quarterly Journal of Speech*, 55 (April 1969), 161-68.

9. Peter Gay, *Style in History* (New York: McGraw Hill, 1974), pp 97-99, 106-14. See p. 109 in particular for discussion of Macaulay's "affection for Ciceronian antithesis and Augustan balance" in a *History of England*.

10. *Catalogue of the University of Wisconsin 1881-1882*, p. 55. The 1883-84 catalogue reads the same.

11. Turner's University of Wisconsin transcript is in Box 53.

12. *Wisconsin State Register*, 30 April 1881, and the *University Press* of the same date.

13. Cicero *Orator* 403-10.

14. See the evaluation of Lysias in the reprinting of R. C. Jebb, *The Attic Orators From Antiphon to Isaeos*, I (New York: Russell and Russell, 1962), pp. 160-73.

15. Billington, *Frederick Jackson Turner*, p. 18.

16. In Wayland Maxfield Parrish and Alfred Dwight Huston, "Robert G. Ingersoll," *A History and Criticism of American Public Address*, I, ed. William Norwood Brigance (New York: McGraw-Hill, 1943), pp. 368-69.

17. *Ibid.*, p. 364.

18. For a text of this address and another brief appraisal of Ingersoll, see Wayland Maxfield Parrish and Marie Hochmuth, *American Speeches* (New York: Longmans, Green and Company, 1954), pp. 409-46.

19. For a definitive list and discussion of the syntactical sources of style, see Carpenter, "The Essential Schemes of Syntax," pp. 161-68.

20. In Parrish and Hochmuth, *American Speeches*, pp. 415-16.

21. *Ibid.*, pp. 422, 420.

22. Robert G. Ingersoll, "Decoration Day Address," in *American Public Addresses 1740-1952*, ed. A. Craig Baird (New York: McGraw-Hill, 1956), pp. 172, 177, and 174. This particular draft was delivered in New York City on 30 May 1888; Baird notes, however, that Ingersoll gave a widely publicized and similar address in New York City on Memorial Day in 1882, *ibid.*, p. 169. This earlier version might have been the one Turner wanted to read, or he may have decided to find a draft of Ingersoll's noted eulogy upon the death of his brother, 2 June 1879. In Baird, pp. 177-79.

23. See Gordon F. Hostettler, "The Political Speaking of Robert M. La Follette," in *American Public Address: Studies in Honor of Albert Craig Baird*, ed. Loren Reid (Columbia: University of Missouri Press, 1961), pp. 115-16.

24. See Hostettler, *ibid.*, and Carroll P. Lahman, "Robert M. La Follette," in *A History and Criticism of American Public Address*, II, p. 945.

25. The story, dated 3 May 1879, is titled "A Portage University Student Enthusiastic Over the Oratorical Contest." Although merely signed "F," the author surely is Turner. Admittedly, this issue of the newspaper which carried Turner's story about La Follette also carries a text of a speech by Ingersoll, whose style therefore was known to Turner at this exact time.

26. For more detailed discussion of the psychological process of identification, see my essay "The Stylistic Identification of Frederick Jackson Turner with Robert M. La Follette: A Psychologically Oriented Analysis of Language Behavior," *Transactions of the Wisconsin Academy of Sciences, Arts and Letters*, 63 (1975), 102-15.

27. "F.J. Turner 1881 Commonplace Book," HEH, TU vol. 3.

28. The Commonplace Book lists all books read by Turner that year as well as in 1880-81.

29. For a more detailed discussion of these psycholinguistic precepts, see P.C. Wason, "The Processing of Positive and Negative Information," *Quarterly Journal of Experimental Psychology*, 11 (May 1959), 92 and 102-103 as well as "Response to Affirmative and Negative Binary Statements," *British Journal of Psychology*, 52 (May 1961), 139; Davis Howes and Charles Osgood, "On the Combination of Associative Probabilities in Linguistic Contexts," in *Psycholinguistics*, ed. Sol Saporta (New York: Holt, Rinehart and Winston, 1961), pp. 226-27 and 219; George Miller, *Language and Communication*, rev. ed.

(New York: McGraw-Hill, 1963), pp. 174-87; and Charles Osgood, "Psycholinguistics," in *Psychology*, ed. Sigmund Koch (New York, 1963), 6, pp. 290-92. Or, for the digest of this material, see Carpenter, "The Ubiquitous Antithesis" or "The Essential Schemes of Syntax."

30. John P. Hoshor, "American Contributions to Rhetorical Theory and Homiletics," in *History of Speech Education in America*, ed. Karl R. Wallace (New York: Appleton-Century-Crofts, 1954), p. 142.

31. Adams Sherman Hill, *The Principles of Rhetoric* (New York: Harper and Brothers, 1878), p. iv.

32. For an overview of the teaching of rhetoric at this time, with particular attention to Hill's text and the emphasis on style, see Ronald F. Reid, "The Boylston Professorship of Rhetoric and Oratory, 1806-1904: A Case Study in Changing Concepts of Rhetoric and Pedagogy," *Quarterly Journal of Speech*, 45 (October 1959), 239-57.

33. Hill, *Principles of Rhetoric*, p. 242.

34. *Ibid.*, p. 131. As Hill admits, his analogy here is derived from Richard Whately's *Elements of Rhetoric* (1828).

35. *Ibid.*

36. Italics are mine, to help identify the bases of the antitheses; ellipses represent words crossed out by Turner.

37. From Turner's father, 19 April 1883, Box A.

38. *Wisconsin State Journal*, 19 May 1883.

39. *University Press*, 19 May 1883. The text of the oration is published in the *University Press* of 26 May 1883. In contrast to the prestigious and longer established Athena and Hesperin, Adelphia was a small and relatively newly formed literary society. *University Press*, 17 May 1881.

40. This sobriquet is supplied by Joseph Schaefer, "The Author of the 'Frontier Hypothesis'," *Wisconsin Magazine of History*, 15 (1931), 86-89. A text of Turner's "Architecture Through Oppression" is published in the *University Press*, 21 June 1884. (Author's note: these observations about Turner's oratorical endeavors in high school and college reflect my reactions to similar, personal experiences. As a senior at Western Reserve University in 1954, I won the Woodward Prize for Oratory, which enabled me to participate in that year's contest of the Northern Oratorical League (formed in 1890 by Western Reserve, Northwestern, and the universities of Iowa, Michigan, Minnesota, and Wisconsin). I delivered my oration for that contest—for which I won first place—from the stage of the large lecture room in Bascom Hall at the University of Wisconsin, a site undoubtedly familiar to Turner.)

41. *Wisconsin State Register*, 23 June 1883.

42. For a description of Turner as a teacher of rhetoric and oratory, see Goodwin R. Berquist Jr., "The Rhetorical Heritage of Frederick Jackson Turner," *Transactions of the Wisconsin Academy of Sciences, Arts and Letters*, 59 (1971), 28-30.

43. Turner's longhand draft of his eulogy of Frankenburger, 8 February 1906, Box 55.

44. *Dial*, 8 (May 1887), 7-10.

45. "Notes for an Address Before the Lincoln Centennial Association," File Drawer 14A.

46. To William F. Allen, 31 December 1888, Box 1.

47. Turner's personal copy of *The Winning of the West* is the Huntington's Rare Book 139455; "The Hunter Type" folder is in File Drawer 15B.

48. To Turner, 10 and 26 April 1895, Box 2. In heavily underscored descriptions, Turner himself saw Roosevelt as embodying those frontier ideals, an *"all-around American"* who became what he did because he *"lived* the West, as well as studied it." In "Impressions of Theodore Roosevelt as a little boy and a young man, by his sister, Corrine Roosevelt Robinson," ca. 1920, in Box 56.

49. "Notes on Dante," in File Drawer 15B.

50. To Max Farrand from Dorothy Kinsley (Turner) Main, 21 March 1933, Box 50. For other indices of Turner's enchantment with this verse, see *Sunday Times* (London) 25 March 1923; Joseph Schafer to Max Farrand, 29 June 1933, Box 50 A; and Max Farrand, "Frederick Jackson Turner at the Huntington Library: A Memorial," typescript manuscript in Box 49.

51. Turner to Wilson, 24 December 1894, Box 1; and letters from S.S. McClure and John S. Phillips, both of *McClure's Magazine*, 19 and 9 October 1896, Box 2. Although he often promised publishers to write those accounts and infuse them with the "vitality" of his own "proper literary presentation," Turner rarely delivered. See for instance Turner's description of a projected book about George Rogers Clark, in a letter to Houghton, Mifflin and Company, 21 January 1901, in Box 3.

52. Frederick Jackson Turner, *Reuben Gold Thwaites: A Memorial Address* (Madison: State Historical Society of Wisconsin, 1914), pp. 41-43.

53. Turner to Kenneth Colgrove, 1 June 1915, Box 25; and to Arthur H. Buffington, 15 February 1917, Box 27.

54. Grace Lee Nute, "Frederick Jackson Turner," *Minnesota History*, 13 (June 1932), 159-61.

55. Kennth Burke, *A Rhetoric of Motives* (New York: George Braziller, Inc., 1955), pp. 19-23, 55-99.

56. Jerome Kagan, "The Concept of Identification," *Psychological Review*, 65 (1958), 304.

57. Eleanor E. MacCoby and William C. Wilson, "Identification and Observational Learning from Films," *Journal of Abnormal and Social Psychology*, 55 (1957), 76-87; David J. Hicks, "Imitation and Retention of Film-Mediated Aggressive Peer and Adult Models," *Journal of Personality and Social Psychology*, 2 (1965), 97-100; Albert Bandura and Althea Huston, "Identification as a Process of Incidental Learning,: *Journal of Abnormal and Social Psychology*, 63 (1961), 311-18; Albert Bandura, Dorthea Ross and Sheila Ross, "Transmission of Aggression Through Imitation of Aggressive Models," *Journal of Abnormal and Social Psychology*, 63 (1961), 575-82; and Robert S. Albert, "The Role of Mass Media and the Effect of Aggressive Film Content Upon Children's Aggressive Responses and Identification Choices," *Genetic Psychology Monographs*, 55 (1957), 252.

58. Walter Weiss, "Effects of the Mass Media of Communication," in *Handbook of Social Psychology*, 2nd ed. by Gardner Lindzey and Elliot Aronson (Reading, Massachusetts, 1969), V, pp. 98-100.

59. For additional discussion of this outlook toward identification, see William J. McGuire, "The Nature of Attitudes and Attitude Change," in *Handbook of Social Psychology*, 3, pp. 180 and 187. The early Freudian interpretation of identification regarded this element of vicarious reinforcement as a matter of "unconscious inference." See W. W. Meissner, "Notes on Identification," *Psychoanalytic Quarterly*, 39 (1970), 565.

60. Frederick Jackson Turner, "The Significance of History," in *The Early Writings of Frederick Jackson Turner* ed. Fulmer Mood (Freeport, New York, 1969), p. 44.

61. Hill, pp. 5, 65, 67, 85, 129, 132, and 142.

62. Turner's 33 page typewritten manuscript, with longhand revisions, is in File Drawer 15 A. This file drawer also contains several pages of what is apparently a still earlier draft, which was adapted for the address to the Madison Literary Club. Although delivered on 9 February 1891, Turner's note on the title page suggests it was drafted in the main during January 1891.

63. Billington, *Genesis*, p. 145.

64. *Ibid.*, pp. 142, 147-51.

65. George Louis Buffon, "*Discours sur le Style*," trans. in Lane Cooper, *The Art of the Writer* (Ithaca: Cornell University Press, 1952), pp. 146-55.

66. After Edmund Gosse, "Style," in *Encyclopedia Britannica*, 11th ed., pp. 1055-58.

67. Billington, *Frederick Jackson Turner*, pp. 99-103.

68. In *The Genesis of the Frontier Thesis*, Billington quotes liberally from "American Colonization" to show parallels with the conceptualization in Turner's 1893 paper for the American Historical Association. See pp. 53-56.

69. Billington, *Genesis*, p. 3.

70. For further discussion of Turner's neo-Lamarckian metaphors, see William Coleman, "Science and Symbol in the Turner Frontier Hypothesis," *American Historical Review*, 72 (1966), 22-49.

71. This excerpt from the frontier thesis, and all others utilized herein, are from the version which appeared originally in the *Proceedings of the State Historical Society of Wisconsin* (Madison, 1894), also reprinted in Fulmer Mood, *The Early Writings of Frederick Jackson Turner* (Freeport, New York, 1969), pp. 185-219.

72. See also my "Style in Discourse as an Index of Frederick Jackson Turner's Historical Creativity: Conceptual Antecedents of the Frontier Thesis in His 'American Colonization,'" *Huntington Library Quarterly*, 40 (1977), 269-77.

73. Billington, *Genesis*, p. 56. Billington also suggests that the *Aegis* essay was cannibalized from earlier lectures.

74. "Problems in American History" is reprinted in Mood, *Early Writings*, pp. 71-83.

75. As reprinted in Mood, *Early Writings*, p. 185.

76. From Albion Small, 9 November 1892, Box 1.

77. To Woodrow Wilson, 16 July 1893, Box 1.

78. See Billington, *Genesis*, pp. 161-63.

79. *Ibid.*, pp. 160-61. See this section for a description of Turner's typical procrastination when preparing an address, or see also Billington's "Frederick Jackson Turner: Non-Western Historian," *Transactions of the Wisconsin Academy of Sciences, Arts, and Letters*, 59 (1971), 9-10.

80. See Charles E. Osgood, "Some Effects of Motivation on Style of Encoding," in *Style in Language*, ed. Thomas A. Sebeok (Cambridge: M.I.T. Press, 1966), pp. 296-97.

81. See Lloyd I. Bitzer, "The Rhetorical Situation," *Philosophy and Rhetoric*, 1 (1968), 1-14.

82. *Ibid.*, 1, 6-7.

83. Billington, *Genesis*, p. 3.

84. Turner's autobiographical letter to Constance L. Skinner, 15 March 1922, MSE 902 in the Turner Collection at the State Historical Society of Wisconsin, typically cited as SHSW, TU.

85. Turner to Arthur M. Schlesinger, 18 April 1922, Box 31 A.

86. Billington, *Gensis*, p. 170.

87. *Ibid.*, pp. 166-67.

88. These reactions, including the newspaper's misspelling of Turner's initials, are in Billington's note, p. 167.

89. *Ibid.*, p. 171.

90. *Ibid.*, p. 172.

91. *Ibid.*, p. 174. See also the brief description of early reaction to the address in Mood's introductory essay, "Turner's Formative Period," in *Early Writings*, p. 39.

92. For a valuable, annotated bibliography of Turner's publication, see Mood, *Early Writings*, pp. 233-37.

93. Charles A. Beard, "A Review of *The Frontier in American History*," *New Republic*, 25 (16 February 1921), 349.

94. See for instance Billington, *Genesis*, pp. 3-4; Harvey Wish, *Contemporary America*, rev. ed., (New York, 1955), pp. 46-47, 517; Max Lerner, *America as a Civilization* (New York, 1957), p. 34; and Richard Hofstadter, *The Progressive Historians* (New York, 1969), pp. 47-164. For valuable bibliographies of studies about Turner and his influence, see Billington, *Frederick Jackson Turner*, pp. 565-69; or Wilbur R. Jacobs, *The Historical World of Frederick Jackson Turner* (New Haven, 1968), pp. 262-74.

95. For further discussion of this Neo-Lamarckian impetus, see Coleman, "Science and Symbol."

96. Billington, *Frederick Jackson Turner*, pp. 186-87.

97. Billington, *Genesis*, pp. 3-4. Billington avers that with the possible exception of Charles A. Beard's work, Frederick Jackson Turner's discourse "did

more to vitalize the study of American history than any other interpretation."

98. After C.K. Ogden and I.A. Richards, *The Meaning of Meaning* (New York, 1923), pp. 123-26, 149, and 158-59. See also I.A. Richards, *Practical Criticism* (New York, 1929), pp. 176 ff.

99. Hofstadter, pp. 84, 119-20, 126.

100. Billington, *Genesis*, pp. 174-75.

101. Letter to William F. Allen, 31 December 1888, Box 1.

102. This operational definition of style is derived from Rulon Wells, "Nominal and Verbal Style" and Charles E. Osgood, "Some Effects of Motivation on Style of Encoding," both in *Style in Language*, ed. Thomas A. Sebeok (New York, 1960), pp. 215 and 293.

103. In the *Wisconsin State Register*, 17 February 1866; 26 April, 3 May and 9 August, 1873; and 20 April 1878.

104. Compare, for instance, the parallelism in the successive repetitions of "It was...." on pp. 79 and 217, in Mood, *Early Writings*.

105. The rhetorical appropriateness of antitheses for articulating main themes or morals in discourse is discussed in my commentary, with Robert V. Seltzer, "Situational Style and the Rotunda Eulogies," *Central States Speech Journal*, 22 (Spring 1971), 11-15.

106. In Mood, *Early Writings*, p. 72. This essay appears originally in the *Aegis* of 4 November 1892, pp. 48-52. Turner's personal copy at the Huntington Library bears the following notation: "This (with the Fur Trade thesis) constitutes the beginnings of my writings on the frontier, as a symbol of the westward movement (and) its reactions on the East and the Old World." While this document is the first published statement, my earlier statement herein argues that the "American Colonization" address was a prior pivotal factor in the conceptual evolution of the frontier thesis.

107. Actually there are several places in the 1892 essay which are almost antithetical, but they do not have the balance and apposition of his 1893 effort. Although the frontier hypothesis is considerably longer, its number of antitheses can be compared to the extent to which these conformations appear in some contemporary discourse. See Carpenter and Seltzer, "Situational Style and the Rotunda Eulogies," as well as our commentary "On Nixon's Kennedy Style," *Speaker and Gavel*, 7 (January 1970), 41-43. See also Carpenter, "The Ubiquitous Antithesis."

108. Beard, "A Review."

109. See Daniel J. Boorstin, *The Genius of American Politics* (Chicago: University of Chicago Press, 1953), pp. 163-64.

110. David Noble, *Historians Against History: The Frontier Thesis and the National Covenant in American Historical Writing Since 1830* (Minneapolis: University of Minnesota Press, 1965), pp. 3-4.

111. *Ibid.*, p. 16.

112. Billington, *Frederick Jackson Turner*, pp. 185-86.

113. Cushing Strout, *The Pragmatic Revolt in American History: Carl Becker and*

*Charles Beard* (New Haven: Yale University Press, 1958), p. 1.

114. I have utilized this approach in other studies attempting to explicate the rhetorical effectiveness of historical writing. See my "Alfred Thayer Mahan's Style on Seapower: A Paramessage Conducing to *Ethos,*" *Speech Monographs,* 42 (August 1975), 190-202; or "The Historical Jeremiad as Rhetorical Genre," in *Form and Genre: Shaping Rhetorical Action,* ed. Karlyn Campbell and Kathleen Jamieson (Speech Communication Association, 1977), pp. 103-17. The public's responses utilized herein also constitute the bases of my "Frederick Jackson Turner and the Rhetorical Impact of the Frontier Thesis," *Quarterly Journal of Speech,* 63 (April 1977), 117-29.

115. See Carpenter, "The Essential Schemes of Syntax," p. 167.

116. *Washington Star,* 24 March 1923. This and other newspaper reactions cited herein are among the extensive clippings in File Drawer 15 D.

117. *Detroit Saturday Night,* 8 January 1921; and Carl Becker's review in *The Nation,* 3 (10 November 1920), 536. Only dated 1920, the promotional announcement is in File Drawer 15 D, too.

118. See for example the discussions in David Krech and Richard S. Crutchfield, *Elements of Psychology* (New York: Alfred A. Knopf, 1958), p. 103; Edwin G. Boring, Herbert S. Langfeld and Harry Porter Weld, *Foundations of Psychology* (New York: John Wiley and Sons, 1948), p. 218; and Howard Kendler, *Basic Psychology* (New York: Appleton-Century-Crofts, 1963), p. 215.

119. See for example M. H. Short, "Some Thoughts on Foregrounding and Interpretation," *Language and Style,* 6 (Spring 1973), 97; and Irene R. Fairley, "Syntactic Deviation and Cohesion," *Language and Style* 6 (Summer 1973), 216.

120. Aristotle *Rhetoric* 1404b. This translation by Lane Cooper (New York: Appleton-Century-Crofts, 1932).

121. In the commentary on this passage by E. M. Cope, *An Introduction to Aristotle's Rhetoric* (London: MacMillan and Company, 1867), pp. 283-84.

122. *Ibid.,* pp. 282-83, 286. See also the translation and commentary by John H. Freese on Aristotle and *The "Art" of Rhetoric* (London: William Heinemann, 1959), pp. 350-51.

123. John P. Seward, "A Neurological Approach to Motivation," *Nebraska Symposium on Motivation,* 4 (1956), 199.

124. William H. Dember, *The Psychology of Perception* (New York: Holt, Rinehart and Winston, 1960), p. 348. See also Dember and Robert W. Earl, "Analysis of Exploratory, Manipulatory, and Curiosity Behavior," *Psychological Review,* 64 (1957), 92. For other discussions of this concept of novelty, see Ernest R. Hilgard, *Introduction to Psychology* (New York: Harcourt, Brace and Company, 1953), p. 296; Jerome S. Bruner and Leo Postman, "On the Perception of Incongruity: A Paradigm," in *Readings in Perception,* ed. David C. Beardslee and Michael Wertheimer (Princeton: D. Van Nostrand Company, 1958), pp. 648-62; and D. E. Berlyne, "Attention to Change," *British Journal of Psychology,* 42 (1951), 269-70 and "Novelty and Curiosity as Determinants of Exploratory Behavior," *British Journal of Psychology,* 40 (1949), 68-80.

125. A wide range of commentary has addressed itself to this point. See for example Donald E. Broadbent, *Perception and Communication* (London:

Pergamon Press, 1958), pp. 84-86.

126. I surveyed the extensive commentary about novelty and attention in my "Schemes of Syntax as Attentional Factors of Advantage in Discourse," (Ph.D. diss., University of Wisconsin, 1966).

127. *Supra*

128. Miller, p. 89. For additional discussion of norms for repetition in the common idiom, see pp. 88-95 and 120-24 as well as Colin Cherry, *On Human Communication* (New York: Science Editions Inc., 1957), pp. 101-108 and 115-20.

129. Comparisons of type-token-ratios are meaningful, of course, only when language segments of similar lengths are utilized. See Wendell Johnson, "Studies in Language Behavior: I. A Program of Research," *Psychological Monographs*, 56 (1944), 1-2.

130. "A rose is a rose is a rose is a rose" has a TTR of .27. In the context of novelty and attention, consider this observation by Gertrude Stein about her often-quoted line: "Now the poet has to work in the excitingness of pure being; he has to get back that intensity into the language. We all know that it's hard to write poetry in a late age, and we all know that you have to put some strangeness, something unexpected, into the structure of the sentence in order to bring back the vitality of the noun. Now it's not enough to be bizarre; the strangeness in the sentence has to come from the poetic gift, too. That's why it's doubly hard to be a poet in a late age. Now you have seen hundreds of poems about roses and you know in your bones that the rose is not there. All those songs that sopranos sing as encores about 'I have a garden; oh, what a garden!' Now I don't want to put too much emphasis on that line, because it's just one line in a longer poem. But I notice that you all know it; you can make fun of it, but you know it, now listen! I'm no fool. I know that in daily life we don't go around saying 'is a...is a...is a...is a....' Yes, I'm no fool; but I think that in that line the rose is red for the first time in English poetry for a hundred years." See Gertrude Stein, *Four in America* (New Haven: Yale University Press, 1947), p. v.

131. See George A. Miller and Noam Chomsky, "Finitary Models of Language Users," in *Handbook of Mathematical Psychology*, ed. Robert Luce, Robert Bush, and Eugene Galanter (New York: John Wiley and Sons, 1963), pp. 471-75. See also Noam Chomsky, "On the Notion 'Rule of Grammar,'" and Victor H. Yngve, "The Depth Hypothesis," both in *Structure of Language and Its Mathematical Aspects*, ed. Roman Jakobson, in *Proceedings of Symposia in Applied Mathematics* (Providence: American Mathematical Society, 1961), 12, pp. 10, 131-36.

132. In traditional rhetorical theory handbooks on style, a specific variation of this technique called for the rhetor to repeat the last item of one segment at the beginning of the next and so on, as in "It was the energy of Africanus that gave him his peculiar excellence, his excellence that gave him glory, his glory that gave him rivals." From Quintilian *Institutes of Oratory* ix. 3. 56. This conformation is known traditionally as *gradatio, klimax,* or *scala.*

133. Jon Eisonson, J. Jeffery Auer, and John V. Irwin, *The Psychology of Communication* (New York: Appleton-Century-Crofts, 1963), p. 250.

134. Carl I. Hovland, Irving L. Janis, and Harold H. Kelley, *Communication*

*and Persuasion* (New Haven: Yale University Press, 1953), p. 59.

135. Claude E. Shannon and Warren Weaver, *The Mathematical Theory of Communication* (Urbana: University of Illinois Press, 1949), p. 96.

136. To Turner from Helen Wengler, 10 March 1921, Box 31; and from Charles Andrews, 6 February 1894, Box 1.

137. *London Times Literary Supplement*, 25 August 1921.

138. From W.H. Shephard, undated, in vol. 1 "Red Book," a collection of letters from students and friends upon Turner's leaving the University of Wisconsin to teach at Harvard.

139. See for instance: *Boston Transcript*, 19 November 1920; *New York Churchman*, 2 April 1921; *Pacific Christian Advocate*, 5 January 1921; *New York Times*, 17 March 1932; and a commencement address at Bradley Polytechnic Institute by Christian C. Kohlsaat, 24 June 1898, in the *Peoria Journal* of that date. See also Arthur H. Buffington to Turner, 30 December 1920, Box 30; and Lewis Stilwell to Charles Edwards, 26 April 1924, in vol. 11 "Blue Book," a collection of letters upon Turner's retirement from Harvard.

140. Poem by Homer C. Hockett in vol. 2 "Blue Book." See also Kohlsaat's Commencement Address, *ibid.*, and the reference to the "virile" democracy of the frontier, in a review in the *Harvard Alumni Bulletin*, 23 (16 December 1920), 267. Turner drew a line marking off this reference to virility.

141. In the "Bookshelf" supplement to *The Atlantic*, 127 (January 1921), 4-6. In some recent-bound volumes of *The Atlantic*, this supplement is excluded. Turner's copy, however, is in File Drawer 15 D.

142. Becker, review in *The Nation*.

143. *Milwaukee Sentinel*, 30 January 1921.

144. *Boston Post*, 18 December 1920.

145. Arthur P. Whitaker to Turner, 27 October 1921, Box 31; and the notebook of George W. Bell for History 17, "The History of the West," during the 1910-11 academic year. In File Drawer 14 D.

146. Edwin Black, "The Second Persona," *Quarterly Journal of Speech*, 56 (April 1970), 112-13.

147. *Ibid.*, 113.

148. *Ibid.*, 119.

149. See Ernest G. Bormann, "Fantasy and Rhetorical Vision: The Rhetorical Criticism of Social Reality," *Quarterly Journal of Speech*, 58 (1972), 405, 398.

150. See Billington, *Genesis*, pp. 78-83; and Wish, p. 2.

151. Theodore Roosevelt to Turner, 10 February 1894, Box 1.

152. James A. James to Lawrence Larson, 22 May 1910, and William V. Pooley to Turner, 12 May 1910, both in vol. 1 "Red Book"; George W. Stone to Turner, 4 February 1921, Box 31; and David Kinley to Turner, 24 August 1896, Box 2.

153. *St. Louis Post Dispatch*, 2 April 1935; and Phillips F. La Follette to Joseph Schafer, 12 August 1933, Box 50 A. Italics are La Follette's.

154. *Boston Evening Record*, 22 August 1896; *Boston Herald* 15 November 1920; and the *New York Times*, 7 November 1920.

155. *Pacific Christian Advocate*, 5 January 1921.

156. *New Haven Journal Courier*, 13 July 1932.

157. Lerner, p. 34.

158. Turner cut out this excerpt form a 1904 issue of the *Portland Oregonian* and marked it for use in a lecture to be entitled "The New Era." In File Drawer 15 D. Such success stories were an important basis of much popular literature around the turn of the century, but that image prevailed even later, perhaps the closest parallel being in Edna Ferber's *Come and Get It*, describing the financial growth of a Wisconsin lumber family and their ultimate move toward the eastern establishment.

159. George W. Bell's Notebook for History 17, File Drawer 14 D.

160. *Chicago Tribune*, 30 August 1896; *Boston Herald*, 22 August 1896; and the *Times* (Lowell, Massachusetts), 7 September 1896. Although these reactions are in reviews of Turner's article, "The Problem of the West," in the September 1896 *Atlantic Monthly*, they still reflect the frontier thesis conceptualization that permeated that particular essay as well. See also the *New York Evening Post*, 4 December 1920; and Lloyd William Brooke to Caroline Mae Turner, 13 March 1933, Box 50.

161. Letters from Theodore C. Smith, the History Department of Williams College, June 1910; and Rosa M. Perdue, 23 April 1910; both in vol. 1 "Red Book."

162. A typed copy of "Reminiscences of F.J. Turner by August C. Krey," to Ray A. Billington, 18 April 1960, Box 52.

163. For a detailed description of the Board's activities, see George T. Blakely, *Historians on the Homefront: American Propagandists for the Great War* (Lexington: University of Kentucky Press, 1971).

164. Turner to Max Farrand, 5 May 1917, Box 28.

165. Edgar E. Robinson to Turner, 27 April 1918, Box 28.

166. Turner to Stephen Slaughter, 12 October 1918, Box 28. In this letter, Turner displayed a keen sense of international politics, recognizing how "the hellish spirit of the Germans in retreat" was forcing Americans into a punitive frame of mind to seek "revenge" at the peace table.

167. Turner's longhand copy of Aubert's remarks in *Transactions of the Illinois Historical Society*, 24 (1924), 84. In File Drawer 15 D. Turner had marked off the reference to the trenches with red lines.

168. *Ibid.*

169. Robinson, *ibid.*, and Arthur H. Buffington to Turner, 13 December 1920, Box 30.

170. Guy Emerson to Turner, 29 September 1919, Box 29.

171. Guy Emerson to Turner, 2 January 1919, Box 29.

172. Guy Emerson to Turner, 23 June 1920, and Lois Rosenberry to Turner, 7 November 1920, both in Box 30.

173. Box 30 contains over a dozen such letters to Turner. See in particular the correspondence from A. Lawrence Lowell, 18 October 1920; Frederick Merk, 23 June 1920; and Ulrich B. Phillips, 16 December 1920. See also the plea in the *Historical Outlook*, 10 (March 1919), 156.

174. Michael C. McGee, "In Search of 'The People': A Rhetorical Alternative," *Quarterly Journal of Speech*, 61 (October 1975), 247, 239-40.

175. *Ibid.*, 241.

176. Charles McCarthy to Turner, 23 June 1910, in vol. 1 "Red Book."

177. *Supra*

178. Aristotle *Rhetoric* 1356a.

179. *Ibid.*, 1378a

180. For further discussion of more recent research about *ethos*, see for example Hovland, Janis and Kelley, *Communication and Persuasion*, pp. 19-55; Erwin P. Bettinghaus, *Persuasive Communication* (New York: Holt, Rinehart and Winston, 1968), pp. 101-21; C. David Mortensen, *Communication: The Study of Human Interaction* (New York: McGraw-Hill Book Company, 1972), pp. 142-59; Bert E. Bradley, *Fundamentals of Speech Communication: The Credibility of Ideas* (Dubuque, Iowa: William C. Brown Company, 1974), pp. 64-81; and Kenneth E. Andersen, *Persuasion: Theory and Practice* (Boston: Allyn and Bacon, 1971), pp. 217-46.

181. From Theodore Roosevelt, 10 February 1894, Box 1.

182. To Turner from Charles M. Andrews, 6 February 1894, Box 1.

183. Josiah Strong, *Our Country: Its Possible Future and Its Present Crisis* (New York: Baker and Taylor Company, 1885), p. 1.

184. *Ibid.*, p. 129.

185. *Ibid.*, pp. 144-53, 159-80. For instance, Strong says the Anglo-Saxon has "an instinct or genius for colonizing. His unequaled energy, his indomitable perseverance, and his personal independence, made him a pioneer. He excels all others in pushing his way into new countries....Nothing more manifestly distinguishes the Anglo-Saxon than his intense and persistent energy...which...is peculiarly American." See p. 173.

186. *Ibid.*, p. 222.

187. Bettinghaus, *Persuasive Communication*, p. 107.

188. *The New York Churchman*, 2 April 1921 and the *Wisconsin Alumni Magazine* (no date), p. 74. Both reviews are in File Drawer 15 D; Turner himself had marked off the section in the *Wisconsin Alumni Magazine* which he had cut out.

189. From Anna Y. Reed, 23 May 1910, in vol. 1. "Red Book" and Thomas M. Liams to Caroline Mae Turner, 16 March 1932, vol. 5.

190. Samuel Eliot Morison to Caroline Mae Turner, 27 March 1932, vol 5. See also letters with a similar tone to Charles W. Edwards from Lewis D. Stilwell, 26 April 1924, vol. 2 "Blue Book" and to Caroline Mae Turner from Annie Kempton Roach and John U. Nef, both undated, in vol. 5.

191. Henry Nash Smith, *Virgin Land: The American West as Symbol and Myth* (Cambridge: Harvard University Press, 1970), pp. 120, 12.

192. *Ibid.*, p. 4.

193. Joseph T. Klapper, *The Effects of Mass Communication* (New York: The Free Press, 1960), p. 51.

194. Paul F. Lazarsfeld, Bernard Berelson, and Hazel Gaudet, *The People's Choice* (New York: Columbia University Press, 1948), p. 151.

195. Elihu Katz, "The Two-Step Flow of Communication: An Up-To-Date Report on an Hypothesis," *Public Opinion Quarterly*, 21 (1957): 77. See also Elihu Katz and Paul F. Lazarsfeld, *Personal Influence: The Part Played by People in the Flow of Mass Communicationss* (Glencoe, Illinois: The Free Press, 1955), p. 286.

196. Katz (1957), *ibid.*, p. 63; and Bernard Berelson and Gary A. Steiner, *Human Behavior: An Inventory of Scientific Findings* (New York: Harcourt, Brace and World, 1964), p. 550.

197. Berelson and Steiner, *ibid.*, and Katz, *ibid.*

198. See Klapper, *Effects of Mass Communication*, pp. 34-36. For another overview and critique of research about the "two-step flow of communication," see Frederick C. Whitney, *Mass Media and Mass Communications in Society* (Dubuque, Iowa: William C. Brown Company, 1975), pp. 56-58, 412-15, and 446-47.

199. *New Haven Journal-Courier*, 13 July 1932. The clipping is in Box 57.

200. *Minnesota Daily*, 7 June 1900. The clipping is in Box 54.

201. *Ibid.*

202. Samuel Becker, "Rhetorical Studies for the Contemporary World," in *The Prospect of Rhetoric*, ed. Lloyd Bitzer and Edwin Black (Englewood Cliffs, New Jersey: Prentice-Hall, 1971), pp. 25-26.

203. Paul B. Sheatsley and Jacob J. Feldman, "A National Survey on Public Reactions and Behavior" and Wilbur Schramm, "Communication in Crisis," both in *The Kennedy Assassination and the American Public*, ed. Bradley S. Greenberg and Edwin B. Parker (Stanford: Stanford University Press, 1965), pp. 152-53, 16. Both analyses are cited in Becker, "Rhetorical Studies."

204. Richard A. Cherwitz, "The Contributory Effect of Rhetorical Discourse: A Study of Language-in-Use," *Quarterly Journal of Speech*, 66 (February 1980), 33-50. See in particular pp. 33, 39, 44-45, and 50.

205. Smith also suggests that at the time *The Green Berets* was made we had conquered a continent and were looking beyond Hawaii (and earlier the Philippine Islands) to where "the East is west of the West"; and this particular film is "a sadly revealing metaphor for our hankering after lost frontiers." I heartily recommend a reading of Julian Smith, *Looking Away: Hollywood and Vietnam* (New York: Charles Scribner's Sons, 1975), particularly pp. 5, 27-29, 92-94, and 128-30. Another interpretation of film's attitudinal impact at this time deals with *Patton*. Many people, particularly those whom Richard Nixon counted among his "Silent Majority," perceived General Patton's speech before the flag at the opening of the motion picture to be articulating in the 1940s what *should* have been our Vietnam policy in the 1970s: win. See Ronald H. Carpenter and Robert V. Seltzer, "Nixon, *Patton*, and a Silent Majority Sentiment about the Vietnam War: The Cinematographic Bases of a Rhetorical Stance," *Central*

*States Speech Journal*, 25 (1974), 105-10.

206. See for example John Morton Blum, *V Was For Victory: Politics and American Culture During World War II* (New York: Harcourt, 1976).

207. Henry Nash Smith, p. 120.

208. Charles U. Larson, *Persuasion: Reception and Responsibility* (Belmont, California: Wadsworth, 1973), pp. 140-42. The cultural myth about the wisdom of the rustic complements what Larson refers to as another societal predisposition of the faith in the "possibility of success." Many Americans *do* seem to favor an attitude often expressed as "if you follow the advice of the common man and use common sense, with sincerity and hard work, you will be a success." *Ibid.*, pp. 142-43.

209. For a brief overview and analysis of Carter's television ads, see L. Patrick Devlin, "Contrasts in Presidential Campaign Commercials of 1976," *Central States Speech Journal*, 28 (Winter 1977), 238-49; for a more detailed account of presidential campaign images, with particular attention to "the candidate as farmer" and "sturdy yeoman," see William Burlie Brown, *The People's Choice: The Presidential Image in the Campaign Biography* (Baton Rouge: Louisiana State University Press, 1960), pp. 83-92.

210. *Jacksonville Times-Union and Journal*, 5 August 1978, p. C6.

211. *Washington Star*, 24 March 1923, in File Drawer 15 D.

212. Gordon S. Wood's review of *History of the Westward Movement*, in *The History Book Club Review* (July 1978), 3-7.

213. *Ibid.*

214. Frederick Merk, *History of the Westward Movement* (New York: Alfred A. Knopf, 1978), pp. 616-17.

215. Italics mine. As a long time reader of *The History Book Club Review*, and a fairly regular purchaser of its selections over the years, I do not recall having received such a notification about any other book.

216. Bormann, "Fantasy and Rhetorical Vision," 398-99. Much of Bormann's concept of a rhetorical vision evolves from his examination of research in small group behavior, most notably the work of Robert Bales, *Personality and Interpersonal Behavior* (New York: Holt, Rinehart, 1970). Careful observations of communication interactions in groups suggest that certain dramatizations articulated by one person "would chain out through the group. The tempo of the conversation would pick up. People would grow excited, interrupt one another, blush, laugh, forget their self-consciousness. The tone of the meeting, often quiet and tense immediately prior to the dramatizing, would become lively, animated, and boisterous, the chaining process, involving verbal and nonverbal communication, indicating *participation in the drama*" (italics mine). Moreover, the kind and degree of arousal are "partly in the message as well as in the people participating in a fantasy chain"; for "whether an individual's aroused physiological state is interpreted as hate, fear, anger, joy, or love is partly determined by the drama that accompanies the emotional state." See Bormann, 397, 406.

217. *Ibid.*, 397, 399. Much of Bormann's thinking here is founded upon stud-

ies of the persuasive role of myth in communication as well as more well known "balance theories," all illustrated with a brief discussion of how Hitler applied this rhetorical strategy so successfully.

218. The Associated Press wire service carried the story; one of the newspapers carrying the item was the *Gainesville Sun*, 21 April 1978, p. 2A. A telenet computer search of the *New York Times* Information Bank indicates that paper itself did not carry the story, perhaps suggesting (in one interpretation at least) that to New Yorkers an appeal for a return to frontier ideals is so common as to be no longer newsworthy.

219. Samuel Becker, pp. 22-24, 33.

220. *Ibid.*, p. 25.

221. For any further, brief discussion of "figure" and "ground" in the context of communication, see Broadbent, *Perception and Communication*, p. 60.

222. I have discussed the functional relationship between style and emphasis (and hence memorability) in several essays. In the pragmatic context of political persuasion, see my "The Ubiquitous Antithesis," 428-29; or "The Problem of Style in Presidential Discourse," in *Concepts in Communication*, ed. Jimmie D. Trent, Judith S. Trent, and Daniel J. O'Neill (Boston: Allyn and Bacon, 1973), pp. 118-19.

223. I found only one reference to a person's character attributes in Turner's several notebooks from his undergraduate American history courses, in vol. 13.

## A. Prize Winning Orations

WINNING ORATIONS are personal triumphs. For in achieving victory for oratory on the public platform, the contestant attains a recognition and personal satisfaction of substantial magnitude. After all, the winning contest oration demands both a creative effort and an artistic performance. And winning demonstrates conclusively the orator's superiority in several dimensions of behavior.

Intellectually, the orator must master a conception—first by formulating and structuring the cognitive substance of discourse and then by polishing its stylistic form for final presentation. And the latter endeavors with language invariably lead to a heightened ego involvement with the oration as discourse. For with each change in syntax and lexicon, the orator's personality becomes more deeply ingrained within that statement. Furthermore, with each word substitution and every recasting of word order, the style becomes a more complete reflection of the orator as an unique individual, distinct from the other orators in the contest, indeed differentiated in a positive way from all other high school or university peers. Finally, with each successive reading during stylistic polishing, the discourse as an entity becomes more firmly embedded in the mind of its creator.

Of course the memorization process for the contest adds to the orator's intellectual involvement with the discourse. In the contest situation, the oration must be delivered from memory—faultlessly. So for many hours before the event, the speaker sits with that manuscript as created and adapted, reading it over seemingly endlessly, trying to achieve absolute mastery of recall over the words and their progression. Prior to the contest, the orator likely will be found reciting the statement again and again, aloud in solitude or silently in the presence of others. The contestant becomes preoccupied with achieving total and unfaltering memorization. And each preparatory reading and recitation make the substance and form of the oration even more salient in the consciousness of its creator. Indeed, many prize-winning orators know the experience of being able to deliver their speeches faultlessly from memory even a year or two after the last presentations, so well learned are they.

Physically, the winning of an oratorical contest demonstrates the speaker's prowess in managing voice and body for a persuasive delivery. In all likelihood, the orator's gestures and bodily movements are rehearsed, even before a mirror. Thus, the physical activity of the speaker during the contest has been approved not only by an oratory coach but the most severe and demanding critic of all—the orator himself. Moreover, every nuance of vocal variety is carefully rehearsed. Variations in pitch are perfected to avoid monotony and suggest feeling; vocal quality is managed to help evoke appropriate meaning; force is varied to achieve emphasis by progressive increases in volume; and rate is altered artistically not only to aid audience comprehension but to help project the orator's emotion, with which listeners might empathize.

Young Turner clearly was capable of such an artistic performance. Recall that his April 1881 delivery of Marc Antony's "Address to the Romans" was judged "the finest declamation and the best rendered that has been heard from the Assembly Hall stage." Indeed, all his life Turner seemed attuned to the ways in which prowess in delivery affected audiences. Even in the seminal 1891 address on "American Colonization" to the Madison Literary Club, Turner saw fit to mark a margin at one point with the reminder "pause."

In that 1891 address, the intended pause accompanied a stylized passage quoted from Charles Kingley's *Westward Ho:* "It was the men of Devon, whom we shall learn one day to honor as they deserve, to whom she [England] owes her commerce, her colonies, her very existence." In addition to evincing Turner's fondness for a statement relying upon rhetorical parallelism through the repetition of "her," as well as the alliterative "commerce" and "colonies," the passage incorporates a distinct *asyndeton*, that quality of terseness achieved by the omission of conjunctions. While reading that passage now, one can almost hear Turner building to an emotional climax with each successive, clipped segment delivered somewhat louder and somewhat faster—and then deliberately pausing to allow the effect to take hold with his audience. More important for appreciating the eloquence in Turner's winning orations, imagine how the young man's rhetorical style was combined with a dramatic delivery in this similar excerpt from "The Power of the Press," his high school commencement address:

> The great Creator speaks, and the world arises from chaos. Eden is lost. Israel is chosen of God. The centuries roll on.

The *brevitas* would befit any Attic orator conforming to the classical style which suggests that a persuader's emotion is evinced by terseness. Again, one can almost hear a much younger Turner building to a rhetorical climax suggestive of passion. Indeed, in many ways, the eloquent style of Turner's winning orations allowed him to demonstrate his mastery over the physical aspects of delivery, as one can conclude now by reading those statements aloud.

And those victories also allowed Turner to demonstrate what might have been the most personally satisfying prowess of all: the capability of the young man to master his own emotions. Contest orators know the heightened feelings before competition—the combination of optimistic expectation for winning and pessimistic fear of a poor showing. Outwardly composed, the orator awaits his turn to speak. Inwardly, the stomach may feel something of that sense of uneasiness; the palpitations of the heart are more pronounced; and the palms are sweating. And no matter how many contests are part of the orator's past experience, successively more significant competitions are likely to stimulate the same emotional responses.

Once the orator begins speaking and warms to the task at hand, however, the symptoms of uncertainty soon disappear. Indeed, the audience which may have been a blurred mass before the speaker's eyes becomes with each successive sentence more a group of distinct faces, differentiated and recognizable. Anxiety abating, physical uneasiness tends to dissipate. In control of emotions, the speaker then can experience that exhilaration of oratory, from being "out front" and "in control." And when a total endeavor of creative effort and artistic performance is recognized by an award of first place, the orator knows a sense of deep, personal satisfaction.

For Frederick Jackson Turner, the winning orations had to be among his most rewarding triumphs. Admittedly, he would cannibalize one oration for passages in the next. For example, in high school's "The Power of the Press," Turner said this:

> Standing one day in a great library, I looked upon the army of books resting in the long line of shelves. A feeling of awe and solemnity seemed to pervade the place. Here in the dusk and twilight reigned Wisdom and Knowledge. This was their kingdom. It needed no incantation to call up the great ones of all ages and lands. From these books rose the "kings of Thought" as from a grave.

Then, in his later University of Wisconsin Junior Prize oration, Turner utilized virtually the same statement:

> I stood one evening in a vast library. As the soft twilight floated through the tinted panes, a feeling of solemnity and awe seemed to pervade the place, and, as the dusk increased, there seemed to steal from out the dim corridors, those mighty kings of thought....

The point is that with each use of a previously effective passage in a new rhetorical endeavor, with equally successful results, Turner's techniques for eloquence became more firmly entrenched in his compositions. Therefore, in understanding and appreciating the persuasiveness with which the frontier thesis was articulated, Turner's winning orations of a decade and more earlier are invaluable. They evince the tendencies for eloquence which, *because* they were rewarded with favorable recognitions, became so much a part of the historian's later discourse. And any reading now of those oratorical triumphs should be accompanied by an examination of the model which Turner emulated, La Follette's "Iago." As presented in the appendix, this one statement more than any other—by the historian's own admission—may be *the* pivotal factor to which can be traced all of Turner's eloquence and ultimate rhetorical impact upon our national self-consciousness.

# THE POWER OF THE PRESS

About four centuries ago was born in the brain of John Guttenberg, an idea destined to be the propagator of learning, of Christianity, and of civilization, and thus to sway the future of the world. In the year 1438, John Guttenberg invented the art of letter press printing, or printing sheets with movable types. This, although one of the simplest, is at the same time one of the greatest of all human inventions. It was conceived just as the world was emerging from the long night of the Mediaeval Ages. It rose from that darkness like the sun from the mists of morning, and shed the blessed light of education upon the world. Today that glorious sun, the Press, has reached its zenith, and we bless it for the present fulness of our civilization, and feel that it will never set and leave the world in the darkness of former times.

There have been other ages of civilization, when poets sung and orators spoke in words of eloquence. Greece reached a civilization, in some respects as great as our own, but Greece fell, and her learning was almost blotted out. She lost her intellectual greatness because she could neither transmit or disseminate her education; for, although manuscript writing was in vogue, yet to secure the works of the learned was difficult in the extreme to those not possessed of wealth. These manuscripts were found in isolated libraries and in the homes of the rich, but among the masses they could not be. For these reasons Greece could not diffuse her learning, and education belonged to the comparatively few.

Today we may talk with all the great ones of earth. We have only to go to our books, and poets of every age will sing their sweetest songs, philosophers discourse in words of wisdom, historians show how empires have risen and decayed, orators persuade by their power and eloquence, and God Himself will point the path of rectitude in that first and greatest book ever published.

He who now gives a truth or a grand conception to the world, knows that mankind will possess it forever. His fame rests on no vague tradition, for the works which gained him honor have been baptized in the immortality of the Press.

But the importance of the Press in the transmission of ideas is not less than the power which it exerts today. It is an instrument of unspeakable good in the diffusion of education, upon which our whole social and political fabric depends. In our own country, especially, is education a political necessity, for here the people rule themselves, and a government of the ignorant *by* the ignorant is but a short remove from anarchy. That there is yet a want of education among the lower classes of the

117

nation, is shown by the rise in our midst of Communism, that fell child of ignorance and crime, which threatens destruction to all the institutions of the land. With the aid of the Press, however, that great and long wished for reform—the education of the masses—becomes not only a possibility, but even a probability.

The wonderful influence of the Press in shaping the morals and customs of a people, is a subject of magnitude too great for present discussion.

Of all political powers the Press is the most important. Who can doubt that the stirring sentences of the Declaration of Independence spurred on the colonists to battle and to victory? That that wonderful work, "Uncle Tom's Cabin," did, in a great measure, awaken the North to a knowledge of the outrages therein portrayed, and a consequent abolishment of slavery? With every great reformation since its rise the Press has been indissolubly connected.

One of its departments, from its power, deserves especial mention. Of all the offspring of the types, there is none whose influence is wider than that of the Newspaper, which has been described as a "ticket of admission to the great Globe Theater, whose dramas are written by God Himself, 'whose scene-shifter is Time, and whose curtains are rung down by Death!'" Aside from its great value as a disseminator of news, the daily press is one of the greatest of civilizers and public teachers, and is a necessary adjunct of every free government.

When there is perfect freedom of the Press, the people will make known their power through it, and will resist all tendency toward oppression. This is recognized by all governments, and, as a consequence, liberty of the Press is found only in countries ruled by the people. The more despotic a monarch, the greater restrictions does he place upon the utterances of the Newspaper; while, on the other hand, as the freedom of the Press increases, so does the freedom of the people. It was a remark of Burke's that there were three estates in parliament, but in the reporters' gallery there sat a fourth estate greater than them all.

Among the many laments of that class of people which bemoans the fancied decay of the good and the grand of past ages, there is none more commonly indulged in than the wail over the decay of oratory. That the world could furnish from its wealth of undeveloped genius, a Cicero or a Demosthenes, should occasion demand them, need not be doubted. But the former measure of power and influence held by the orator, has been irrevocably consigned to a new power, which unites to all his greatness the ability to speak to an audience of such magnitude as the orator of the past never dreamed—to the audience of the whole civilized world—and to place its utterances in a form that can last forever. This is the glorious province of the Newspaper.

When the South declared its intention of seceding, many able discussions took place in Congress, but the Press was the power that fired the Northern heart, and, by showing the country's peril, caused the brave Boys in Blue to go forth to fight for the preservation of the Union. The present financial questions are more ably treated by our great papers than in our very legislative halls. While thus the orator of former times has disappeared, still we confidently trust that his mission has descended to a power which exerts a far greater influence.

Before the Press there opens up a glorious future. It is one of the grandest of Possibilities! Before it all arbitrary ranks and man made nobilities must fall, and the people educated by its power shall rule the nations of the earth. Truly, there was something more than human in Guttenberg's idea! The invention of printing was almost divine in its character.

Standing one day in a great library, I looked upon the army of books resting in the long line of shelves. A feeling of awe and solemnity seemed to pervade the place. Here in the dusk and twilight reigned Wisdom and Knowledge. This was their kingdom. It needed no incantation to call up the great ones of all ages and lands. From these books rose the "kings of Thought" as from a grave.

> When Agamemnon sinks into the tomb
> The beggar Homer mounts the monarch's throne.

Here the Ocean of Centuries was rolled away. The Past became the Present. Homer and Aristotle, Shakespeare and Bacon stood side by side, and by their genius ruled the minds of men. The "baptism of ink" has descended upon the past, and again Babylon is beautiful, Troy is besieged, Athens reigns by her learning, and again Rome's glories shine. The Press commands, and the great events of the world's history are re-enacted. The panorama passes before our gaze. The great Creator speaks, and the world arises from chaos. Eden is lost. Israel is chosen of God. The centuries roll on. Persian magnificence gains supremacy. Alexander goes forth to conquer the world. Caesar is victorious and is killed. And now a greater than Caesar walks the earth. The Savior of Mankind comes to bless the world. We hear the cruel cry of "Crucify Him!" and we see Him bleeding on the cross. The scene moves on. Now the barbarian clans overrun the earth, and all is ruin and desolation. The clouds pass away, and again the sun of Civilization shines

119

forth. Washington appears, and our country gains her lawful place among the nations. Napoleon startles the world by his genius. Civil war rages in our Union, and Lincoln steps forth to save the land and die the martyr's death. The curtain falls upon events transpired, and leaves us with the existing.

Thus has the Press joined the Past and the Present and made them one. But is this all? Nay, more; for as we turn the leaves of *one* book, the Future is unveiled to our mortal gaze, and as the printed page is read, the New Jerusalem rises in its divine beauty and our eyes have seen the glory of the Lord!

"O, Past and Future, so far separated, yet so near, so strange, yet so well known, by what miraculous power do I know you! Books are the true Elysian fields where spirits of the Dead converse, and into these fields a mortal may venture unappalled.—What king's court can boast such company? What school of philosophy such wisdom?"

A text of this oration is printed in the *Wisconsin State Register*, 6 July 1878. Turner's copy is in his scrapbook, in Box 55. The oration was delivered on 28 June 1878.

# THE POET OF THE FUTURE

"Beneath every literature there is a philosophy. Beneath every work of art there is an idea of nature and of life; this idea leads the poet."

If we inquire into the literatures of the past, we shall always find, standing as an epitome of the essential character of his era, a great poet. The greatest poets are the flowering of the genius of their age, and their beauty makes the age immortal.

In yonder library, all times are contemporaries; there Babylon again is beautiful; there rise the towers of Ilium; there is Athens, "ever tripping through the purest atmosphere;" within that room again Rome's glories shine, and there the wild Norse viking sings his war song. We open the lay of Beowulf, and as we read the poet's page, the walls grow unsubstantial and stretch away in the somber forests and rugged homes of the wild north land; we feel the salt gusts of the sea, the dampness of the wilderness is about us, and we hear the symphony of the wind among the pine trees. We are back again in the fierce, rude youth of our race, of which these songs are poetic crystallizations. Would you know Italy in the middle ages? You will find her embodied in the burning pages of Dante. Would you know England in the fourteenth century? In quaint Dan Chaucer's lisping lines that past it is still alive. In Shakespeare we find the record of an age awakening, broad and passionate. Milton is the talesman that shows us the Puritan age. Pope mirrors his times—cold, critical, artificial. It is ever so; from the Iliad of Homer to the Faust of Goethe, each period has given birth to a great poet who is the "very age and body of the time."

Has the present such a poet? In whom has our own age burst into song? Lyric and story flow sweetly from the lips of Longfellow and Tennyson; but in the greatest art there is something deeper than this. Morris and his school, false to their great mission, blind to the age in which they live, have found the lyre of some minstrel of the past, and it breathes remembrance of its ancient harmony, as the shell murmurs of its ocean home. They call themselves the "idle singers of an empty day," and of all our poets, none are like those

> —grand old masters,
> —the bards sublime.
> Whose distant footsteps echo
> Down the corridors of Time.

They all play the lute, and we wait for the master who shall sweep the organ keys. For dare we call this age of ours an "empty" one? At the

121

question the great nineteenth century, so rich in thought and action, rises like a Titan to give strong voiced denial. Its myriad inventions, its schools, its newborn knowledge of nature, all cry "No!" And the whole race of common people struggling up from degradation as old as all the past,—like the lion in Milton, "pawing to get free his hinder parts," proclaims the progress, the grandeur of our times. The age is magnificent: it is the poets who are lacking.

But the spirit of genius never dies, for the law of correlation of forces is as true in the mental as in the physical world. All the arts are but different manifestations of the same spirit of genius. The chivalry of the middle ages has now become poetry; it was poetry then, for there is a poetry of action. "Life," says Emerson, "may be lyric or epic." Here then is the key to our times. That spirit, which in the past has found expression in an epic, such as Homer's, or a drama, such as Shakespeare's, now turned into a new channel, again awaits poetic utterance.

The two great features of the present are science and democracy. The former, following the line marked out by Bacon, investigates nature and her laws, and when a truth is found, applies it to mankind. Science has given to things a new beauty and a poetry. It has swept aside the ancient's firmament, and set us floating on the shores of infinity. It has taught us that the "world globes itself in a drop of dew." It makes the useful beautiful. If the Venus of Milo, chiseled in cold marble, endures as an expression of the genius of the Greek, the locomotive, binding the east and west in bonds of steel, thundering over the prairies and climbing mountains higher than the clouds, an embodiment of power and action—a being whose muscles are iron, whose blood is steam, whose breath is fire, and whose brain is a man—the locomotive is a type of our grand civilization. Science has found a poetry in that "grand epic written by the finger of God upon the strata of the earth." Studying the growth of a violet it has learned the law of development; a deeper poetry lurks in the leaves of botany than in all the petty conceits of a whole school of rhymers. The old Greeks beheld the stars and used them to turn a hexameter. The astronomer of the nineteenth century finds in those circling worlds, a sublimity of law and a hint of infinity. By science, the world has been re-discovered, filled with life, with meaning, with divinity. Nature is calling for her poet!

Side by side with science has walked democracy,—the offspring of many centuries, and yet in its youth. In the past mankind has lain under the domination of the few. Although here and there little masses of men had sprung up and reached a civilization that was intense, yet that civilization was narrow. Athens boasted of her freedom, but Athens was a city of many serfs and few free, and even she was but a little beacon glimmering in the awful waste of an ignorant and oppressed mankind. The spirit of individual liberty slumbered in the depths of the German forest. In the dark ages these rude savages poured into civilization. Subdued to the ideas of the past, they, too, fell under the rule of the kings; but their pristine love of freedom, smouldering through the long ages, at last burst into flame. Our times have seen a new invasion, not of arms but of mind. Just at the dawn of this century, our country took its stand among the nations, self-governed, and proclaiming the equality of men. The French revolution, that awful upheaval of past oppression, that drowning of old wrongs in blood, terrible as it seemed, was prophetic of a new and glorious era. Over all the world we hear mankind proclaiming its existence, demanding its rights. Kings begin to be but names, and the sons of genius, springing from the people, grasp the real scepters. The reign of aristocracy is passing; that of humanity begins. Democracy is waiting for its poet.

The highest genius of our times rests in the men expressive of these ideas; in men like Darwin, Spencer, Watts, Lincoln. In the fulness of time, the facts for which these names stand, will demand musical and enduring expression. The age will demand a mouthpiece, and at its bidding will arise the poet of the future. In vain should we attempt to gauge the song of that poet who turning from the past shall find all fresh, fair, and inspiring in the present. His song will appeal, not to our country alone, but to all countries. He will find beauty in the useful and the common. In his lap science will pour her glorious jewels and bid him to give them the setting of his song. In his ear humanity will whisper deep, inspiring words, and bid him give them voice. He will unite the logic of the present and the dream of the past, and his words will ring in the ears of generations yet unborn, telling them the grandeur of today which boils and surges with awakening life. He will reflect all the past and prophesy the future. As surely as our age transcends all others, so surely will his song rise above all the singers of the past.

I stood one evening in a vast library. As the soft twilight floated through the tinted panes, a feeling of solemnity and awe seemed to pervade the place, and, as the dusk increased, there seemed to steal from out the dim corridors, those mighty kings of thought, whose potent sway forbids the ages of the past to die. With spectral steps they glided together,—blind old Homer with the fillet around his locks; Dante, sable-stoled and stern; Shakespeare with his god-like brow, and all the tuneful throng. With intent and waiting faces they seemed to peer into the mists of the future; for they feel the coming of the master to whose

123

genius they shall bow: in whose rich organ tones shall sound the splendor of the present, the divinity of man and nature.

A text of this oration is published in the *University Press*, 14 (number 35), 26 May 1883.
The oration was delivered on 18 May 1883.

# ARCHITECTURE THROUGH OPPRESSION

To an American standing in some venerable city of the old world, the architecture seems strangely different from that of New York or Boston. About him rise spires, pinnacles and minarets; his step resounds along the naves of vast cathedrals and his heart is thrilled with strange emotion at the sight of

> High embowed roof
> And antique pillars massy proof,
> And storied windows richly bright,
> Casting a dim religious light.

His eye wanders among the wilderness of beautiful carvings and mouldings until he stands bewildered at these treasures of the mediaeval past. He searches for the secret of these works of architecture, and he learns that Nature furnished the designs. "The groves were God's first temples!" Filled with memories of the forest, man wrought in stone the effect it had on him, and wondrous palaces and Parthenons begemmed the earth. In America we have giant cathedrals, whose spires are moss clad pines, whose frescoes are painted on the sky and mountain wall, and whose music surges through leafy aisles in the deep toned bass of cataracts or winds about in aeolian harmonies breathed from the forest harps. But in America where nature yet displays these grand suggestions, we build our buildings common, angular and plain. The palaces and cathedrals of the old world belong to a different age from ours. Our times are plebeian; it is visible in our architecture.

The history of humanity has been a romance and a tragedy! In it we read the brilliant annals of the few who seemed born to reap the fruits of the earth. For them were the glories of wealth, for them the glitter and glamour of life, and for them this "blossoming in stone." But the tragedy of humanity! Millions groaning that one might laugh, servile tillers of the soil, sweating that others might dream; drinking the logwood of life, while their masters quaffed its nectar. Many are the historians who have painted the glories of the past; few there are that tell the "lamentation and the ancient tale of wrong." It was from the extortion of the despot that the magnificent mosques of the Orient were built. When the freedom of Rome had departed and her peasantry had been crushed into serfdom, then the rich and cultivated nobleman adorned his villa with the gems of art, and Italy was decked with splendid palaces. Many a castle on the Rhine remains to furnish quaint old legends, and to tell a story of the robber baron who, spider-like drew within that strong walled seat of his the fruit of the common people's toils.

Art is a glorious gift to man; these works of architecture are a splendid contribution from those who were actors in life's romance, but how ill they suit with the state of the common men in the times in which they rose! When we think of the countless masses who wore the fetters of oppression how dark a shadow their anguish casts about these miracles of stone and marble that their sorrows helped to build. Gloriously rise the spires and minarets of many a mediaeval cathedral, but even by its side was built the hovel of the serf, and as the solemn wail of the *miserere* steals along the stately aisles, seems to bear a burden from the men worn out with toil and slavery! How heavy, gloomy, and how awful stand the pyramids upon the sands of Egypt, telling of—

> The detested task
> Of piling stone on stone, and poisoning
> The choicest days of life
> To sooth a dotard's vanity.

And the deep-wondering, placid face of the Sphynx gazes toward the heavens in a kind of enquiry of how long the children of the earth must be oppressed. So it has looked for centuries, in mute trusting appeal against man's inhumanity to man.

Art is too divine a thing to live by the throes of the people. The civilization of the past, which was the condition of art's existence, left it sadly marred by the incompleteness, the distortion of that civilization. But now the world begins to see that true progress, true enlightenment, means the progress, the enlightenment of all. In this wave of democratic utilitarianism, that is sweeping over the earth, art may seem engulfed, refinement destroyed, and men may shudder as the wave seems about to hide forever all that remains of the ancient idea of the Beautiful. But the fear is groundless! In the very breadth and depth of the inundation lie the possibilities of a grander future. The Greek upreared the Parthenon and sneered at the world as barbaric. The Nineteenth century is striving to build humanity into a glorious temple to its God,—his only fitting temple. When the greatest happiness of the greatest number shall have become something like a reality, when life's tragedy shall cease to clash with life's romance, and the squalor of the hovel shall no longer mar the cathedral's beauty,—then again may "music freeze into marble," and forests blossom into stone.

A text of this oration is published in the *University Press*, 15 (number 39), 21 June 1884.
The oration was delivered on 18 June 1884.

## B. Eulogies and Occasional Addresses

OCCASIONAL ADDRESSES are so named not because they are delivered occasionally. Rather, they are so designated because they are delivered in conjunction with some occasion which, in effect, dictates their themes and content. Thus, on the Fourth of July, an American orator likely will talk about patriotism and the virtues of the United States as a country. Of course the eulogy is the most constrained species of occasional oratory, generally calling forth a speech typically praising the deceased's attributes and then articulating some moral for the audience.

In the Aristotelian paradigm of rhetorical genres, such speeches would be in the category known also as demonstrative or epideictic oratory. In essence, the epideictic speaker is engaged primarily in a rhetoric of display. For the audience is not called upon to render a judgment about the past, to decide whether something did or did not happen. Nor is the audience primarily a judge of the future, rendering some decision, likely as a deliberative body, about the desirability of some policy or course of action advocated by the speaker. Instead, this audience is in effect a judge of the present. Being in attendance upon that particular occasion, they probably agree with the speaker's themes or the praiseworthiness of the deceased. Their act of judgment is of that moment and reserved for the value of the aptness with which the orator articulates the subject matter dictated by the occasion. In effect, then, the epideictic orator demonstrates the ability to say well what the audience most likely believes already.

Turner's eulogies fall easily into the category of epideictic oratory. Appropriate to praising the life of a teacher of oratory, the 1906 eulogy of David B. Frankenburger is brief, again perhaps reflecting what Turner knew of classical rhetorical theory and its recommendations that the deep emotion of the speaker was communicated most effectively through terseness in the discourse. Heretofore unpublished, Turner's text is in longhand, clearly displaying the extent to which he was willing to delete words, phrases, and even longer passages to achieve that basic *brevitas*.

The 1913 eulogy of Reuben Gold Thwaites was a far more

lengthy and carefully detailed composition. Certainly the appropriate way of praising a fellow historian would be with a more extensive, biographical treatment. In addition, the fact that the eulogy was to be published by the Wisconsin State Historical Society undoubtedly motivated Turner to develop the more careful and complete statement (in all likelihood, Turner even may have expanded his spoken address for the purposes of that publication). Today's reader can detect some passages relying on Turner's typical style in discourse, as in the rhetorical parallelism in the following description of Thwaites as a person:

> *He found* in the State itself a ready response to the claims of history; *he found* among the able and unselfish leaders of the Historical Society helpful hands to smooth many a path and carry many a load—the ablest men in Wisconsin's public life were friends of the Society. *He found* support in the University. *He found* an enlightened appreciation in the legislature and the press. *He found* in his associates on the staff of the Society, who gladly merged their personality in his, most loyal and efficient aid in his many-sided task.

In addition to its style in discourse, however, the Thwaites eulogy evinces still other factors of value for today's reader. Turner's text offers an understanding of Thwaites as a prime mover in the development of the Wisconsin State Historical Society. But far more significantly for this volume, that eulogy also provides additional insights into what Turner the historian perceived as praiseworthy in the historical endeavors of others, in this case the capabilities of Thwaites for characterization in discourse. Previously published in 1914 by Wisconsin's State Historical Society, the eulogy is included here for more ready access by those seeking a fuller understanding and appreciation of Turner's eloquence.

In his other occasional addresses, the historian from Wisconsin seemed willing to depart from the more traditional conventions for epideictic oratory. That is, Turner often took the opportunity of an occasion to advocate what in effect was a policy, a deliberative course of action, or a general behavior by his audience. This tendency is particularly evident in three addresses given in conjunction with occasions involving educational institutions: an 1895 commencement address to the graduates of Madison High

School, an 1896 dedication address for the new school building in his home town of Portage, and an 1897 after-dinner address to a meeting of University of Wisconsin alumni. So although published elsewhere in two different places, these three speeches are brought together in this volume to suggest another facet of Turner's rhetorical behaviors.

For a commencement address at Madison High, the typical orator likely would have praised the school and some virtues which its graduates might take with them to apply generally in later life. Instead, Turner used the occasion to speak specifically about Madison as a city and then to advocate a mode of civic patriotism in which his listeners should engage (albeit with ecological considerations of which any contemporary environmentalists would be proud!). Similarly, the dedication address at Portage did not deal with that town's school or specific scholastic system but rather with Turner's wider view of public education, even at the university level. So today's reader of this address can learn of the historian's views on educating people for political citizenship as well as practical, economic insights for greater success in life. Turner also utilized the event to advocate a high school extension program to involve the intellectual interests of entire communities. And in the after-dinner address to University of Wisconsin alumni, Turner delivered no paeon to that school and its graduates. Instead, his brief speech advocated a specific policy for the University of Wisconsin: increased future support for scholarship among the faculty and growth of a graduate program.

The heretofore unpublished address to the alumni on football also suggests Turner's tendency to use an occasion to advocate future policies. In this case, the after-dinner speech at Keely's Restaurant on the night of 31 January 1906 is a bold indictment of brutality and professionalism in the football program at Wisconsin. Believing that the sport had to be de-emphasized to restore the intellectual life of the university, Turner's discussion of abuses concluded with his offering three resolutions concerning the more appropriate place of the sport at the Madison campus. Turner's longhand notation at the bottom of his typed draft indicates that the resolutions were adopted unanimously (for detailed discussion of the historian's role in the football controversy, see Billington, *Frederick Jackson Turner*, pp. 263-80).

As a collective entity, these occasional addresses also illustrate some of the constant elements of Turner's eloquence. And of course today's reader of the three speeches on education, in particular, can discern easily ways in which the historian borrowed from one speech to develop another. For example, from 1883's "The Poet of the Future," Turner took a reference to "Dante, sable-stoled and stern," an alliterative compound wording very much consonant with Aristotle's view of a stylistic quality suitable for epic description (*Rhetoric*, 1406b). "Dante, sable-stoled and stern" then appears in 1895's "The High School and the City." That latter address began with a quotation from Thomas Jefferson: "If a nation expects to be ignorant and free in a state of civilization, it expects what never was and never will be." In turn, 1896's dedication at Portage begins with the same quotation. The peroration of the address at Portage includes Bacon's admonition to "remember that the learning of the few is despotism, the learning of the many is liberty and that intelligent and principled liberty is fame and wisdom and power." While displaying Turner's preference for the antithesis between the "few" and the "many," the statement also includes another stylistic feature characterizing eloquent oratory in moments of functional urgency, that rhetorical heaping of the conjunction "and" *(polysyndeton)*. And to develop his thesis in 1897's commencement address on higher education to University of Wisconsin alumni, Turner utilizes the same quotation!

These notations of Turner's rhetorical cannibalizing are *not* intended to suggest a paucity of ideas or inventiveness on the part of the historian from Wisconsin. He was a busy man. Not only a dedicated teacher, Turner was deeply involved in other dimensions of university life, including demanding committee responsibilities. And throughout all of these activities, Turner tried to continue as a productive scholar. Always in demand as a lecturer and speaker, however, the historian had a sense of obligation to fulfill those ample opportunities to create rhetorical discourse (indeed perhaps too many opportunities). With so many demands upon his time, Turner simply could not find fresh material for every address. So the historian developed a pattern. With extensive and highly successful rhetorical experiences from which to draw, and under pressure of time, Turner tended to take elements which were effective in previous endeavors and utilize them appropriately in successive attempts. And this tendency is emphasized here as a major, causal factor accounting for the final form of what is known today as the frontier thesis.

*Frederick Jackson Turner*

# EULOGY OF DAVID B. FRANKENBURGER

Out of the depths of our grief come brokenly words of love for our friend, words of thankfulness that he lived, words of serene assurance that he has entered into that rest which God gives to his beloved.

What his life meant to his associates, what it meant to the great body of students who through nearly thirty years came into affectionate touch with his instruction and with his uplifting sympathy, we all know. He was a teacher. But he taught his students more than the formal art of expression. Those of us who in our plastic years came under his influence will never forget that rare, questioning smile; that invitation to the best and the highest lying like the seed within our souls. He had the glad expectancy, the appealing sympathy that like God's sunshine drew forth the bud and the blossom of our best endeavor. No member of our faculty was more absolutely bound up in the University of Wisconsin. His life was one of unselfish devotion to his students. Others might teach classes, he taught the individual. To this ideal he gave unstinted of his time and his energy. No timid student ever brought his imperfect work to him without going away heartened by encouragement, aided by helpful suggestions, and above all inspired to do something better.

This attitude toward his students was a part of his attitude toward life. Rejoicing in what was excellent today, he yet awaited the fuller revelations—new truth, new beauty and new good. When he talked of these things, his face was aglow with expectancy.

To such a soul how thin and insubstantial became the veil between the lesser life in the body and that real life eternal and abundant which now is his.

And so we who as his colleagues respected and admired him, we who as his students drew inspiration from his strong and gentle spirit, we who as alumni knew his steadfast interest in our welfare and who wove his gracious personality into those recollections that embody for us the University of Wisconsin, come to him this afternoon with flowers, with tears, and with love. But through our sorrow ring the lines of his favorite Emerson: "Saying, *What is excellent, As God lives, is permanent; Hearts are dust, heart's loves remain, Heart's love will meet thee again.*"

Delivered at the Unitarian Church, Madison, Wisconsin on 8 February 1906. The longhand text is in Box 55. The concluding quotation is from Emerson's "Threnody." The correct punctuation of line three should be "hearts' loves remain."

# REUBEN GOLD THWAITES

*A Memorial Address*

## By Frederick Jackson Turner

On October 22, 1913, the day before the annual meeting of the State Historical Society of Wisconsin, Reuben Gold Thwaites, its Superintendent, who for twenty-seven years had guided its activities, passed from our midst.

So abundant was his vitality, so buoyant his energy, so great, so enduring were his contributions to history, and so deep in our affections had he fixed himself, that it is almost impossible to believe that we shall see him no more, no more rely upon his strong and gentle hand to guide the destinies of this Society, no more rejoice in the companionship of one of the most lovable spirits of our time. The heart aches at the loss. But he died in the fullness of his powers: for him there was no long decay, no saddened realization of failing strength or dimming spirit for the work with which he was intrusted.

> With a cheery smile and wave of the hand,
> He has wandered into an unknown land.

Aptly quoted by the editor of *Public Libraries* in a notice of Dr. Thwaites's death.

He had already paid in full the obligations of the scholar and the administrator. He did a man's work, and left an indelible impress not only on this Historical Society and the State of Wisconsin, but upon the historical activities of the nation. Even the briefest record of his life tells a story so rich in achievement, usefulness, and service that it is an inspiration.

He was born in Dorchester, Massachusetts, May 15, 1853, the son of William George and Sarah Bibbs Thwaites, natives of Yorkshire, England, who had come to Massachusetts three years before. His early schooling was at Dorchester, and in the fall of 1866 he came to Oshkosh, Wisconsin, where for six years he worked on the farm, taught school, and prepared himself in the studies usually pursued in the colleges of that period. Only a boy of unusual ability, initiative, and ambition could have carried out such a program. By 1872 he was on the staff of the Oshkosh *Times*, for which he reported the Democratic presidential convention in Baltimore that year. In 1874-75 he was a special student in Yale College, taking graduate courses in English Literature, Economic History, and International Law. Among his instructors was William

133

Graham Sumner, eminent in the field of economic history, historical biography, and sociology, who doubtless influenced this young student as he did so many others. While pursuing these studies young Thwaites supported himself in part by newspaper correspondence. Returning to Wisconsin, he removed to Madison and became, in 1876, managing editor of the Wisconsin *State Journal*, a leading organ of the Republican party under the editorship of David Atwood. For a time he also supplied a chain of prominent eastern newspapers with Wisconsin news.

The necessary emphasis upon haste in a daily newspaper, often harmful to a writer, does not seem to have left its scars upon Mr. Thwaites. Rather his conscientiousness, his natural accuracy combined with facility, and his efficiency in the organization of work, turned this experience to his advantage. He learned how to think quickly and to act, how to condense, to select the essential, to watch with discriminating eye the play of the political forces about him, to study human nature intimately, and to report what he saw. As reporter of legislative proceedings and political conventions he acquired a wide acquaintance with the public men and journalists of the state which afterwards served him well in his task of popularizing the work of the Society and of securing legislative aid for its development. Moreover, he trained himself in the technique and art of typography, proof-reading, and printing, by actual contact with these phases of the printing office. He became an expert in the material making of a book, as the works which he afterwards edited amply illustrate.

During this decade in which Mr. Thwaites found in newspaper work the outlet for his energy, he by no means lost the scholar's fondness for books nor the literary taste which had been his from his early youth. Even while a newspaper reporter in Oshkosh he had shown historical interests, and as early as 1876 he published a sketch of the Indian Chief, Oshkosh, followed the next year by a history of Winnebago County, Wisconsin. He was one of the early members of the Madison Literary Club. His visits to the State Capitol, where the Historical Library was housed, often brought him into touch with Dr. Lyman C. Draper, that devoted man who watched like a father over the growth of the organization that he loved. Naturally shy and retiring, Draper could be bold and insistent for the Society, and it is one of the tributes to his insight that he recognized in this young editor a man of exceptional promise in the field of history and administration.

So it happened that the veteran, anxious to complete the books for which he had been collecting material during his long life, picked out this young man of thirty-one as the man to train as his successor. In

1885 Mr. Thwaites began the work of Assistant Corresponding Secretary of the Society, and on January 6, 1887, Dr. Draper wrote his letter of resignation closing with these words: "It is no small gratification to me to feel assured that the laboring oar of the Society's success will fall into hands so competent by his culture, his tastes, his industry, and his habits as the gentleman you have approved, and whom you will, I doubt not, choose as my successor. I earnestly entreat for him your confidence and encouragement, and devoutly pray the Good Father to spare him many years, that he may honor himself by faithful and successful labors for the Society." With this "benediction" from his predecessor Reuben Gold Thwaites began the great work of his life as the responsible executive officer of the State Historical Society of Wisconsin. Dr. Draper died four years later at the age of seventy-six, leaving to the Society the splendid results of his lifetime of collecting. He had done all that he could have done for this Society. It was a work of self-sacrificing devotion, the chopping of an historical clearing in the frontier state; it was more than that: his work had caused the Society to be recognized at home and abroad as the strongest in the West, and the Library had already become a noted one. But the times demanded a new man and new methods.

In 1884, after the failure of Dr. Draper to secure an appropriation of fifty thousand dollars for an independent building, the Society had moved into new quarters in the recently constructed South Wing of the Capitol. Disappointed, Dr. Draper had urged that the Society should seek private endowments in order that it might no longer be, as he said, "dependent upon or hampered by any alliance with the State," and in his final report in 1887 he declared: "We need a large general fund, so as to cease being a pauper on the State treasury."

It was at just about this time that the new tendencies appeared which finally brought fame to Wisconsin for its generosity and wisdom in supporting public institutions designed to lift the State to higher levels in all directions, intellectual as well as material. Not to have realized this opportunity can hardly be made a matter of reproach to Dr. Draper. It needed a younger man, with sympathy and insight into the great popular forces that were forming in those days, to perceive and take advantage of this ground swell. Even Mr. Thwaites for a few years adhered to the ideal of a Society based chiefly upon independent endowments, but he soon came to see that the glory and the greatest opportunity of the Society lay in its position as trustee of the State of Wisconsin for the promotion of historical studies. Thereafter he labored with the greatest effectiveness to make the Society worthy of its position as a State insti-

135

tution, freed from spoils and political jobbery by being intrusted to a body of men devoted to the purpose for which it was founded, but nourished by the State and merging its fortunes with the fortunes of the State.

In his first report Secretary Thwaites struck the keynote of his later work. The Society must be modernized, its Library must be given more ample room, for, as he declared, it would pass beyond the limits of its space within fifteen years. He noted also the increased State appropriations for issuing bibliographical lists of its treasures; the beginning of systematic card cataloguing by the most modern methods in place of the outworn system of successive catalogue volumes; and the separation of the *Collections* and the *Proceedings*, reserving the former for historical material, and the latter for the Society's records and historical essays. This was a significant step, emphasizing the distinction between source material and the secondary use of it, but recognizing both as legitimate activities of the Society. The distinction was more sharply drawn as successive issues appeared.

Significant also was the fact that in his first report Secretary Thwaites, so to speak, discovered the State University. He reported that the students formed the majority of the Society's readers. Before many years his statistics of attendance revealed the fact that they constituted ninety per cent of these readers, and that the reading room was inadequate to hold them. From the first he offered new facilities and greater freedom for their work. He opened a seminary room to the advanced students in American history, with full access to the stacks— an unheard of liberality among non-university libraries at that time.

Perhaps I may be pardoned for here recording my own deep gratitude for this hospitality of Secretary Thwaites to the young instructor who led his little band of investigators to this seminary among the Library's collections; to him and to them it was the opening of a new life. From that beginning these students and their successors have sown Wisconsin's seed in universities throughout the Union—all of them bearing in their hearts affectionate remembrance of the open policy and helpful hospitality of this Society and of Reuben Gold Thwaites, the scholar who so generously welcomed young men to the career of scholars.

Through the mass of University readers the Society was extending the influence to the whole State. It became more than a local center, for it made itself useful to what were, in effect, delegates from every county in the Commonwealth. As these young men returned to their homes and as they came to take part in the public life of the State they spread their appreciation of the services of the Society. From this friendly but entirely independent relationship of Society and University were to come advantages not at first foreseen, and a continually closer relationship of the Society to the State.

Nor was it the University students only to whom Mr. Thwaites extended his helping hand. In one of his early reports he noted the increasing interest in American history among the schoolteachers of the State, and their attention to local history, in which he always had a keen interest. The pioneer era was passing away, and the memory of the pioneers and the history of the communities of the State would have to be confided to the coming generation. The Secretary welcomed the demands upon the Society for the volumes of its *Collections* by these schools and proposed the republication of the first ten volumes, embracing the period of Draper's secretaryship, for the first edition was already insufficient to meet these new demands.

Year after year as this response to popular interest grew, year after year as he stimulated and gave intelligent direction to this interest, he reported increasing evidences of friendly relations with the State government, until the movement culminated in the erection of the noble building which since 1901 has housed this Society and the Library of the University of Wisconsin. In preparing the Society to accept this solution, in his study of other libraries and the incorporation of what was best into the interior architecture of the new building, and in the freedom and yet efficiency of his management of the Society's Library and the building, Dr. Thwaites contributed more effectively than has perhaps ever been clearly recognized to the creation of one of America's greatest historical workshops, a workshop that is at the same time a monument of American architecture.

Of the yearly work of Dr. Thwaites for the Society it is impossible to speak in detail. Under his hands the published historical material became more systematic and complete. Knowing the archives in Europe as well as in America, he drew upon the stores of Canada, of Paris, and of London, to illustrate the French period of Wisconsin's history. His persuasive insistence brought into the Library the materials for the foundations of Wisconsin's history from the old fur trading regions of Fox River and Green Bay, Wisconsin River and Prairie du Chien, and the Mackinac center of that trade. He secured and published a mass of material on the Protestant missionaries to Wisconsin, on the early schools, the beginnings of mining, lumbering, and other early industries of the State, and on the foreign groups which transformed the Wisconsin of the Frenchman, the Southerner, the New Englander, and the New Yorker into the Wisconsin of to-day. Papers of political leaders, bankers, and professional men of all kinds came increasingly into the Society's possession.

Its interests were broadened and deepened in all directions. Gaps in its Library were filled so that it became representative of all the great interests of American history in general and the Middle West in particular. The newspaper collections were systematized and opened into new fields. In concert with University professors he welcomed to the Library its great collection of labor literature. To the pamphlet collections he added data exhibiting the activities of political parties, church organizations, and all the homely varied social activities that too often escape the notice of historical societies. His doctrine that the rubbish of one generation may become the indispensable means of understanding its civilization by a later generation led him to a catholicity of view the importance of which the future will attest.

He visited remaining Wisconsin Indian tribes in their old homes, interviewed their chiefs, and incidentally was obliged to be host in his turn to delegation after delegation of these Indians, who, so to speak, camped out in the Society's rooms and claimed and received his personal largesse of board and small coin for days at a time. At his summer home in Turvillwood the gypsy Winnebago, up to a few years ago, still made annual hunting camps, and here he often talked with them. Thus he touched hands with the men of the Stone Age, fraternized with the survivors of the fur trade, with the pioneers, the politicians, and the journalists of the day, with the men of affairs and the scholars.

He issued circulars of instruction on the mode of organizing local historical societies, collecting materials, and building up historical museums. He gave his hearty encouragement and co-operation to the modernizing of the museum into a valuable educational agency of the State. He prepared syllabuses of Wisconsin history for study clubs and schools, and lectured to communities all over the State. Now helping in person to form a local historical society, now giving an address at the dedication of some monument or the marking of some trail, and illuminating the annals of the locality by his own acquaintance with its antiquities and by his wider knowledge of the history of the State of which its own history was a fragment, he strengthened in the localities the historic sense, and in the genuine Wisconsin spirit he made the Society's activity co-extensive with the State. Quoting with approval Woodrow Wilson's remark, "The world's memory must be kept alive or we shall never see an end of its old mistakes," Reuben Gold Thwaites mediated between the Wisconsin of the past and the Wisconsin of the present.

The Wisconsin Historical Society and its publications became a model looked up to by a multitude of western states. The systematic and accurate presentation of the materials in the ten volumes of the *Collections* which he edited; the twenty-six volumes of the *Proceedings;* the invaluable annotations drawn from the editor's own rich information and from the carefully organized stores of the Library; the scholarly papers of Dr. Thwaites himself; the efficient contributions of the staff of historical assistants whom he trained and guided in their work; the care and wisdom with which he brought to the Society's annual meetings speakers both from Wisconsin and beyond its borders, whose addresses set new models for historical study and suggested new fields of investigation—all this was the work of a really great organizer of historical industry.

And how carefully he performed the fiscal duties of his office, bringing to the service of the Society day after day that minute and painstaking accuracy which he applied to his personal business. No legislative investigation could ever find anything but praise for the financial records of the Society. He was efficient before the days of scientific management. He had the responsibility of the physical care of a great library building and it became a model of good housekeeping. He supervised the purchase of books and all the operations of the Library itself, and he so husbanded its inadequate funds that it grew from 118,000 titles to 352,000, threefold what he found it. He brought its needs year after year to the attention of the State with such clarity of exposition and such tactful dealing with men that it grew in the goodwill of the legislators.

Let us not do more than justice to Dr. Thwaites. He found in the State itself a ready response to the claims of history; he found among the able and unselfish leaders of the Historical Society helpful hands to smooth many a path and carry many a load—the ablest men in Wisconsin's public life were friends of the Society. He found support in the University. He found an enlightened appreciation in the legislature and the press. He found in his associates on the staff of the Society, who gladly merged their personality in his, most loyal and efficient aid in his many-sided task.

And yet, when all this is said, it remains that he found them, convinced them, trained them, led them, and retained their trust and affection. With quick and sympathetic intuition he caught and utilized what was best in their suggestions and in them. With quiet, but none the less effective, skill and persuasiveness he bound them to himself for the service of the Society. He so organized these forces that men and women saw in him their natural leader and helpful friend for securing the results in which all were interested. Such gifts of administration are as rare as they are important.

His ability and breadth of interest, his broad humanity, caused other agencies for public good to enlist his aid, for it is the busy man who is appealed to for effective work. He was an active member and vice-president of the influential Free Library Commission, and in many ways he helped to broaden the usefulness of the State Historical Library, to spread libraries throughout the State, and to promote efficiency in the training of librarians. He was secretary and editor of the Wisconsin History Commission, which under authority of the State has already published nine volumes of valuable original papers and reprints on Wisconsin's part in the Civil War, with a tenth in press. All of these manuscripts passed under his careful editorship. He was lecturer in History in the University of Wisconsin, and for several years an extension lecturer for the same institution.

He wrote the standard history of Wisconsin, the history of the University, the history of Madison, the history of his lodge, the record of the Madison Literary Club. He was active in the service of the City Hospital, the University Club, the Madison Art Association, and the Unitarian Church, and in his will he remembered the hospital and the church and most generously left a tithe of his estate to this Society. Had Dr. Thwaites done no more in his busy life but what he did directly by his work for this Society and for the State of Wisconsin he would have made an enduring place for himself, and would have more than repaid all that Wisconsin had done for him.

Thus, ineffectively and incompletely, I have tried to bring before you the work of Reuben Gold Thwaites of Wisconsin. It was in itself a full life; but, ladies and gentlemen, there was also a Reuben Gold Thwaites of the United States. Let us turn briefly to consider our friend and colleague in this wider aspect of his work as man of letters, librarian, historical editor, and historian. A rapid survey of the successive periods of his life from this point of view is all that is possible on this occasion.

In 1884 and again in 1885 Dr. Thwaites visited New Mexico and Colorado and had some idea of establishing a newspaper in this New Southwest. Indeed he proposed to me, then just out of college, that I should join in the enterprise, and he painted the life of the cattle region and the profit of advertising cattle brands in such terms as have always left a doubt whether it was not a golden opportunity lost! But upon his selection as Secretary of the Society, Dr. Thwaites began a course in the rereading of Parkman's works, visited Canada, and in the summer of

1888 canoed down the Rock, the Fox, and the Wisconsin, and wove into a light but charming narrative the history of these rivers with his own observations of scenes and men along them. The next year appeared his *Historic Waterways*, in which he printed this experience, and the summer found him again in Canada and the eastern cities.

In 1890 his first history of Wisconsin came from his pen, under the title *The Story of Wisconsin*. In the succeeding year he published a brief history of *The Colonies*, the first volume of a series in which Woodrow Wilson and Professor Hart, of Harvard, were his co-workers, and this excellent manual became so widely used as a text for colleges that its author gained a reputation beyond his State. In the summer of the year of its appearance he traveled in Europe, studying libraries and archives there and writing his graphic and readable little book, *Our Cycling Tour in England*. In 1894, he took another canoe voyage, this time down the Ohio, the results of which appeared in his *Afloat on the Ohio*, republished as *The Storied Ohio*. In preparation he read most of the previous travels on this famous river from the early days. As he tells us, his purpose was to gather "local color," to "see with his own eyes what the borderers saw; in imagination to redress the pioneer stage and to repeople it." For all of its freightage of history the little craft floated lightly and captivatingly; the voyager painted with loving and skillful touch the scenery, described with his quick appreciation, wit, and human sympathy the life and conversation of the dwellers along the river, and at the same time interested his readers in the daily experiences of his little band of contemporaneous explorers.

This trip illustrated much that was fundamental in Dr. Thwaites's character and work. He based his history firmly on a knowledge of the geography of the country, and he was a minute and conscientious observer of nature. He saw his characters, not as lay figures, but vividly and dramatically as real people. He had an unusual appreciation of the humorous and a knack for keen but kindly characterization. When he told a story he was at once the center of an interested and delighted group, for it was a work of art, the result of psychological appreciation, of sympathetic and lively interest in his fellow-man. He had the gift of dramatic narrative.

Moreover, he believed that the historian should bring to his work an appreciation of the romance in history. As expert in editing as the most technical and dry-as-dust of his brethren, he never read a document or penned a note that he did not see the picturesque, the human scene behind the bare record; ever behind the document there was the pageant. He faithfully gathered the often dreary and dismal records of fur trader and explorer and presented them in well ordered and scientifically edited volumes. But when all is done, he writes: "Piled high with bales of peltries, and propelled by gaily appareled savages and voyageurs, with black-robed priests for passengers, the flotillas swept down the broad rivers in rude procession, paddles flashing in the sun, the air rent with barbaric yells and the roaring quaver of merry boating songs." The history of institutions, of industrial development of laws and governments, appealed to him less than the history of individual achievement. The narrative of action and the documents on which it was based gained his most loving attention.

In 1895 appeared the edition of Withers' *Border Warfare*, under the editorship of Draper and Thwaites, a valuable repository for the historian, enriched by Dr. Thwaites from his own learning as well as from Dr. Draper's treasure-house. Had Thwaites been content to follow in the footsteps of his predecessor, utilizing his collections and editing the mass of material on the Revolutionary era, he would have found ample opportunity and appreciation for his work. But he was too independent to limit his activity to this task. In the end his interests turned to earlier periods and to exploration rather than to border warfare.

In the years between 1896 and 1901 he published his monumental edition of the *Jesuit Relations* in seventy-three volumes. His reviewer in the *American Historical Review* declared that it would "mark an epoch in the historical literature of North America because of the abundance and value of the documents reproduced and the vast erudition utilized by the editorial staff." The editor gathered about him a band of skilled transcribers, proof-readers, translators, local antiquarians, and bibliographers. He gained the co-operation and trust of the most eminent Catholic authorities on the subject, visiting Canada and, in 1897, Italy to this end; he added greatly to the existing sources on the work of these devoted missionaries in America; and produced what will probably be the definitive edition of the *Relations*—the invaluable *monumenta* of American exploration in the era of New France. Among the most useful features of this work was its classified index, extensive in its scale, and accurate in its treatment. For the first time was the American library method applied on a large scale to the service of the historian. To his associate editor, the late Miss Emma Helen Blair, Dr. Thwaites gave generous praise for efficient aid in editing this great work.

Thus, during the period of the campaign for the new library building and the years of its erection, Dr. Thwaites had given to the world an enduring evidence of his scholarship and organizing power, and had brought to the Society a renown which extended to the Old World.

After the completion of the *Relations* there followed from his busy pen a series of volumes, including well written and scholarly biographies of Marquette and Daniel Boone, a reprint of Hennepin, and a volume of historical essays under the title, *How George Rogers Clark Won the Northwest*.

In 1904, following a trip to Yellowstone Park, he issued his *Rocky Mountain Exploration*, a book which prepared the way for two other monumental publications which appeared in the years between 1904 and 1907. These were the first edition of the *Original Journals of Lewis and Clark* in eight volumes, and reprints of *Early Western Travels* in thirty-two volumes. Of these works I may not speak at length. In the former, Dr. Thwaites met and conquered difficulties in a way that proved him an editor of the very first rank. He ferreted out from their concealment missing documents necessary to complete the journals; deciphered the difficult writing and spelling of these historic frontiersmen, who first crossed the continent within the limits of the present United States; mastered the problem of correlating and printing the several journals of the expedition; drew upon all of his resources of typographic and editorial skill to give an absolutely faithful reproduction of the originals; enriched them with a wealth of historical and geographical annotation; and contributed a monographic introduction setting forth the development and historic significance of this epic of American transcontinental exploration.

In his reprints of *Early Western Travels* his skill in annotation was again revealed; but perhaps the most important contribution of Dr. Thwaites in this series was the exceedingly complete and well analyzed index which opened to the historical student the wealth of information which was contained in these accounts of travelers, who in the years between 1748 and 1846 pushed westward until their later representatives reached the far Northwest and the far Southwest. Not only were many of these travels rare, but they had never before been brought together by means of an adequate index for the service of the economic and social historian. Together they present a picture of the irresistible tide of American settlement flowing into the wilderness, of societies forming in the forests, of cities evolving almost under our gaze as we see them through the eyes of these travelers in successive years.

As America grows older, more and more it exhibits a tendency to turn back to the heroic age of its explorers and pioneers. In historical pageants, mural decorations, sculpture, poetry, in all the aesthetic use of historic symbols may be seen this growing appreciation by the nation of its remoter past. By these editions of the *Jesuit Relations* (the early sources of the history of Canada and the Middle West), *Lewis and Clark* (the historical fountain for the states between the Missouri and the Northwest Coast), and the *Early Western Travels*, Dr. Thwaites made himself the editorial authority to whose sources the student must turn if he would study this stage of American development.

And while Dr. Thwaites issued these works he also gave to the world his useful résumé in the American Nation Series of *France in America*, and his edition of *Lahontan*. With the assistance of Dr. Louise Kellogg he issued in later years volumes of valuable annotated documents from the Draper manuscripts and other sources entitled *Lord Dunmore's War, The Revolution on the Upper Ohio*, and *Frontier Defense on the Upper Ohio*.

In 1909 he published his excellent *History of Wisconsin* in the American Commonwealth Series, and in 1912, with the collaboration of Superintendent Kendall, a *School History of the United States*.

I am informed by Miss Nunns, long his right hand in administration, that when death removed him he was planning to begin work on the history of the fur trade, a subject for which no man was better fitted, and that he intended to widen the collections in the field of that far Southwest to which as a young man he had thought of removing.

Often in his reports Dr. Thwaites called the attention of the Society to the importance of keeping in touch with sister institutions in other parts of the country and particularly with the great national associations devoted to history and to library management. He himself regularly attended these associations, and in 1900, the year of the completion of the library building, he was honored by the presidency of the American Library Association and was made chairman of the Historical Manuscripts Commission of the American Historical Association. Four years later he became a member of the Council of the latter Association. In many ways he was one of the most important contributors to its activities, and particularly in fostering the relations between the Association and state-supported historical societies similar to that of Wisconsin.

To many state and local historical societies in various quarters of the Union he was called to lecture on the early history of the West, or to describe Wisconsin's method of fostering historical studies throughout the State. He became an envoy extraordinary to other states to extend Wisconsin's influence. The University of California called him to lecture at its summer session, and again to report on the value of the Bancroft Collection of sources on the history of the Rocky Mountain and Pacific states. Following his advice, California acquired this noble collection, thus making Berkeley the center for the study of that vast section, as Madison is for the Alleghany Mountains and the Mississippi

Valley. He lectured also in Oregon, where he was welcomed as the editor of the sources of the early history of the Pacific Northwest. He represented the American Historical Association and delivered one of the leading addresses in Annapolis at the Canadian celebration of the anniversary of the settlement of the Annapolis Basin. In the East he was made a member of the American Antiquarian Society, to whose publications he contributed a scholarly paper on the early press of the Ohio Valley, and he was honored with membership in the ancient Massachusetts Historical Society. In the West the Mississippi Valley Historical Association made him its president in 1912. Already Wisconsin at its jubilee celebration had given him the honorary degree of Doctor of Laws.

In the course of a little over a quarter of a century, Dr. Thwaites wrote some fifteen books and edited and published about one hundred and sixty-eight additional volumes. To this total of one hundred and eighty-three volumes, which makes an average of about seven for each year, should be added something like one hundred articles and addresses. Of course his worth is not to be tested by the number of volumes—most of these were annotated or reprinted collections of documents; but to have been the responsible editor for so great and so substantial an historical output, while carrying arduous administrative duties, implies an activity beyond the power of most men of letters and science.

Looking back over his record of achievement, considering these extensive and scholarly contributions to American history, which compelled the recognition and respect of his associates throughout the United States, one cannot fail to see how profoundly important all this was to the State Historical Society of Wisconsin. When Dr. Thwaites published a document, made an annotation, addressed a local historical society, dedicated a monument, or marked a trail in the State, he did it with that fullness of knowledge, that large recognition of the significance of his subject, which came from an extensive and thorough study of the whole process of exploration and pioneering in the United States. The forces of American history flowed through the history of the locality and the State when he spoke.

He brought to the altar of this Society his laurels from the nation. They were laurels of love for the man as well as tributes to the scholar's worth. When he died, this note of affection was struck not only by the country press from many a Wisconsin town, not only by the city press of the Northwest, but in publications and letters from all over the United States.

145

At a recent meeting of members of the Council of the American Historical Association a letter was drawn up and signed by men among the most distinguished in the historical activities of the nation, expressing in the sincerest and warmest terms their sense of personal loss, their love and admiration for Dr. Thwaites as a man and as an historical scholar.

Short in stature, but with a compelling personality, his cheery, winning spirit shining out behind his twinkling eyes, always ready with a joke or a story that impressed a point upon his hearers; alert, decisive, receptive, helpful, a man of honor and of character, active in the Unitarian Church and respected and trusted by the Catholic clergy; an author whose style was graphic, lively, and so carefully disciplined that it concealed the care with which he worked out each sentence; a writer with imagination, a conscientious scholar, and a man of affairs, Dr. Thwaites combined in himself most unusual qualities.

He was married in 1882 to Miss Jessie Turvill, and to them was born a son, Fredrik T. On most of his happy summer outings where travel was both recreation and the search for new material, he was accompanied by his family. In their companionship he found a happiness that remained with him through life.

Wherever he went, whether among the Indians of Wisconsin or of the Arizona Pueblos, the French fur traders, or the scholars of the great national associations, he was greeted with a quick recognition that here was a rare man, a man to be welcomed as a friend. We who lived in daily contact with him may not have known how wide was the circle of his friends, for he disliked to talk of himself and of his achievements. But we know how richly he deserved that friendship, for we who saw him at his daily work, who knew him in his home, we, too, leaned on him, trusted him, and loved him.

This Society has been fortunate in the length of service of its great executive officers. Draper and Thwaites span the whole active life of the Society, which is nearly as old as the state itself. If we consider the years of Dr. Draper's superintendency of public instruction and of the Civil War, during which the publications of the Society were suspended, each of these men gave to the Society about the same length of service, substantially a generation. Draper was the founder; Thwaites was the great historical editor and modernizer, the builder of a new type of state historical society.

In the years to come, on the basis of the structure they reared, this Society will become increasingly the home of historical students. Here are the priceless materials for the history of that vast Middle West, whose ideals are shaping the nation. To understand the economic, political, and social development that followed the era of explorer and pioneer requires the work of many students and will extend into later generations. Other men will succeed to Dr. Thwaites's office and, if they do their full duty, mindful of his example, they will open new avenues of progress to this Society and will explore new fields of history.

Happy, thrice happy, they, if in the times to come their names shall be spoken with the respect and the affection with which we speak the name of Reuben Gold Thwaites.

This eulogy is published by the State Historical Society of Wisconsin (Madison, 1914).

*Frederick Jackson Turner*

# THE HIGH SCHOOL AND THE CITY

"If a nation expects to be ignorant and free in a state of civilization, it expects what never was and never will be."

These are the words of Thomas Jefferson, the American exponent of the rule of the people. It would be *superfluous* to dwell on the obligation of the state to educate. Perhaps it is not superfluous to point out the obligation of the student toward the power that educates him. That it is the duty of the state to support education in no way diminishes the debt due to the state from those who are the especial recipients of her bounty. Next week the graduates of the University of Wisconsin will assemble on the University hill, and look across the city to the white dome of the state house. *There* is the symbol of their real alma mater—the mother whose generous hand opens the gates to the treasure house of learning. To her they owe the service of good citizenship. Patriotic, intelligent devotion to the state of Wisconsin is the right return for the bounty of the state.

Today the city of Madison graduates from her high school this class of young men and young women. It may be taken for granted that they realize that they owe to the nation and the state a patriotic return for the benefits conferred upon them; but do they realize that they owe a particular return to the city of Madison?

The patriotism which this occasion calls for is preeminently civic patriotism, loyalty and gratitude to the city which has educated them. This type of patriotism is too little felt in America. There are germinal indications of the feeling. Americans point with pride the price of local real estate; they rejoice in belonging to a boom town, they glory in platting suburb after suburb, they vie with their rivals on the census list, they struggle with each other for the possession of the normal school or the home for the feeble minded. But of deep seated devotion to the city as an institution there is but little.

To the man of the ancient world, civic emotion rose spontaneously, with overmastering power. Think for a moment what the city meant to the Greek. To him the city was founded by a god or a divine hero. Within its walls the gods made their abode. As generations went and came the city was peopled by ancestral deities as well. The city of the present was but a phase of the immemorial city, running back through ancestral deities to the god who founded it, running on through the generations to come.

Into this divine companionship the man was born. And here he lived. To lose his citizenship was to become a homeless wanderer, a man without a nation. The spell of religion was cast about the city. To pollute the waters was to offend the gods who there had their abode. To defile the city in any way was to call down the vengeance of an offended deity. On the city height, the acropolis, rose noble buildings, simple and stately, devoted to the gods. Up the rocky summit wound the solemn procession. In the open theater were performed supreme efforts of dramatic genius. On the rocky height orators addressed the whole body of citizens. Under the open sky philosophers walked and talked. As one looks back in imagination to a city like Athens, bathed in translucent atmosphere, abode of men like Phidias, Demosthenes, Socrates, Pericles, Aeschylus, standing for a great ideal of freedom, fronting the hosts of oriental power, lighting the torch of liberty, intellectual and political—that unquenchable flame that still burns and beams wherever civilization is—one is tempted to wish that he too were an Athenian, living in the city of the Violet crown, sharer in a common life, artistic, religious, political. The man of Athens knew what civic pride meant. His country was bounded by the city wall. Even in the days of her imperial glory, Athens was a city bearing rule over other cities, not the capital of a wide domain. This gave intensity to politics, and patriotism, concentrated on this one glorious city, burned with a fierce intensity. And Athens, the eye of Greece, the supreme type of the Hellenic city, was one of a noble sisterhood in the ancient world, where city and nation were one. Even Rome, the eternal city which spread its ring wall until the civilized world lived within its limits, still illustrates the devotion to the city. As the Roman household had its altars and its household gods, so the city of Rome had its temple of Vesta and its vestal virgins guarding the sacred city fire that was to Rome what the household altar was to the family. Her citizens worshipped at a civic shrine and gloried in the Roman name. Rome had no Phidias to raise a Parthenon, nor chisel perfect forms from marble, but she became the mistress of the world. Hear the words in which her poet Virgil celebrates her glories:

"Others I grant shall with more delicacy mould the breathing brass; from the marble draw the features to the life; plead causes better; describe with the rod the courses of the heavens, and explain the rising stars: to rule the nations with imperial sway be thy care. O Romans, these shall be thy arts: to impose terms of peace, to spare the humbled, and to crush the proud."

In the middle ages we have again the splendid spectacle of the city-state. You recall at once the imperishable glories of Venice, the bride of the Adriatic, Florence the home of art and letters, where the mighty Petrarch whispered the magic word beauty in the ear of sleeping Eu-

149

rope, where the divine Dante, sable-stoled and stern, walked the streets with his deep unfathomable song in his heart, and on his brow the bitter scorn of fate, where Savonarola raised his prophetic voice. The man of Florence knew what civic pride meant. And so, too, civic spirit can be seen in the cities of mediaeval Germany, surrounded with huge walls and moats, and battlements. Within these grim defenses, the citizens built those miracles of architecture, the cathedrals, whose lofty spires rose over the landscape, a perpetual memorial of the devotion of a whole city. And as the chimes of bells rang from the city's towers, they made sweet music in the ears of the burghers who called that city home, and aroused emotions of civic pride that the modern man can hardly understand.

It is not difficult to explain the lack of civic patriotism in America. In part it is due to the general spirit of individualism. The ancient and the mediaeval city were the outcome of social effort, of combined sacrifice and of pleasures found in exalting the glory of the city, rather than the individual glory of the citizens. And this social effort is not the characteristic of American life. Here the aim has been to build up the individual citizen. Government has been pictured as a necessary evil and taxation a thing to be endured. It is not easy to bring Americans to make liberal expenditures for the promotion of the interests of the whole. Again patriotism in America has been a divided thing. In colonial days it was England the mother country that aroused the patriotism of the people. Then men gave to their new states the devotion formerly given to England. As the national feeling grew it came to struggle with the patriotism toward the state, and the affections of the citizens "perceived a divided duty." And at best devotion to the nation has overmastered devotion to the states. In all this shifting of the object of patriotic sentiment, the city has steadily lost ground, and the sentiment of patriotism itself has suffered. Again the city is a mere *local government*. It is an administrative division in sharp contrast with the old city-state which sent its ambassadors, marshalled its army, fought with rival cities, made laws, and developed *intensity* of political activity because of the very *concentration* of this activity. Think, too, of the way population shifts in America. The citizen of Boston today may be a dweller in Tacoma in a fortnight. Cities themselves spring from the ground in a generation,— busy, populous, made up of men who come and go. Contrast this with the Greek city where families had dwelt for twenty generations.

It is not easy to arouse enthusiasm for mushroom cities, nor for a city in continual change.

Add to these explanations the fact that American cities lack individuality—and picturesqueness. The idea of *defense* was prominent in the ancient city. On the hill tops were the ring walls to which the shepards and tillers of the soil fled for refuge. Little by little the city grew about these citadels, and was picturesquely crowned with temples, or fortresses. In the modern America the conditions of *trade* have preponderated in forming the cities. At the junction of railroad systems on the plains, at the confluence of rivers, at a harbor on lake or ocean, have been built the cities of America, and the result is as monotonous and uninteresting as could have been expected. The *business* basis of the city explains not only its unpicturesqueness but the neglect of its government as well. In American cities the energetic and intelligent citizens have been so devoted to amassing wealth that they have attended to their own business blocks, and their own residences, and let the general management of the city fall into the hands of the less worthy.

But there is I think ground for hope of better things in the American city.

With the passing away of the days when there were unlimited opportunities for individual activity there is coming to America an increase of the social sense, an increased feeling of social responsibility. No longer are there millions of acres of free lands, mines to be pre-empted, great railroads to be built. Population becomes denser. There are signs that co-operation is beginning to supersede individuality.

Movement of population too is likely to *decrease* in this country. As the conditions of life become more stable men will live their lives in one city, and their children will follow them. Thus city life will gain continuity; and one generation will be the more ready to build for its successors, when its successors are likely to be its own children. As wealth accumulates, as Americans cease their feverish rush for exploiting the country, and begin [to] look for means of life as well as means of livelihood, they will more and more combine their activities to make the city a worthier place. We may expect more and more the development of public libraries, museums, art galleries; public control of transportation, lighting, water, and so on.

In the direction of better *city government* there is already to be traced a healthy spirit of reform. Civic federations are forming, men are giving scientific study to European systems of municipal government, and municipal activity. College settlements are working in the city slums. Men of wealth are endowing institutes of learning, and of practical arts for the development of a richer life among the common people. In a hundred ways the last few years have shown most encouraging signs that men are coming to realize their civic responsibility and the need of

151

applying community of effort to the development of the city.

The old city-state is gone forever. City and nation can never again be one. The glories of Athens, of Rome, of Florence, as municipal republics are the precious possessions of history. But they can never be repeated. Nor is it altogether a matter for regret. The very intensity of rivalry within such little states which made such a brilliant life possible brought with it equally intense antagonisms, and bitterness of faction. What was gained in variety and individuality of life was partly lost by an unworthy narrowness and provincialism.

We should strive to retain what was best in the old city life. The patriotism that belongs to one's *country* is not the feeling that we have or should have for the city; but the patriotism that consists in pride in the peculiar excellencies of the city, the patriotism that demands a pure and intelligent administration of city government, the patriotism that resents any violation of the municipal rights of the citizen, the patriotism that makes a man give freely to the support of improvements in his city, this we may well possess.

Let us congratulate ourselves upon living in a city which is so well designed to call out these worthy sentiments. If many American cities are lacking in individuality, in attractiveness, it is not so with ours. Stand on one of the hills that surround her, and count the glories of Madison. On either hand lie her matchless lakes, silver in the sunshine, golden in the moon light, opalescent, rainbow like at sunset hour. If a man is stirred by beauty he will be stirred by these lakes of ours. And there between them stands the capitol, emblem of her queenly position in Wisconsin, with its stately dome of white visible from afar. On another height rises the University. Within a decade this has grown from a little college into rivalry with the greatest Universities of the country. We shall soon count her students by the thousands. Other cities give bonuses for little schools. Madison has but to open her doors to this stream of students from all parts of the state, —from *many* states. Hospitality, mere self interest, indeed, demands that we give these guests of the city the best of sanitary conditions the best conditions of urban life in all ways.

Here too is our Historical Library, soon to be housed in fitting form near to the buildings of the University. From the Alleghanies to the Pacific there is no such library in American history as this. It has but three or four rivals in the country. As years go on, and as the nation becomes interested in her past as well as in her present and her future, Madison will be sought by increasing numbers of scholars for this priceless possession.

But it is needless for me [to] continue this enumeration. We are indeed happy in such a city. Beauty, political life, learning have here taken their abode. Let us see to it that we do our work as citizens.

These lakes of ours like crystal beakers brimming full should sparkle unpolluted. When Longfellow wrote of our limpid lakes with sylvan deities, he could hardly have expected us to empty into these lakes the city sewage. Here at least we might borrow from the city religion of the Greek, and shrink from the anger of the offended deities of the waters. We ought to drive away the spectres from our marshes. Intelligent and patriotic action would drain them and remove the menace to the city health. We ought never to allow the central part of our city to be overhung with smoke, and the air choked with its odors. Here in our country town we have a right to pure air as well as pure water. We ought to have here the cleanest city in Wisconsin, the best schools, the best government, and we might have all of these if we had but a little of the spirit of civic patriotism. Here is our home; let us make it worthy of the beauties with which nature dowered it.

Members of the graduating class, you have received the bounty of this beautiful city. Repay these gifts by patriotic, disinterested, vigorous citizenship. You owe to Madison a filial devotion. In a large degree the city will reflect the ideals of those who year by year pass from the high school to active citizenship. Let those ideals be high ideals. And remember that it is the wise choice of the highest things day by day that elevates the civic character.

> Daughters of Time, the hypocritic Days,
> Muffled and dumb like barefoot dervishes,
> And marching single in an endless file,
> Bring diadems and fagots in their hands.
> To each they offer gifts after his will,
> Bread, kingdoms, stars, and sky that holds them all.
> I, in my pleached garden, watched the pomp,
> Forgot my morning wishes, hastily
> Took a few herbs and apples, and the Day
> Turned and departed silent. I, too late,
> Under her solemn fillet saw the scorn.

A text of this speech is in Box 54; it also is published in *Frederick Jackson Turner's Legacy: Unpublished Writings in American History,* ed. with an Introduction by Wilbur R. Jacobs (San Marino: The Huntington Library, 1965). The speech was delivered on 14 June 1895.

Frederick Jackson Turner was graduated from the high school at Portage, Wisconsin, in June 1878. At that time the town's school population was small enough so that both high school and some of the upper grammar grades were accommodated in one stern and uncompromising two-story brick structure. At the end of 1895 a new high school building, of modern design and construction, was completed. On January 1, 1896 this building was dedicated in the presence of about four hundred citizens. The dedicatory ceremonies included music and brief remarks by various leading townsmen. The principal address of the day was delivered by the most distinguished alumnus of the high school who was within easy reach: Fred Turner, as his fellow townsfolk always remembered him. Turner was close at hand and often visited Portage, coming over from Madison to see his parents who resided on Franklin Street near the school.

Turner's dedicatory address was printed the following day in the Portage *Daily Register*. This is the only form in which it is known today. The historian gave it no specific title when it was printed in the columns of the home-town newspaper and never cited it in any of his subsequent writings. Up till now it has been a lost piece. For purposes of bibliographical reference in the future it has seemed best to settle on a name for the address. The title decided upon is: Education in a United States without Free Lands. The text as printed here is based upon a photostat of the address as published originally in the Portage newspaper. A few printer's errors and related inaccuracies have been corrected or eliminated.[1]

Turner's celebrated essay of 1893 looked backward and drew conclusions from the historic experience of the American people. In the present address the speaker based himself on the premise that one era of American history had come to an end, and that another, a different one, had commenced. This new era was to be characterized by the absence of free land. How were Americans to equip themselves for survival in this novel oncoming age? The address gives Turner's answer to this principal question.

Professor Merle Curti obligingly consented to look over the text of the address, and from his comments thereon the following observations are taken. This address, he states, displays Turner's readiness to apply his interpretation of American history to an *ad hoc* situation. Here we see the historian using his knowledge to guide social action in the community of Portage. Turner was primarily concerned with the social implications of public education on the high school level. Here he moved in the tradition of Horace Mann and spoke the same language that John Dewey had already begun to use. Like many other social Darwinists of the age, Turner emphasized the role of intelligence in social evolution. Organized intelligence above the common school and below the university is necessary for the proper adjustment of mankind to the ceaseless struggle for existence. The high school must help to prepare graduates with an effective and usable knowledge of the social studies; these possess a utilitarian function in our social order and are instruments of adjustment in the strife of evolution. "Turner wanted the high school to do for the hinterland of Portage—for the larger Portage community—what the University was doing for the State; he wanted it to be a community center, a social and intellectual force. This notion is especially significant. Insofar as I know, he was breaking new ground here, for the idea of the modern community high school was hardly envisioned even by the most advanced educational leaders in 1896. In 1898-99 Dewey was to do something with this concept, and in *Democracy and Education* (1916) he was to refine the concept."[2]

With these introductory remarks one makes an end of exegesis. Now let the reader turn to the address itself, observing as he reads the extent to which a prediction based upon a historical analysis made in 1896 has been borne out in the course of half a century.

*Frederick Jackson Turner*

# DEDICATION AT PORTAGE HIGH SCHOOL

Thomas Jefferson, the foremost advocate of the rule of the people in his time, declared: "If a nation expects to be ignorant and free in a state of civilization, it expects what never was and never will be." Jefferson realized that democracy meant more than the right of a people to rule itself. Unless democracy was to obstruct progress, destroy the accumulated gains of civilization, and ultimately to fall beneath the ruin it had wrought, democracy, he saw, must train itself for the exercise of its powers.

Acting in consonance with this idea, Jefferson not only broke the power of the aristocracy of Virginia; at the same time he proposed measures of popular education, whereby the masses would "be qualified to understand their rights, to maintain them, and to exercise with intelligence their parts in self government." The educational system which he advocated included common schools, academies, and a university. He was not able to carry out his scheme in its completeness; but he did create the noble University of Virginia, and as president of the United States he urged that the general government should found a national university.

Thus the prophet of our early democracy saw the importance of education in a republic. "If a nation expects to be ignorant and free in a state of civilization, it expects what never was and never will be!" Washington too, uttered the same sentiments, in these words: "In proportion as the structure of a government gives force to public opinion, it is necessary that public opinion should be enlightened."

But in the days of Washington and Jefferson the danger of an ignorant democracy was not a serious one. The dangers they apprehended were not very real. No conspiracy to overthrow popular government could have gained serious headway. Moreover, the democracy of that day was a limited one; it did not include all members of the community. In the south the negro did not vote; in the north great respect was paid to leading families, and throughout the union a majority of the states imposed a property qualification on the franchise, whereby large portions of the masses were excluded from the right to vote. But there existed a more effective check upon dangers arising from the rule of the people than either of these facts.

Early American democracy could afford to rule wastefully, and ignorantly, and yet the results were not very serious. Americans had a safety valve for social danger, a bank account on which they might continually draw to meet losses. This was the vast unoccupied domain that stretched from the borders of the settled area to the Pacific ocean. Endowed with such untold natural resources, with a continental sweep of fertile lands, forests, pasture grounds and mines, democracy could make mistakes and never be aware of its errors. No wonder Americans exulted that Uncle Sam was rich enough to give us all a farm. No wonder that they scorned to study methods of government and regarded office as the spoils of political war, and believed that in America the ability to govern came by instinct. Thus the early American democracy, when it did achieve command in the days of Andrew Jackson, was fashioned under conditions of free land and complete mobility of labor. The poor boy could go west and grow up with the country. For generations America was another name for opportunity. No grave social problems could exist while the wilderness at the edge of civilization opened wide its portals to all who were oppressed, to all who with strong arms and stout heart desired to hew out a home and a career for themselves. Here was an opportunity for social development continually to begin over again, wherever society gave signs of breaking into classes. Here was a magic fountain of youth in which America continually bathed and was rejuvenated. Out of this freedom of opportunity came the self-made man, the man who with quick eye to the main chance, and with coarse, courageous strength, seized his own.

Such a nation might make mistakes, and could make them without gravely feeling them. It cared not for European history, political systems, or industrial ideas, for these were foreign to it, and seemed to offer no advantages to this American world so unlike that across the Atlantic. The United States gave itself to the task of developing its vast domain, and almost forgot the existence of Europe. The nation became what John Randolph called it, "the mammoth of the American forest."

At last this land animal has toiled across the continent, and looks on the waters of the Pacific ocean. Behind him lies a changed world. Where were dense forests and wild wastes of prairie, are waving grain fields, innumerable hamlets, and busy cities; the whirr of the mill wheels sounds in the place where sounded the roar of the cataract. The public lands are taken up. Uncle Sam is no longer rich enough to give us all a farm. Ever since 1790 the census maps had shown for each decade the line of frontier settlement, but in 1890 the superintendent announced that there was no longer a frontier of settlement. The continent is crossed; the wilderness is won; America is transformed.

We find conditions of complex life, inequalities of wealth, and dense settlement comparable to those of Europe. Its problems become our problems. We have our labor troubles, as Europe has. We study her methods of municipal government to adapt them to our cities. We cease to be an isolated nation, and we find ourselves again taking to the water, building a navy and meeting European competition. We have our fisheries question, our Hawaiian question, our interoceanic canal question, our Samoan question, our Cuban question, and but yesterday the secretary of state threw our gauntlet in the face of England, Germany and France, and declared that the United States is practically sovereign in both Americas and that its fiat is law. In a word, ladies and gentlemen, American democracy has entered on a new career.

It can no longer entrust its destinies to untrained men with safety. In domestic affairs the struggle for existence becomes intense; Labor fronts Capital; in the homogeneous American society of our fathers, fissures begin to open between classes, fissures that may widen into chasms. In place of the old equalities of wealth we have Vanderbilt's country home in the woods of North Carolina, costing $6,000,000, circled with forty miles of pleasure grounds, on the one side, and on the other squalid tenement houses where children never see the flowers. In the relations of America with other nations, the old recklessness in choosing public servants will no longer do. For our congressmen, our administrators, we need men trained in the widest knowledge of political science. We need thoughtful, intelligent constituencies. If we do not have them we shall quickly learn the lesson of the survival of the fittest.

Certainly it needs no prophet to point out that if education was important to the old, comfortable, American democracy, it is now, with our influx of emigrants, our domestic dangers, and our critical foreign relations, a matter of life and death. Knowledge is always power, but to a democracy it is the condition of existence. "Remember," said Bacon, "that the learning of the few is despotism—the learning of the many is liberty, and that intelligent and principled liberty is fame, wisdom, and power." These are golden words; they should be written in every legislative hall in the land. In the principle of popular education is, perhaps, the greatest hope of the civic salvation of the American people.

Let us enquire then more particularly just what part public education plays in the conservation of democracy, and this will enable us to see the importance of the high school in the educational system. In the first place the public school acts as a cement to keep the various classes together. Here wealth and poverty sit side by side; study from the same books; and learn to understand each other. The democracy of the school room is complete and the aristocracy of intellect is the only privileged class recognized. No one can estimate the importance of this practical contact between classes. If the people ever break it down by crying out against expenditures necessary to make the public schools as good as the best, if public schools become weakened and fall into the hands of the poor alone, the gravest of blows will have been struck at peaceful democracy.

Again public education is essential to a democracy in order that the people may be enabled to rule wisely. When the question of extending the suffrage was being agitated in the second decade of this century, one of the fears most commonly expressed was that the pressure of wealth under intelligent direction would enable the unscrupulous to control the laboring men. The danger anticipated from the influence of great moneyed interests in political affairs was not a fanciful one, and if wealth were to monopolize education, the populace will certainly suffer. On the other hand an ignorant populace is a pliant tool in the hands of the unscrupulous demagogue, ready to tear down, unable to build up, and falling like a blind Sampson beneath the ruins of the temple of state.

In the third place a democracy needs public education, because where competition is sharp and the struggle for existence keen, we need to husband all our resources; we must know how to use them well. Our schools should include studies not now a part of them, studies that shall make more intelligent farmers, by teaching more scientific and economical modes of agriculture and farm management; studies that shall foster manual skill. Our education must be framed for the farmer and the artisan as well as for the business and the professional man.

And in the next place American democracy requires that this same education, which is useful for promoting the industrial power of the individual, should be applied also to the affairs of the nation. With the increasing complexity of social and industrial relations we can less and less afford untrained legislation on such important topics as the tariff, currency, and industrial relations. We must have an intelligent democracy capable of choosing wise leaders and of understanding their utterances.

We must have an educated democracy capable of grappling with the conditions arising from our changed foreign relations. We must have men who know European and South American history, who understand the political institutions and forces at work there, who understand international law. We must have men who can wield the whole energies of the state most efficiently and forcibly, if we would win honorable peace, and opportunity for this people to pursue the path of national development.

But finally, in a democracy, we need education as a means of life, even more than as a means of livelihood. It ought to come into all our homes,

159

widening the horizon, opening to the common man the knowledge of the best that has been done and thought in the world, unrolling to him the record of the ages gone by with marvelous march of events, making him see life as an unfolding from the past, from which it cannot break loose, spreading before him nature's infinite book of secrecy, enabling him to read in the common life about him the wonderful lessons of science. When such elements of culture are brought down from the few to the many, a new day will have dawned for democracy.

Now let us ask what educational instrumentality is best qualified to meet these requirements in the training of youth in a democracy. At the outset it would seem obvious that many, if not all, of the advantages of education, for democracy at least, would be lost if this education were relinquished into private endowments. Wealth would monopolize, or at least direct, the higher education, and we should have all the evils of class opposition and of an ignorant populace led by ignorance or demagogy.

If we are limited therefore to the public educational system, let us consider which portion of the system is best suited to disseminate education among the masses. It has been estimated that taking the count as a whole, three-fourths of the students who enter in the primary grades cease school life at eleven years of age, and that nineteen out of twenty do not enter the high school. If this estimate be even remotely close to the fact, it is seen that more attention should be paid in our elementary schools to the studies that promote good and intelligent citizenship. But it would be hopeless to do much more than equip such young students with the ability to read and write and reckon, to kindle right aspirations, and to awaken interest in the child mind. What can be done, should be done, but, after all, democracy can not be rightly equipped for defense through the work of the elementary schools.

Turning to the university we find it a matter of congratulation that those who enter the institution represent all classes, and are able to bring back to the service of the people the results of the highest training. The importance of such institutions cannot be ever estimated. The university fosters the search for pure truth; it aims not merely [at] knowledge of the time, but to widen that knowledge, to add new truths by investigation, to teach what is the best, and so it reacts on the whole educational system. It is the educational work shop, the intellectual observatory. It sends teachers to the high schools, teachers who have caught the inspiration and the insight of university ideals and methods. Its graduates mingle with the citizens of the state and thus extend the advantages of the university. Its publications, its extension lectures, its

160

agricultural institutes spread this influence still more widely. It is a training school for just that kind of political and economic knowledge that the new conditions demand. The University of Wisconsin comes closer to the people than does any other university in the world.

But as the youthfulness of the pupils in the elementary schools makes it difficult for them to exert a determining influence upon the development of American democracy so the fewness of the numbers of those that attend the higher institutions of learning, such as the university and the normal schools, places a check upon their direct influence on the great mass of the people. There is needed a school, which takes from the primary grades their best pupils, and brings them under the influence of men trained in these higher institutions. Such a school would contain pupils who had mastered the elements of education, and who were sufficiently advanced to hear and profit by the words of the best writers and thinkers. This is the foundation of the high school. It is the clearing house of the American school system, the receiving and disseminating center of education. The first free high schools were founded at the very time when America passed definitely into the hands of the common people, at the close of the first quarter of the present century. They have grown with the growth of democracy. It is estimated that five-eighths of the high school pupils of the country are children of the laboring classes. This percentage ought to be greatly increased.

But even as it is, the function of the high school as "a discoverer of talent and genius," as it has been called, is very clear. Here the son of the wielder of the pick axe and the spade as well as the son of the banker or broker, tests his intellectual power, and is encouraged to continue his career to the highest institutions if he has ability and ambition. The high school multiplies the nation's chances for getting the best for the public service. It helps to break down social barriers, and to keep open the doors of preferment to poor as to rich. It is a feeder to the university. But its main purpose is to send the boy and girl out into active life, equipped with something more than the rudiments of education. As the great distributing center for ideas to the young, its place in our educational system is of profound importance. That this importance is recognized may be gathered from the fact that one half the state constitutions specify the high school as objects of legislation and general interest.

Now, if the high school holds this important relation to the community, we may enquire how it may be made to fulfill its mission more completely.

In the first place we should give more attention there to the subjects that make for good citizenship, to history, and to the creation of the

161

historical modes of thought, for these train the judgment and cultivate progressive conservatism; to the study of government, not only the constitution of the United States as it exists on paper, but to the actual workings of the machine (as in the nominating conventions, and in the process of congressional legislation by speaker and committees). Nor should we limit the study to our constitution; the pupil ought to know something of the governmental machinery of other nations. He should be taught to read and understand the daily press in its reports of congress, of the market, of contemporary European history. The high school student should also be given a training in economics whether by formal text book, or in connection with his historical and political studies. He should know something of the financial and industrial questions of the time. In short greater emphasis should be laid on the studies that qualify men to make right returns for the bounty of the state, by giving to the state more intelligent service.

And lastly, the influence of the high school should be enlarged by high school extension. It should spread its influence throughout the community, and the surrounding country district. It may do this in many ways. In the first place it should make its work so valuable and so attractive as to attract more pupils from the ward schools and from the country districts. This room should be too small to hold its members. In the next place each high school in our smaller cities should have a large and carefully selected library, open for consultation, under certain restrictions, to the whole community. Here should be not only books, but current magazines, newspapers and public documents. A small but well chosen collection of photographs of works of art and foreign architecture might well be added at a moderate cost. A good library would do more to keep pupils at the high school and to multiply its power than any other one thing except the good teacher.

Another feature of high school extension should be the promotion of clubs which should have their home here. The high school hall is the proper place for literary clubs, travel clubs, clubs to debate governmental measures, and clubs to discuss industrial questions. Such clubs centering in the high school would not only stimulate the intellectual interests of the whole community, they would also react on the pupils of the high school and make them see how closely their own work is related to life. When pupils begin to see a connection between their studies and the busy activities of the outside world, the effect is marvelous.

This hall should also be made use of in securing educational lectures, lectures not only from outsiders, but lectures in the line of the pupil's study by Portage men and women who have given particular attention to some line of work. In a word, ladies and gentlemen, this building should be the intellectual center of your city. It should be a harmonizing, stimulating, enriching force in your midst. It should reach out to every family in the city. "Remember that the learning of the few is depotism, the learning of the many is liberty and that intelligent and principled liberty is fame and wisdom and power." By working with such ideals you shall make this building something more than well proportioned iron and brick and wood. So shall this house become a bee hive filled with the honey of ideas and with each new swarming from the hive new elements of strength will be added to the community.

The passage from the old building to the new will be a symbol of progressive intellectual change.

> Build thee more stately mansions, O my soul,
> As the swift seasons roll!
> Leave thy low-vaulted past!
> Let each new temple, nobler than the last,
> Shut thee from heaven with a dome more vast,
> Till thou at length art free.

A text of this speech is in Box 54; it also is published in *Agricultural History*, 23 (October 1949), 254-59, with the accompanying analysis by Fulmer Mood.

## NOTES

[1] Mrs. Ruth Swenson, librarian of the Portage Free Library, has been kind enough to compare the typescript copy prepared by the editor of *Agricultural History* with the original text in the Portage *Daily Register*, Jan. 2, 1896.

[2] The editor desires to thank Professor Merle Curti for his penetrating and instructive comments which, as printed in conjunction with the text, enhance its value and contribute markedly to its interpretation.

*Frederick Jackson Turner*

# THE UNIVERSITY OF THE FUTURE

Fellow graduates:

A noble past is an inspiration to a university; but even such venerable institutions as Columbia, Yale and Harvard, Princeton and Pennsylvania are learning that they cannot live by traditions alone. They see that they must adjust themselves to changed conditions of today. Pennsylvania and Columbia are in important respects almost as modern as Chicago and Leland Stanford. Princeton's sesquicentennial was the occasion of her proclaiming a new policy with her new name; Harvard's stately educational structure has been haussmannized by the genius of President Eliot, and Yale,—if Yale rest content with muscular glory and the most splendid trophy room in America, she will never rank among the universities of tomorrow.

The question is less of the University of yesterday than of the University of tomorrow.

Wisconsin has her own brief past—brief in years, long in stages of development. A past, that, as we have heard, from the venerable Nestors of our alumni had its own charms, its own inspirations, its noble men. But our catalogue of 1870 is twin sister to the catalogue of a Dakota or Wyoming college of 1897. Hardly more than a quarter of a century marks the educational transition from the frontier college to the University of today; and the question is imperative: what of the University of tomorrow? I believe that the universities of the middle west have a splendid opportunity. Into this region while it was still prairie and forest poured the children of the Atlantic states, carrying with them ideals of democracy, equality, freedom of opportunity for all men. The wilderness taught them audacity in social development. In the old centers of settlement society is becoming less plastic, the tendencies toward social stratification are accentuated and the problem for the Middle West is can these early American ideals be conserved and adapted to the changed conditions of contemporary society. It is the mission of the State University of tomorrow to grapple with this problem. It must not servilely aim to imitate the universities of the East. It must proudly conserve what is best and original in its own experience, it must seek with independence for the best in the older institutions, and it must build freely and fearlessly. It must express the highest creative power of the center of the republic.

The State University is the very outcome of democracy. Institutions on private foundations may influence democracy from the outside; but the State University *is* democracy in its higher educational aspect. From

164

this fact flow its great opportunity and its gravest danger. As the plain people come more and more into self consciousness and into determination to exert their power, they expose the university to two dangers. On the one hand there is the danger that democracy may not realize that education—the highest education—is essential to its own safety. The man who would turn the University over to the leisure classes and to the generosity of wealthy men alone should ponder Bacon's golden words:

"The learning of the few is despotism, the learning of the many is liberty, and intelligent and principled liberty is fame and wisdom and power."

*But* whatever be the *immediate* future it is safe to say that democracy will come to recognize the need of the University as essential to its own security. The greater danger is that democracy will wish to level the University down to its own ideals. If the State University of tomorrow is to be representative of the ideals of the masses, its day is done. A sapping process will have been at work upon the University ideals. Palpable and showy results will be called for in place of the subtler contributions of culture. Buildings, numbers, victories will take the place of educational power. The worth of the professor will be reckoned by the length of his office hours and by the size of his classes rather than by his contributions to knowledge.

In the face of this danger the duty of the University is clear. It was recently set forth with dignity and power by President Adams in his baccalaureate. Its duty is to find and to hold high and helpful ideals, to stand for them so persuasively, so imperatively that its sons and daughters will be the leaders of thought in this democracy. Ideals and leadership! These are the watch words of the hour. With them the future is secure. Without them, all victories on the athletic field, all budgetary glories, all lofty buildings and all crowds of students are but food for powder.

I have faith in the University of tomorrow. I believe that it will remain the unprejudiced sanctuary for the finding of truth in the midst of contending parties; that it will broaden and deepen its investigations into the fields of nature and of society; and that it will render its discoveries indispensable to democracy.

I know of no more encouraging indication in this direction than the recent growth of graduate studies. Ten years ago we had but four graduate students; in six years they had grown to more than forty and today there are seventy. But the growth in numbers is not so significant as the growth in the spirit of investigation—that search for new truth by professor and student, that creative work which is the truest function

165

and most useful service of the University.

By developing our forces of devoted graduate students we shall raise the scholarly ideals of the undergraduates with whom they mix; we shall send out a band of missionaries to the schools, the pulpit, the press, and the forum of the state, men who shall stand for the most careful research, the highest ideals, the noblest achievement of the University of tomorrow. It is for the alumni to foster and support this great work. Other institutions have recognized the power of graduate work more fully than have we. Cornell and Pennsylvania each have about forty fellowships and scholarships; Harvard has a hundred. We have ten.

Let us build the University of tomorrow. Founded on the high school and the Normal school, working gladly together,—expressing and directing the great democracy of the Middle West,—seeking the goal of spiritual power rather than that of material success, the University of tomorrow will be worthy of this place in which its lot is cast.

A text of this speech is published in Jacobs, *loc cit*. Turner's manuscript is in File Drawer 15 B.
The speech was delivered on 23 June 1897.

# TO THE ALUMNI ON FOOTBALL

The importance of athletics in university life is recognized by everybody. The only question is how to keep the system clean and in right relation to the purpose of the university. Before the Civil War, athletics were but slightly known in American colleges. "Noble athletic sports," wrote Edward Everett in 1856, "manly out-door exercises, which strengthen the body and bring man into a generous and exhilarating communion with nature, are too little cultivated in town or country."

Since then the pendulum has swung far in the other direction. The gospel of the strenuous life is now ascendant, and there is less danger that we shall have pale and ascetic students in their cloisters, lacking a physical basis for the intellectual life.

Fierce college rivalry, the development of the coach, the production of experts fighting for victory on the football field, have shifted the problem. As a result of specialization, new dangers to the welfare of college life have appeared. We now face conditions produced by these great waves of excitement raised by the struggle for college championship. The popular interest in victory has transformed college athletics. The ideal of widespread sport among students generally is replaced by the ideal of collecting from all over the country a winning aggregation. There is an increasing tendency for the college student to take his exercise vicariously; to turn over the athletic field and athletic activities to a few highly-developed gladiators, fighting for the honor of the college in a game in which the average undergraduate has no share, unless it be to aid in organized cheering on the bleachers, in the midst of a vast crowd drawn by the love of a spectacle. For over two months of the college year (for nearly three in the opinion of President Angell) the interest of the undergraduate is dominated by football. So fierce is the rivalry, so well-disciplined is the excitement, that it is almost disloyalty to the college not to give one's self up to the prevailing interest. Enthusiastic alumni, carried away by the desire to see the college victorious and in violation of solemn agreements between the colleges, in violation of the certification which the player must make, and the faculty endorse, collect or subscribe funds to maintain in college, not the lad whose abilities mark him out for a career of scholarship and service to the state, but the athlete, whose prowess will help to make a winning team. The football giant is the Hero. The press exploit his weight and his features in the sporting column alongside of O'Brien and Fitzsimmons. The high-school boy is breathless over his greatness. The absurd idea spreads among students that football is the test of the ex-

167

cellence of a university and the proper means of advertising it. Human
values are put in wrong perspective, and the fundamental purpose of the
university is lost sight of. College ideals are distorted, while the high
schools imitate and exaggerate the evils of the situation among the younger generation.

No one doubts that the "major sports," like deep-sea sailing or hunting big game, have the touch of danger, the call to courage, that meets a
response in American character. But when the gladiators fought lions in
the Roman arena, the vast populace which filled the Colosseum and
shouted itself hoarse at the spectacle was getting precious little exercise
and was developing its courage in very doubtful fashion. So also the
undergraduate on the bleachers shouts for an eleven which is not an
outgrowth of normal athletic life in the University but largely brought
in to win games.

Football has been passing away from the position of a game played by
the undergraduates as a general sport on their own grounds. It has
become a business, carried on far too often by professionals, supported
by levies on the public, bringing in vast gate receipts, demoralizing student ethics, and confusing the ideals of sport, manliness, and decency.
Coaches and managers scour the country for material. Faculties are kept
busy playing a game of hide and seek with the man who sells his athletic
skill for personal gain, and who pretends to uphold the honor of the
university. The decent men of the elevens, for thank God they still
exist! play side by side with the professional, and obscure the moral
wrong of it all. Faculties are deceived into certifying the eligibility of
mercenaries and the faculty cloak is made to cover the evil practises. It
has become almost impossible to prevent the importation of professional
athletes, whose interest is to make their football skill pay, and for whom
misguided enthusiasts outside of the college furnish the funds for support. The public has pushed its influence inside the college walls, and is
demoralizing student sentiment, exalting fictitious heroes, condoning
brutality, setting up false ideas of the true honor of a university, and,
making it impossible for faculties and for the clean and healthy masses
of the students to keep athletics honest and rightly related to a sane
university life. The offenders are not numerous, but they are very active
and noisy. Let us frankly concede that these evils started in good intentions, or in laxities, fostered by the desire to win, excused by the belief
that our neighbors were doing worse things. They grew by what they
fed on. Abandoned by some when they realized the real tendency of the
evils, the corruption has become increasingly difficult to ferret out, and
for that very reason, has become increasingly corrosive in its effect upon

the ideals of impressionable young men, a menace to upright character, a danger to the career of men who are to go out as leaders in the world of business and of public service. Tammany Hall methods have no legitimate place in the education of college men. They are certain to bear a bad harvest in later years.

I am not describing conditions peculiar to one college. In different ways, and in different degrees, the evils are common to the whole system.

Is it any wonder that the faculty of Wisconsin, impressed by the evils in the situation, called a halt, proposed a truce, a breathing space, a lull in the bitter rivalries, mutual distrust and suspicion, so that the universities might cease to point the finger of scorn at one another and might strive to build a more normal, rational, and moral athletic life in right relations to the activity of the university as a whole?

There has never been an intention on the part of the faculty to take a final decision without affording time for the expression of student and alumni sentiment. But leadership and final responsibility belongs to the faculty. In all the universities the movement for reform was led by those who, from long experience on faculty athletic committees, are most intimately in touch with the situation. It is a striking and significant fact that the old friends of football and the most experienced members of the faculties are clearest in stating the existing evils and in insisting that if the game is to continue changes are imperative.

In the unanimous words of the conference of the big nine representatives, made up almost entirely of experienced chairmen of athletic committees and expressed by one of them who was once himself a football player: "It is not, to our minds, a question between suspending the game as an intercollegiate sport or cutting away its evils."

We are, I think, agreed that evils exist. The question of how to make football a proper game, in proper relations to university life, is the essential one.

The conference believed that, while the old game should be abolished, it was desirable to try the experiment of playing a reformed game under certain regulations; and that suspension was the only alternative if these failed; that drastic action would be warranted; but that it should not be taken if genuine reforms are practicable.

The members of the faculty cannot be expected to turn from the work for which the university was founded, and make themselves detectives and police in order to support a game which is becoming obnoxious to the moral and intelligent people of Wisconsin who pay for the university. If, in a modified form, it is to stay it will be because alumni and

169

students cooperate with the faculty in keeping the game decent and a fit part of university activities.

The overwhelming unanimity of the press of the country, in general, and of Wisconsin, in particular, shows that the attitude of the faculty is in entire accord with public sentiment. Whatever extreme football enthusiasts among students or alumni may think, the sober judgment of the men who pay for the university sustains the faculty in its determination to call a halt to present conditions. The masses of the students and of the alumni are discontented with present football evils. We are fighting to sustain the higher mission of the university, determined that it shall not fall behind the moral sentiment of the community, that it shall not forget its obligation to the taxpayers of the state of Wisconsin.

At the same time, the faculty recognizes that students have a right to rejoice in the days of their youth, to glory in the strength of body as well as of mind. It understands the student desire to cheer for Wisconsin in the territory of Michigan, to wave the cardinal in defiance to the maroon. Intercollege athletics are not yet to be abolished; that has not even been discussed. But the brutality of the game must go, mercenary professionalism, immorality, deceit, and corruption of student sentiment must go, and, in their place, must come a game that students can play, a game kept subordinate to the intellectual life of the university, a game that leaves no slimy trail across the campus, no stain on the fair name of our alma mater. Having come to know the conditions, it is the right and the duty of the faculty to take vigorous action. Football will surely go, if students and alumni deceive themselves in the belief that the faculty will bear alone the burden of keeping the game free from taint and of restraining it within the bounds of moderation. They will cut it out, root and branch, if the forces of demoralization continue to vitiate the university atmosphere.

Resolved, first, that the Madison alumni of the University of Wisconsin approve such reforms in the game of football as will free it from professionalism and brutality, and they pledge their support for sustaining the purity of athletics in Wisconsin.

Resolved, second, that in case such reforms can be effected we are in favor of the continuance of intercollegiate football.

Resolved, third, that we have confidence that the faculty will deal with the subject in the spirit of sympathy with the legitimate interest of the student body in clean athletics, and in due recognition of the faculty's primary obligation to keep the University true to the purpose of the taxpayers of Wisconsin in establishing an institution for the promotion of education and good citizenship in the state.

A longhand draft and a polished typescript, with some additional revision, are in Box 55. Turner's longhand note on the copy as delivered says, "Passed by an overwhelming majority."
The speech was delivered at Keely's Restaurant in Madison on 31 January 1906.

## C. Academic Addresses

THE ROSTRUM offered Turner many rhetorical opportunities for the initial conceptual casting and the final stylistic polishing of his historical writings. Indeed, in several instances, the foundations of published essays are attributed by Turner himself to discourse created as commencement addresses, dedication speeches, as well as guest lectures at other institutions and before civic or honorary societies. For example, Turner delivered the commencement address at the University of New Hampshire, 13 June 1922; that discourse was the foundation of an important, subsequent essay, "Sections and Nation," published as the lead article that fall in *The Yale Review*.[1] The Huntington Library's text of the address bears Turner's note on the cover of its folder, "this was by modification made into my article 'Sections and Nation.'"[2] Similarly, Turner's "Social Forces in American History" had a rhetorical evolution. As published in 1911 in *The American Historical Review*, the statement was prepared as his presidential address to the American Historical Association on 28 December 1910, with still other oratorical antecedents in several Phi Beta Kappa addresses, particularly one of 10 June 1907.[3]

Other oratory came into print as chapters in Turner's 1920 book, *The Frontier in American History*. Thus, his 1910 commencement address at the University of Indiana as well as a 1909 Phi Beta Kappa speech at the University of Kansas became Chapter Ten of that work, "Pioneer Ideals and the State University"; a 1914 commencement address at the University of Washington became Chapter Eleven, "The West and American Ideals"; a 1918 dedication speech at the opening of the building housing the Minnesota Historical Society became Chapter Thirteen, "Middle Western Pioneer Democracy"; and of course his "Social Forces in American History" reemerged as Chapter Twelve.[4] So when the frontier thesis appeared as Chapter One of *The Frontier in American History*, the inclusion of this essentially oratorical effort was consonant with the rhetorical tone created in part by other chapters in the book. Clearly, preparations for the public platform in academia provided ample opportunities to develop

173

statements which later came into print as part of the legacy of his historical writing.

Most of these academic addresses are easily accessible today in other anthologies.[5] The heretofore unpublished speech of the most interest, however, is the earlier analyzed statement on "American Colonization" to the Madison Literary Club since in this 1891 address are some conceptual antecedents of the frontier thesis. The influence of Turner's rhetorical adaptations for an audience upon his own historical creativity has been explicated in the prior discussion and what remains is to present this rhetorical endeavor in the final form which evolved from the historian's efforts to achieve eloquence.

The capstone to this anthology without question must be the frontier thesis itself. Although "The Significance of the Frontier in American History" has been reprinted many times, it should be read again, as evidence of a distinct style evolving from Turner's predilection for achieving rhetorical impact by emulating the oratorical prowess of Robert M. La Follette. When read as the oration which in effect it is, the frontier thesis can be regarded essentially as the culmination of a long sequence of successful oratorical efforts on the part of its creator. And when read as well with an understanding of that statement's profound impact upon the popular mind for several decades, the function of the historian as persuader can be appreciated more fully. Surely the persuasiveness of history is seen more clearly through a composite, evolutionary view and analysis of these speeches—and of the eloquence of Frederick Jackson Turner.

## NOTES

[1] *The Yale Review*, 12 (October 1922), 1-21. This essay is readily available in the reprintings in *Frontier and Section: Selected Essays of Frederick Jackson Turner*, ed. Ray A. Billington (Englewood Cliffs: Prentice-Hall, 1961), pp. 136-53; as well as *The Significance of Sections in American History*, ed. Max Farrand (New York: Henry Holt and Company, 1932), pp. 315-39.

[2] In File Drawer 14A.

[3] The original publication of "Social Forces in American History" is in *The American Historical Review*, 16 (January 1911), 217-33; a text of Turner's preceding 1907 Phi Beta Kappa address is in Box 55; his notes for the speech are in File Drawer 14C.

Billington discusses Turner's Phi Beta Kappa addresses, noting in particular how the historian would extract themes from one speech and utilize them subsequently for rhetorical efforts at other universities on other days, even weeks or years later. Billington also suggests that the "Sections and Nation" essay may have had oratorical antecedents even before the commencement address at the University of New Hampshire—in Phi Beta Kappa addresses in the spring of 1922 at the universities of Michigan and Chicago. See his *Frederick Jackson Turner*, pp. 196-97, 306, and 380.

4 "The West and American Ideals" was published originally in *The Washington Historical Quarterly*, 5 (October 1914), 243-57. Billington has an insightful account of this particular speech, describing with still another example Turner's tendency to procrastinate. As early as October 1913, Turner agreed to deliver the speech; he started west on 4 June 1914, arriving in Seattle on the fifteenth or sixteenth of that month, a day or two before the commencement—with the address still untouched and the notes from which it was to be developed mislaid. Billington suggests the address was hastily written in a hotel room; and "in that one inadequately prepared address Turner provided his future critics with enough unsubstantiated generalizations to keep them busy for years." See his *Frederick Jackson Turner*, pp. 448-49.

5 Again, see Billington, *Frontier and Section;* Farrand, *Sections in American History;* and of course Turner, *The Frontier in American History.* See also *Frederick Jackson Turner's Legacy: Unpublished Writings in American History*, ed. with an Introduction by Wilbur R. Jacobs (San Marino: The Huntington Library, 1965).

*Frederick Jackson Turner*

# AMERICAN COLONIZATION

The colonizing spirit is one form of the nomadic instinct. The immigrant train on its way to the far west or the steamer laden with passengers for Australia is but the latest embodiment of the impulse that took Abraham away from Ur of the Chaldees and sent our Aryan forefathers from their primitive pasture lands to Greece and Italy and India and Scandinavia. The motives of migration are many but the underlying spirit, the capacity upon which they operate, is the instinct for moving. The *völkerwanderung* had hardly resulted in the downfall of Rome and the rise of the feudal system, when the crusades followed, and the last scene in the crusades was the first scene in the exploration of the New World.

There have been various types of colonizing states. Phoenicia was the first great colonizing power. From island to island, and from cape to cape these traders planted their posts in the Mediterranean, bringing arts and the alphabet to Greece, sowing the seeds of civilization in Carthage and in Spain, and sending rivulets of eastern culture through the river valleys into central Europe. Even Africa received her trading posts, and Phoenician sailors rounded Cape Good Hope over twenty centuries before Vasco da Gama. Her colonies were pre-eminently commercial; the germs of them were factories placed among primitive peoples, and sustained by barter. At first Phoenician ships made only occasional visits; then, as we read in the Odyssey, they sometimes anchored and traded for a whole year, at last the permanent factory was established. Pirates and slavers though they were, at first, the trading colony which the Phoenicians developed was an institution of far reaching importance. It blended races and civilizations; it fostered the custom of depending on outside nations for certain provisions; it impregnated the primitive people of the Mediterranean lands with the higher life of the old East; it made them dependent on this higher civilization and thus it prepared the way for their growth.

Carthage, the daughter of Phoenicia, developed the restrictive system. The rivalry of the Greeks, who had been to school to Phoenicia, endangered her profitable commerce. In the absence of competition a trinket goes as far in trade with barbarians as a more valuable consideration, but rivalry destroys this advantage. Appreciating this Carthage laid a firm hand on her possessions and excluded other nations.

But Greece was the real successor to the colonizing energy of Phoenicia. The states of Hellas sent out colonies to the eastern shore of the Mediterranean, occupied the islands of the Aegean, and settled cities in southern Italy, whose flocks and fields soon gave them a material greatness that surpassed that of the parent states. Greek colonies spread Greek influence along the southern shore of France, circled the Black Sea with settlements, and flecked the Mediterranean with Grecian sails. Unlike Carthage, the cities of Hellas retained no hold on their daughter states. Greek colonization like the swarming of bees, or the departure of an adult son, meant the setting up of a distinct establishment. Indeed the Greek name for colony, *(apoikia)*, signified a leaving of the house. The colonists took with them fire from the sacred hearth, the ties of kinship and of common speech, and the community of culture that we call Greek, but that was all. There was no political connection between the colony and the parent city.

Rome's plantations were primarily designed to extend and defend the Roman territory. Sent out by the state and under its direct control, they were continually watched by the home authorities, and were operated for the benefit of the government. Rome and Carthage on the one hand, and Greece on the other, present the opposite types of colonization.

In the Middle Ages, Genoa and Venice, partly as a result of the crusades, developed a colonial activity in the East, and the former even established a commercial colony in the suburbs of Constantinople.

With the end of the Middle Ages a new colonizing epoch opened. European activity was transferred from the Mediterranean to the Atlantic, and this change transformed both Europe and America.

In the eighth century of our era the hosts of Mohammed had taken Spain from the Goths and had cooped up the Christians in the mountain fastnesses of the northwest of the peninsula. Prevented by the decisive battle of Tours from conquering all Europe, the Saracenic power still extended from the Bosporus across Africa into Spain, while the crusades for Jerusalem were in progress. For nearly eight hundred years the conflict went on in Spain. It heightened in the Spaniards the love of fighting and contempt for labor. To dispoil the infidel and to crush his religion were for centuries the ambitions that were forming Spanish character. Spoliation became the ideal rather than economic activity. At length the Spanish kingdoms were combined in two important ones, and Ferdinand of Aragon had wedded Isabella of Castile. Forced back step by step the Mohammedans retired to the state of Granada in the south. Here the civilization of Islam made its final stand. But all the men and measures that in 1492 found place before the walls of Granada sink into insignificance before a Genoese sailor who brought hither his plans. The problem of the age was a route to India. The sailors of Venice and Genoa, whose eastern trade had been ruined by the Turk,

177

sought the courts of princes whose domains fronted on the Atlantic. Columbus had become a convert to the idea held by Aristotle that the earth is a sphere and that the way to reach India was by striking out boldly to the west of Spain. Inspired with this idea and with the ambition to amass wealth with which to make a crusade for the Holy Sepulchre, he sought the sovereigns before Granada.

If one were to trace the genesis of American colonization he would have to say that the nomadic instinct and the pressure of overpopulation gave birth to the Aryan migrations; and these to the *völkerwanderung*. The last phase of the *völkerwanderung* was the Norman expeditions which merged easily, and to a large extent casually into the crusades and the offspring of the crusades is American colonization. Hardly a better example of the continuity of history could be found.

For countless ages Nature had been preparing America for her new tenant. Stores of metal and beds of coal had been laid down; inland seas had deposited fertile plains; river valleys and mountain chains had fixed highways for settlement; forests had stretched over the land, and waterfalls foretold the rumble of the mills. All was ready for sentient life. American history is the account of how this environment was occupied by a new organization. It is the history of the application of men and ideas to these physical conditions. Much of this history was written down in sybelline leaves in the age of geologic preparation.

Two chains of mountains shutting in a wide valley made the essential features of the surface. In the west these mountains came so close to the sea that the Pacific coast offered small invitation to continuous colonization. In the east the mountains lay farther inland and rivers flowed to meet the ocean—in the north shorter and abounding in water powers near to the coast; in the south longer and more placid, suited to great plantations with a river front before which sea-going vessels might cast anchor. Abundant bays and harbors made the Atlantic an open door. To the vast central valley shut in between the Alleghanies and the Rockies there were various eastern entrances. The system made up of St. Lawrence Gulf and River and the Great Lakes outflanked the mountains on the north and was the key to the continent. It had connection with the tributaries of the Mississippi, and these gave access by way of the rivers and lakes of Canada, to the Arctic and the Pacific; and by the Missouri and Columbia system opened a highway across the plains and through the Rocky mountains to the Pacific. The Gulf of Mexico as well lay open to the colonies who should find this back door route to the midst of the continent. The lowlying southern region in its turn outflanked the mountains, but here the river courses did not so invite exploration.

178

Between these routes were two other entrances to the central basin. The Hudson-Champlain system with its westward stretching tributary, the Mohawk, led the way to the St. Lawrence and the Great Lakes [and was safely approached by Long Island Sound.] The other route was a mountain valley running down from central Pennsylvania southwesterly into western Virginia and broken on its western ridge by Cumberland Gap, near the present boundary line between Kentucky and Tennessee. There were other important roads across the Alleghanies, but these were essential.

From one point of view the colonization of America is modern; its birthplace is Europe in the Renaissance; but America was the scene of colonizing activity ages before the European period. The continent is a vast palimpsest. The glacial epoch left traces of man here and probably in after ages Asia contributed various stocks to the peopling of the New World. Antequarians dispute as to the lines of migration but there is general agreement that the channels and mountain valleys graven in the remote past were the determining elements of the prehistoric *völkerwanderung*. It is generally agreed that successive waves of colonization passed along the Columbia, Missouri, Mississippi, and St. Lawrence route from the west to the east.[1] The story of this prehistoric colonization by Mexican and Peruvian pueblo makers and cliff-dwellers, by moundbuilders, and by the many wandering tribes of wild Indians, would be most fascinating, were anyone wise enough to write it.

The aborigines were to have a profound effect upon the colonization of America. They as well as the mountains and river valleys, would determine the lines of advance. The Iroquois, for instance, planted on the Hudson-Mohawk route, would prevent settlement there, and act as a buffer between the colonists north of the lakes and those to the south. Thus in point of fact western New York was settled later than western Pennsylvania; and thus the New York settlements were protected from French inroads.[2] The lands of Kentucky and Tennessee into which Shenandoah Valley and Cumberland Gap led were unoccupied by Indians in the Eighteenth Century. Here was both a gap in the mountain wall and in the Indian wall beyond it. It was natural that colonization should seek the lines of least resistance—and indeed it was in the Kentucky and Tennessee region that English settlements did first break through the mountains. The Indians tilled cornfields and made clearings along the Atlantic coast, and frequent pestilences in some places so depopulated the villages that the colonists would be able to settle down, cuckoo-like, in Indian nests. The existence moreover of supplies that might be purchased or conquered from the Indians was a most important factor in rendering possible the European occupation of America. The Indians . . .³

In the days of Henry VII while Spain was exploring the West Indies and South America, English commerce was commonplace and simple. Wine brigs sought the coast of Spain and France, small craft ran between the Thames and the Scheldt, codfishers went to the banks of Iceland, to lay in the fish supply for winter months and the coast cities sent out fleets which fished in the channel. It was a prosaic period for England. The daring of the vikings had been outgrown; the daring of the Age of Elizabeth was yet to come. Before the death of the virgin queen, English seamen were to grapple with Spain and win the ocean for themselves. The center of maritime activity was Bristol, located where the Ocean seems to flow right into the very heart of England to meet the waters of the Severn River. Near to it was the land of Devonshire, and these regions in the southwest of England were the nursery of all her subsequent power upon the sea. Today, in the words of Senator Hoar, "England holds all the great routes of commerce. She steps from island to continent, and from continent to island, from fortress to naval station and from naval station to fortress. England has not only laid her hands on those enormous countries and the men who inhabit them but the way she has got control of the great highways, the great roads of commerce, is more wonderful still."

For the opening of the story of how England won the sea we must turn to the heroic age of the Tudors, and particularly to the seamen of Devonshire. Charles Kingley has said in his novel *Westward Ho* "It was the men of Devon, whom we shall learn one day to honor as they deserve, to whom she [England] owes her commerce, her colonies, her very existence."

"For the last seven years," wrote the Spanish ambassador in London in 1498, "the people of Bristol have sent out every year two, three, or four light ships in search of the island of Brazil, and the Seven Cities." These were names then applied to parts of India. In Bristol at this time there lived a Venetian navigator, John Cabot, by name. You will remember that Venice and Genoa, had the trade with China and India in the Middle Ages . . .⁴

. . . it saw Sir Frances Drake dashing into the treasure cities of the Spanish Main, capturing the gold galleons, and "plowing a furrow around the globe." Philip's ambassador to Elizabeth told the truth when he exclaimed: "Your mariners rob my master's subjects on the sea and trade where they are forbidden to go. They plunder our people in the streets of your towns. They attack our vessels in your very harbors, and take our prisoners from them. Your preachers insult my master from their pulpits, and when we apply for justice we are answered with threats."

The fact is that at bottom this period was a war of Calvinism against Catholicism—a war of freedom of thought against the authority of the church, a war of free government against absolute despotism.[5] From his desk in the Escurial, like a spider in his web, Philip II plotted the election of Popes favorable to himself, the extirpation of heretics, the assassination of princes, the conquest of kingdoms. To fringe the Atlantic and Pacific with dependant Catholic states, was his ambition. England was his objective point. By the conquest of that country he could ensure Spain's eternal dominance of the ocean, crush free government, and reinstate the church.[6] He began to collect from all parts of his empire, ships and seamen for such a fleet as should sweep the English from the seas. At last on a summer day of 1588 the watchers on the English hills described in the distance the whitening sails of the Invincible Armada. The fateful day for England and America had come. If this fleet accomplished what it sought, English parliaments were at an end, constitutional liberty was at an end, freedom of religion was at an end; if the Armada won, Shakespeare's plays would probably never be written, nor Milton's epic; if it won Spanish rule, crushing out colonial life and vigor and shaping all into a huge machine would spread over America.[7]

But Hawkins, Frobisher, Drake and Raleigh commanded squadrons. The winds fought for England and the Armada was ruined. The days of Spanish greatness were over, and the ocean was open for the colonizing ships of other states. Within a generation the fleets of Holland plowed Spanish seas and carried on a world wide commerce. In 1609 Henry Hudson steered his Half Moon up the river that bears his name, and in two years more New Amsterdam was planted on the greatest of American harbors. France also, having found unity under Henry of Navarre, sent colonies where her fishermen had gone before. In the same year with Hudson's expedition, Champlain gave his name to the beautiful lake near the head of Hudson River.[8] And English Jamestown was planted and growing in power while the Dutch and French were occupying the north. The struggle for America now lay between these three states.

Up to this point we have found three leading factors in inducing expeditions to the New World: the crusading zeal, the search for a route to India, and the hope of finding another Mexico. The sixteenth century was the age of the fabulous: the mythical straits of Anian furnishing a way across the continent to India were sought after by almost every explorer of the time, and even men like Filbert believed in rivers that ran over pieces of pure gold as big as one's fist. America was reported to be a land where every cottage had pecks of pearls, where banquet halls were built of crystal with pillars of massy gold and silver.

The passage to the more prosaic age of trading companies and agricultural colonies was not a sudden one. The idea of the transcontinental strait long endured. Raleigh's colonists had heard from the Indians that the Roanoke river rose so near the South Sea (Pacific) that its source was often made salty by the waves. Lane the governor of the colony had declared: "The discovery of a good mine by the goodness of God, or a passage to the South Sea, and nothing else can being this country into request to be inhabited by our nation." So we find that John Smith under orders from the London company ascended the Chickahominy, searching for a water route to India. The information which he gave to Hudson of a passage to the north of Virginia sent this explorer up Hudson river. Champlain sought the same fabled strait and when Nicolet came to Wisconsin he believed that he had found the veritable highway to Asia.

To the Jamestown colonists Drayton addressed his ode,

> And cheerfully at sea
> Success you still entice
> To get the pearl and gold
> And ours to hold
> Virginia
> Earth's only paradise.

Although this was at first the ideal of the London company as well as of the poet, there were elements of a different nature involved in the Jamestown colony. The age of Elizabeth so brilliant in its intellectual life, so full of daring and adventure, had nevertheless been an age of economic distress. The peasantry were particularly miserable. There was a large increase of population and a rise in the price of food unaccompanied by a rise in wages. The land owners had been turning their tilled lands into sheep pastures which were found more profitable. Thus men were thrown out of employment, and crime and poverty were abundant. Colonization was urged as a remedy, and the commercial company became the means of American settlement. England's world power began with two trading corporations, the East India company and the London company.

The early history of Virginia, the typical southern colony is the his-

182

tory of the transition from the ideal of exploitation to the ideal of economic growth. Its physical geography fitted it for large plantations widely extended along rivers. The existence of a native product—tobacco—made it an agricultural colony. Even the streets of Jamestown were planted with tobacco, and the government was obliged to compel the cultivation of corn by statute.

The development of the county system of local government which is suited to a sparcely settled district, and the calling of a legislative assembly, mark the political contributions of Virginia, and disclose some of the gains to America from the defeat of the Armada.

But if in respect to self-government the Virginia colonists affiliated themselves to the Greek rather than to the Roman type of colony, their baronial social organization, with slavery at the base of the pyramid, was more like the Roman and the Spanish. The south looked upon labor with contempt. In this respect the Virginia planter had close relations with the Mexican hidalgo.

Thus England made her first plantation in America, a plantation that mirrored the period of its settlement, and so was in a large degree only a transition from the Spanish type. Holland sent a colony soon after. Says Carlyle: "Those Dutch are a strong people. They raised their land out of a marsh, and went on for a long period of time breeding cows and making cheese, and might have gone on with their cows and cheese till doomsday. But Spain comes over and says 'We want you to believe in St. Ignatius.' 'Very sorry,' replied the Dutch, 'but we can't.' 'God! but you must,' says Spain; and they went about with guns and swords to make the Dutch believe in St. Ignatius. Never made them believe in him but did succeed in breaking their own vertebral column forever, and raising the Dutch into a great nation." This is the story in a nutshell! Hardly had the Spanish power been weakened by the combined attacks of England and Holland when the Dutch went east to the Indies and west to America, seeking new avenues for their energy. In the same year that the Spaniards were compelled to make a permanent truce with the Dutch, Henry Hudson, as we have seen, explored the river that bears his name. Thus he found the key to internal communication between Canada and the West and the Middle region. Like the Phoenicians the Dutch were colonizers for the sake of commerce rather than from political considerations. The fur trade furnished not only the beginning but the principal *raison d'etre* of New Netherlands. That the English should seize the region was inevitable, for it interposed between New England and the South. It will not be possible to speak of the other middle colonies, though Pennsylvania especially deserves study. Penn made

183

particular efforts to attract German settlers of the Quaker type.[9] He may well be called the first of our immigration commissioners.

The colonization of the central region resulted in the formation of middle colonies in every respect. As mixed in its nationality as any of the existing states; with a variety of social diversions, the middle class preponderating; varied in its industries, being agricultural like the South, and commercial like New England; possessing the mixed town-and-county form of local government; heterogeneous in its religious sects; characteristically western in the west and in the east a typically eastern colony; it was, in a word, a mediating region—a region which interpreted New England to the South and the East to the West. It was also a pivotal region, a fighting ground for ideas and social forms.[10]

History is the interpretation of the present in the light of the past. Given the South and Middle Colonies alone, we could not explain the present United States. To find a most important determining factor we must examine the Puritan colonies.

The reign of James I was not only a period of economic distress, it was also the era of the constitutional struggle against the doctrine of divine right and against the attempt to impost upon all Englishmen the discipline of the Church of England. "A king is above law by his absolute power" said James; and he also asserted, "I will have one doctrine, one discipline, one religion in substance and ceremony." Plymouth was founded in opposition to the last assertion; Massachusetts Bay in opposition to both assertions. Plymouth marks the fight of Independency for existence; Massachusetts Bay represents the struggle of the landed gentry and the middle classes for the Puritan ideal of civil government—an ideal completely realized in this country and only prophesied by Cromwell in England.

Too much stress can hardly be laid upon the tonic effect of the ethical ideals of the Puritan colonists. They have been abundant fountains of reformatory movements in this country. The Puritan took himself too seriously, but with all his gloominess and bigotry he had a tremendous moral earnestness of the highest value to our civilization.

Respect for labor was another characteristic of the New England colonists. They had no hopes of finding a route through America, nor of exploiting the country. They came to develop America, not by governmental aid, but by their own exertions. Thus they form a sharp antithesis to the Spanish colonists. But the greatest contribution made by them to our national life was the town meeting. Various theories have been advanced as to the origin of the New England towns, but it seems to me that they are the product of three forces: the congregational policy, the revival of the old English town organization, and the peculiar local conditions. The congregational form of church organization was peculiarly adapted to persecuted sects by reason of the isolation which it afforded and this also fitted it for new settlements. Being a self governed body it was sufficient unto itself, and like some forms of animal life it was capable of subdivision without destroying the life of the parts. The congregation had also from the very nature of the case, a democratic tendency. As Fiske has pointed out the congregational system afforded abundant opportunity for theological discussion, which not only sharpened the interests of the Puritans, but also tended to cause separations in the congregations, and thereby to develop new settlements. The close connection of congregation and town is indicated in the religious basis of the franchise and in the use of the meeting house as a gathering place for the political as well as the religious life of the community. Much has been written about the town as a reversion to the old Germanic mark. There are too many analogies between the New England town and the "tun" of our German forefathers to be overlooked. Placed again in a wilderness environment, the descendants of the Anglo-Saxons reproduced many of the characteristics of the early towns. But we must not neglect the local conditions as factors in producing the New England town. The hostile Indians made it desirable for the colonists to settle in communities; nor did the country invite the broad plantations. The region required that men should make their struggle for existence in compact isolated communities. Aside from the self governing characteristics of these towns, their capacity for sending representatives to larger political bodies was of the highest importance. I have spoken of the tendency of the congregation to throw out offshoots; besides this tendency the fur-trade was continually bringing to the knowledge of the New England town the existence of better lands and inviting to new settlements. The first period of New England history has been characterized as the period of *settlement*, when Plymouth and Salem were planted. The second period is that of *budding*, when these parent towns sent colonies to other places. Thus little groups of towns grew up around Plymouth and around Boston; in the same ways the Connecticut river towns were settled; New Haven with a group of neighboring towns, and Rhode Island followed a like process. Had the New England town been like the Greek city this dispersion might have gone on indefinitely. But the capacity of the town for representation saved us from this result. Shortly before the middle of the seventeenth century a movement of combination began. The various towns of Plymouth sent representatives to a general court. The towns of Massachusetts Bay, of Connecticut, of New Haven, and of Rhode Island did the same. Then came the larger federation into the New England Union, in which the separate colonies retained their individualities while uniting for common action. This process was prophetic of the later history of the United States.

It is hard not to dwell too long upon the characteristics of the Puritan colonies. One should say something of their educational system. Consider the value of the stream of culture that has flowed from New England to fertilize America. Its influence is still felt in literature, religion and philosophic thought. There is hardly a community in the United States that has not been quickened by some man or woman who has borne to it the New England love of the intellectual life.

Such were the Puritans.[11] Their small hill-side farms were separated by the forest. To the west were the opposing mountains shutting in the little towns while they developed their intense local life. The short tumbling rivers near to the coast foretold their manufacturing possibilities. To the east was the ocean; whose chilly waters teeming with cod were not so attractive as the warm currents of the south, flowing over pearl beds, yet in those fishing shoals were mines far more profitable than the gold that the Spaniards sought by conquest and by slavery. The Ocean was New England's highway. "The great main," says Weeden, "swept along her shores with all the forces of the world." She became the carrying power of America.

But while this English colonization was going on east of the Alleghanies, on the other side of the mountains and to the north forces were gathering that must be met and conquered unless all this development should go for nothing. The essential features of French colonization are well known. In a previous paper I have presented to the club the essential features of the French colonization, and have tried to show how the birch-canoe of the voyageur was a transforming visitant to the western Indians, making them dependent on the white man. Threading the water labyrinths of the great West the voyageur was also a pathfinder for civilization. But French colonization, like the Phoenician, rested on the factory. Like Spanish colonization, moreover, it was able to dissipate itself over vast regions; the lakes and rivers invited New France continually onward, and the plastic nature of the Frenchman made him the boon companion rather than the enemy of the Indian.

French administration was in all respects akin to the Roman; local life and self government were as obnoxious to Louis XIV and his successors, as to Philip II. At last the English met and overcame the French at the Heights of Abraham. Says Bancroft: "This victory, one of the most momentous in the annals of mankind, gave to the English tongue and the institutions of the Germanic race the unexplored and seemingly infinite west and north."

Two contending types had fought for the mastery of America, the Roman and the Germanic. The first defeat of the former came with the destruction of the Spanish Armada; as a second instance the colonization of Puritan Massachusetts marks the failure of the Stuarts to impose Spanish methods on England; again just a century after the Armada, the same dynasty with Governor Andros as its instrument, attempted to introduce the Roman type into the English colonies by consolidating the settlements and abolishing the town meetings and self taxation; a fourth time the two types met in conflict when the French lost the continent. The American revolution was the last act in the same drama of *libertas* against *imperium*, and here again the struggle came against the efforts of the English government to break with the English spirit and introduce the Roman type. The Declaration of Independence in part an outcome of the navigation laws came at the same time as Adam Smith's protest in his wealth of nations against the restriction system.

On the east of the Alleghanies, therefore, English colonization developed an organism capable of throwing out offshoots of its own. In the period of settlement were produced many of the germs of our national institutions and characteristics.

American colonization did not cease with the planting of Georgia. Indeed, it is only in the present that the colonizing era is coming to a close. I do not hesitate to say that this fact is the key to American history. As the occupation of the New World transformed Europe, so the occupation of the Great West has determined the flow of American energies, been the underlying explanation of political history, and has had profound reactive effects upon the social and economic life of the East. What first the Mediterranean Sea and later the New World were to the Aryan peoples, breaking the bond of custom, and creating new activities to meet new conditions, that the undeveloped West has been to the American descendants of these Aryans.[12]

No great dramatic crises have characterized the colonization of the West. Though there have been such occurrences as the discovery of gold in California, the Mormon colonization of Utah, and the fight for Kansas, yet on the whole the process has been a gradual and steady one. We may group the main facts regarding western settlement under the following topics: colonization by the pioneers of the South and Middle States through Cumberland Gap; colonization by the New England States in the Northwest territory; and the European immigration.

On the outskirts of the Atlantic colonies, pressing continually toward the West dwelt the American backwoodsmen. All along the uplands from Pennsylvania to Georgia, forming a cordon of defence to the colonists of the lower lands lived these pioneers. They had come from various nations. There were French Huguenots driven out by the Revocation of the Edict of Nantes, Salzburgers who had fled from the persecutions of their bishop in the Austrian Tyrol, and Germans from the Palatinate devastated by the Grand Monarch. But of all these backwoods men the dominant stock was the Scotch-Irish. From the first quarter of the 18th century, this nationality stalwart, sinewy both in body and in mind, came in a steady stream. Leaving Ulster the colonists came to America and reached the western frontiers by two channels,— either they came to Pennsylvania and, entering the valleys trending to the southwest, joined the Germans and English that had already found this great highway; or they came to Charleston, and passed across South and North Carolina. The united streams poured across the mountains through Cumberland Gap, and out into the blue grass region of Kentucky and Tennessee. The advance was not a sudden one. The pioneers pushed westward by small groups of families, and the settlements were made about palisaded log forts. They brought with them local self government, and democracy. Among their earliest acts were meetings to draw up written constitutions. This discloses the important fact that the American political institutions, formed before the flood of foreign immigration set in, were able to endure, and to mould the society beyond the mountains. In the period of the Revolution these pioneers went on and won new lands.

Once—in 1738—the Presbyterian synod of Philadelphia had sent a commission to the governor of Virginia, proposing to people the Shenandoah Valley with Scotch Irish who should hold the western frontier against the Indians on condition of being guaranteed freedom of worship. This was the same kind of colonizing proposition that the Puritan veterans of the Revolution made in their camp at Newburgh, on the eve of breaking ranks. They asked of Congress permission to plant a new State in the Ohio region to be a defence against the Indians and the English, on condition that slavery should be excluded from the Northwest. The result of their efforts was the Ordinance of 1787. The most important fact about this Ordinance from the point of view of American colonization was the provision for the organization of the territories with local self government, and a provision for the ultimate admission of these territories as States upon attaining the requisite growth. By this arrangement the United States declared against the Roman type of colony, and settled the destiny of the great West. Marietta, a colony of Revolutionary soldiers of Puritan ancestry was settled in 1783, and in 14 years Ohio was a State.

To restrict the term colonies to political dependencies is plainly to limit the word improperly. We ought to determine whether a migratory movement is rightly to be classed as colonization or not, by the spirit of it. If we find considerable groups of persons of the same nationality settling down in an unoccupied territory, bearing with them the characteristics of the mother country, we shall not go far astray if we term this practically colonization, even though the territory be the property of a civilized state, and even though it is hard to say at what point colonization of this nature becomes pure immigration. As I have pointed out before both are manifestations of the nomadic instinct. Taking this liberal use of the term, we may call much of the European settlement of the West, colonization. The occupation of Kentucky and Tennessee and of the Ohio region, represents that interstate colonization which needs so much to be studied. We can never understand our country properly until we know the materials out of which our Western States have been constructed. We need students who shall neglect Pocahontas and the mention of the first white child in Brown county, in order that they may study where and by what means the characteristics and the population of western states like Kansas, California and Wisconsin were produced. What was contributed by New England? by the Middle State? by Spain? When State and county history shall be studied in the light of world history, we shall begin to know our country better and this is the goal of history—to know the present by the study of its development from the past.[13] But when we have taken account of all the elements that the colonization by the trans-Alleghany organism has furnished, we have still left out of consideration a great body of facts. Every economic change, every political change, every military conscription, every socialistic agitation in Europe, has sent us groups of colonists which have passed on to our prairies to form new self-governing communities, or who have entered the life of our great cities. These men have come to us historical products. They have brought to us not merely so much bone and sinew, not merely so much money, not merely so much manual skill; they have brought with them deeply inrooted customs and ideas. They are important factors in the political and economic life of the nation. The story of the peopling of America has not yet been written. We do not understand ourselves.

Natural conditions have determined the location of those foreign groups. In some of the valleys of Pennsylvania for example, the Germans predominate, in others the Scotch-Irish. Take Wisconsin as a typical western state. Consider the German settlement of our Lake Shore counties, or the Belgian colonization of the Door county peninsula. What better example of a colony could be furnished than the Swiss settlement of New Glarus, organized under the patronage of the parent canton, and set down with its social framework intact in Green county. The Helvetii in the days of Caesar felt restricted in their narrow valley and attempted to settle in Gaul. The later occupants of these Helvetic valleys, moved by a like impulse made a colony in Wisconsin. Roscher, the founder of the historical school of Political Economy in Germany proposed to colonize some western American state with Germans and he suggested Wisconsin as the most promising place with which to begin. Our fellow in history is now investigating German immigration and has found that various societies have been formed among Germans in America to foster this attempt and that newspapers existed to advocate it. Recent events make it worth while considering whether the attempt did not indeed succeed! The German colonies in the West very often represent some particular province as Pommerania or Prussia. It is not remarkable that this spontaneous colonization compelled the German government to develope a colonial policy of its own, in order to divert the stream into lands politically dependent upon Germany. This is one of the keys to the recent activity of Germany as a colonizing power. American colonization has become the mother of the German colonial policy.[14] Nor is it without significance in this connection that Cook's visit to Australia came in the same year as our Declaration of Independence. England found recompense for the loss of her American colonies by new colonies in the Pacific. But enough has been said to indicate the importance of the study of the European colonization of the West. When we remember that in 1880 at least 30.9% of Wisconsin's population were foreign born; that Nevada's foreign born made 41.2% of her population; that California showed 33.9% we begin to realize the extent of this colonization. But a vastly larger percentage would be shown by taking those of foreign parentage. We must admit that in order to know the United States we cannot stop with the colonization of the Atlantic coast.

In conclusion, one question must arise. I have said that the colonization of the United States is now coming to a close. The passive age of her colonization is over. But the term passive does not properly describe the fact, for the United States herself has developed colonizing energy in settling the West. Our organism has been completed. We have a national self-consciousness, a self-sufficing industrial organization. Will not this organism bud as did the trans-Alleghany organism? The law of colonization in our day is stated as follows:

"In lands having a highly developed industry which produce more than the land itself can consume, there is an important incentive to the possession of colonies in the fact that thus they can furnish themselves with consumers of the home product; for the colonists being long devoted to the home production of the raw material furnish at the same time a ready market for the manufactures of the mother country; and this market can be monopolized by the laws of the mother country." In the light of this law, is not the recent Pan American Congress an evidence of the desire of the United States to secure at least substitutes for colonization by attaching South American economic life to our own. As Blaine has said "our manufactures and our agriculture, are overrunning the demands of the home market. Nor would it be an ambitious destiny for so great a country as ours to manufacture only what we can consume or to produce only what we can eat." "The annexation of the Trade" of South America may be the outcome of our colonizing energy. If it be so will the United States succumb to the Spanish type or will Spanish America be regenerated by the economic influence of the Germanic type?[15]

Turner's manuscript is in File Drawer 15 A.
The speech was delivered on 9 February 1893.

## NOTES

[1] Turner had circled the phrase "from the west to the east," and his question mark in the margin suggests that he wanted to study the validity of the assertion that the prehistoric migrations indeed had gone from west to east.

[2] Turner's question marks in the margin at this point suggest he is still uncertain about this assertion, too.

[3] Pages are missing at this point. Of course this reflects the historian's characteristic way of preparing papers, speeches, and articles: Turner often cannibalized previous statements for whole sections which he then inserted to make up new documents.

[4] Pages are missing at this point.

[5] Here is Turner's attempt at successive antitheses—between Calvinism and Catholicism, freedom of thought and authority of the church, as well as free government and absolute despotism. The passage is not nearly as well balanced, though, as in his antitheses in the frontier thesis or his college orations, for instance.

[6] Turner's marginal notation at this point indicates that he has four pages

from another manuscript which he wants to insert here at some later date.

⁷ Although the historian's parallel repetition usually is achieved by repeating at the *beginnings* of successive clauses, this passage shows Turner trying to achieve a rhetorical effect by repetition of the same word or phrase at the conclusions of succeeding sentence elements.

⁸ Here, as in another subsequent usage, Turner has left out "the" before Hudson, an idiosyncracy not consonant with his usual high regard for grammatical correctness.

⁹ The marginal note here suggests that the historian wants to consider changing "German" to "Dutch."

¹⁰ In the margin to his statement about "a mediating region" and "a fighting ground for ideas and social forms," Turner has drawn a sharp line and written in his reaction, "typical of U.S."

¹¹ Previous to this sentence, Turner chose to delete the sentence, "Take an educated, liberty loving people of a sturdy moral nature, with their intellect whetted by theological disputation and place at their service the town meeting."

¹² This is the synthesizing passage to which Turner had added the marginal note "need of studying this." Compare this statement with his frontier thesis peroration: "What the Mediterranean Sea was to the Greeks, breaking the bond of custom, offering new experiences, calling out new institutions and activities, that, and more, the ever retreating frontier has been to the United States directly, and to the nations of Europe more remotely."

¹³ Turner's tendency here toward an antithetical conformation seems to echo his prophetically autobiographical Burrows Prize Oration as a University of Wisconsin junior. As articulated there, the "Poet of the Future" has a distinct duty: "He will unite the logic of the present and the dream of the past, and his words will ring in the ears of generations yet unborn, telling them the grandeur of today which boils and surges with awakening life. He will reflect all the past and prophesy the future."

¹⁴ Question marks in the margin at this point suggest Turner's feeling a need to investigate this further.

¹⁵ Turner's signature, and the date February 9, 1891, appear after this sentence. It is likely that he anticipated answering his concluding rhetorical question, however, for the next sheets in the folder contain a long quotation from "Payne, *European Colonies*" which seems to address itself to the matter of economic influences of colonization.

# THE SIGNIFICANCE OF THE FRONTIER IN AMERICAN HISTORY[1]

In a recent bulletin of the Superintendent of the Census for 1890 appear these significant words: 'Up to and including 1880 the country had a frontier of settlement, but at present the unsettled area has been so broken into by isolated bodies of settlement that there can hardly be said to be a frontier line. In the discussion of its extent, its westward movement, etc., it can not, therefore, any longer have a place in the census reports." This brief official statement marks the closing of a great historic movement. Up to our own day American history has been in a large degree the history of the colonization of the Great West. The existence of an area of free land, its continuous recession, and the advance of American settlement westward, explain American development.

Behind institutions, behind constitutional forms and modifications, lie the vital forces that call these organs into life and shape them to meet changing conditions. The peculiarity of American institutions is, the fact that they have been compelled to adapt themselves to the changes of an expanding people—to the changes involved in crossing a continent, in winning a wilderness, and in developing at each area of this progress out of the primitive economic and political conditions of the frontier into the complexity of city life. Said Calhoun in 1817, "We are great, and rapidly—I was about to say fearfully—growing!"[2] So saying, he touched the distinguishing feature of American life. All peoples show development; the germ theory of politics has been sufficiently emphasized. In the case of most nations, however, the development has occurred in a limited area; and if the nation has expanded, it has met other growing peoples whom it has conquered. But in the case of the United States we have a different phenomenon. Limiting our attention to the Atlantic coast, we have the familiar phenomenon of the evolution of institutions in a limited area, such as the rise of representative government; the differentiation of simple colonial governments into complex organs; the progress from primitive industrial society without division of labor, up to manufacturing civilization. But we have in addition to this a recurrence of the process of evolution in each western area reached in the process of expansion. Thus American development has exhibited not merely advance along a single line, but a return to primitive conditions on a continually advancing frontier line, and a new development for that area. American social development has been continually beginning over again on the frontier. This perennial rebirth, this fluidity of American life, this expansion westward with its new opportunities, its continuous touch with the simplicity of primitive society, furnish the forces dominating American character. The true point of view in the history of this nation is not the Atlantic coast, it is the Great West. Even the slavery struggle, which is made so exclusive an object of attention by writers like Professor von Holst, occupies its important place in American history because of its relation to westward expansion.

In this advance, the frontier is the outer edge of the wave—the meeting point between savagery and civilization. Much has been written about the frontier from the point of view of border warfare and the chase, but as a field for the serious study of the economist and the historian it has been neglected.

The American frontier is sharply distinguished from the European frontier—a fortified boundary line running through dense populations. The most significant thing about the American frontier is, that it lies at the hither edge of free land. In the census reports it is treated as the margin of that settlement which has a density of two or more to the square mile. The term is an elastic one, and for our purposes does not need sharp definition. We shall consider the whole frontier belt, including the Indian country and the outer margin of the "settled area" of the census reports. This paper will make no attempt to treat the subject exhaustively; its aim is simply to call attention to the frontier as a fertile field for investigation, and to suggest some of the problems which arise in connection with it.

In the settlement of America we have to observe how European life entered the continent, and how America modified and developed that life and reacted on Europe. Our early history is the study of European germs developing in an American environment. Too exclusive attention has been paid by institutional students to the Germanic origins, too little to the American factors. The frontier is the line of most rapid and effective Americanization. The wilderness masters the colonist. It finds him a European in dress, industries, tools, modes of travel, and thought. It takes him from the railroad car and puts him in the birch canoe. It strips off the garments of civilization and arrays him in the hunting shirt and the moccasin. It puts him in the log cabin of the Cherokee and Iroquois and runs an Indian palisade around him. Before long he has gone to planting Indian corn and plowing with a sharp stick; he shouts the war cry and takes the scalp in orthodox Indian fashion. In short, at the frontier the environment is at first too strong for the man. He must accept the conditions which it furnishes, or perish, and so he fits himself into the Indian clearings and follows the Indian trails. Little by little he transforms the wilderness, but the outcome is not the old Europe, not simply the development of Germanic germs, any more than the first phenomenon was a case of reversion to the Germanic mark. The fact is, that here is a new product that is American. At first, the frontier was the Atlantic coast. It was the frontier of Europe in a very real sense. Moving westward, the frontier became more and more American. As successive terminal moraines result from successive glaciations, so each frontier leaves its traces behind it, and when it becomes a settled area the region still partakes of the frontier characteristics. Thus the advance of the frontier has meant a steady movement away from the influence of Europe, a steady growth of independence on American lines. And to study this advance, the men who grew up under these conditions, and the political, economic, and social results of it, is to study the really American part of our history.

In the course of the seventeenth century the frontier was advanced up the Atlantic river courses, just beyond the "fall line," and the tidewater region became the settled area. In the first half of the eighteenth century another advance occurred. Traders followed the Delaware and Shawnese Indians to the Ohio as early as the end of the first quarter of the century.[3] Gov. Spotswood, of Virginia, made an expedition in 1714 across the Blue Ridge. The end of the first quarter of the century saw the advance of the Scotch-Irish and the Palatine Germans up the Shenandoah Valley into the western part of Virginia, and along the Piedmont region of the Carolinas.[4] The Germans in New York pushed the frontier of settlement up the Mohawk to German Flats.[5] In Pennsylvania the town of Bedford indicates the line of settlement. Settlements soon began on the New River, or the Great Kanawha, and on the sources of the Yadkin and French Broad.[6] The King attempted to arrest the advance by his proclamation of 1763,[7] forbidding settlements beyond the sources of the rivers flowing into the Atlantic; but in vain. In the period of the Revolution the frontier crossed the Alleghanies into Kentucky and Tennessee, and the upper waters of the Ohio were settled.[8] When the first census was taken in 1790, the continuous settled area was bounded by a line which ran near the coast of Maine, and included New England except a portion of Vermont and New Hampshire, New York along the Hudson and up the Mohawk about Schenectady, eastern and southern Pennsylvania, Virginia well across the Shenandoah Valley, and the Carolinas and eastern Georgia.[9] Beyond this region of continuous settlement were the small settled areas of Kentucky and Tennessee, and the Ohio, with the mountains intervening between them and the Atlantic area, thus giving a new and important character to the frontier. The isolation of the region increased its peculiarly American tendencies, and the need of transportation facilities to connect it with the East called out important schemes of internal improvement, which will be noted farther on. The "West," as a self-conscious section, began to evolve.

From decade to decade distinct advances of the frontier occurred. By the census of 1820[10] the settled area included Ohio, southern Indiana and Illinois, southeastern Missouri, and about one-half of Louisiana. This settled area had surrounded Indian areas, and the management of these tribes became an object of political concern. The frontier region of the time lay along the Great Lakes, where Astor's American Fur Company operated in the Indian trade,[11] and beyond the Mississippi, where Indian traders extended their activity even to the Rocky Mountains; Florida also furnished frontier conditions. The Mississippi River region was the scene of typical frontier settlements.[12]

The rising steam navigation[13] on western waters, the opening of the Erie Canal, and the westward extension of cotton[14] culture added five frontier states to the Union in this period. Grund, writing in 1836, declares: "It appears then that the universal disposition of Americans to emigrate to the western wilderness, in order to enlarge their dominion over inanimate nature, is the actual result of an expansive power which is inherent in them, and which by continually agitating all classes of society is constantly throwing a large portion of the whole population on the extreme confines of the State, in order to gain space for its development. Hardly is a new State or Territory formed before the same principle manifests itself again and gives rise to a further emigration; and so is it destined to go on until a physical barrier must finally obstruct its progress."[15]

In the middle of this century the line indicated by the present eastern boundary of Indian Territory, Nebraska, and Kansas marked the frontier of the Indian country.[16] Minnesota and Wisconsin still exhibited frontier conditions,[17] but the distinctive frontier of the period is found in California, where the gold discoveries had sent a sudden tide of adventurous miners, and in Oregon, and the settlements in Utah.[18] As the frontier had leaped over the Alleghanies, so now it skipped the Great Plains and the Rocky Mountains; and in the same way that the advance of the frontiersmen beyond the Alleghanies had caused the rise of important questions of transportation and internal improvement, so now the settlers beyond the Rocky Mountains needed means of communication with the East, and in the furnishing of these arose the settlement of the Great Plains and the development of still another kind of frontier life. Railroads, fostered by land grants, sent an increasing tide of immigrants into the Far West. The United States Army fought a series of Indian wars in Minnesota, Dakota, and the Indian Territory.

By 1880 the settled area had been pushed into northern Michigan, Wisconsin, and Minnesota, along Dakota rivers, and in the Black Hills region, and was ascending the rivers of Kansas and Nebraska. The development of mines in Colorado had drawn isolated frontier settlements into that region, and Montana and Idaho were receiving settlers. The frontier was found in these mining camps and the ranches of the Great Plains. The superintendent of the census for 1890 reports, as previously stated, that the settlements of the West lie so scattered over the region that there can no longer be said to be a frontier line.

In these successive frontiers we find natural boundary lines which have served to mark and to affect the characteristics of the frontiers, namely: the "fall line;" the Alleghany Mountains; the Mississippi; the Missouri where its direction approximates north and south; the line of the arid lands, approximately the ninety-ninth meridian; and the Rocky Mountains. The fall line marked the frontier of the seventeenth century; the Alleghanies that of the eighteenth; the Mississippi that of the first quarter of the nineteenth; the Missouri that of the middle of this century (omitting the California movement); and the belt of the Rocky Mountains and the arid tract, the present frontier. Each was won by a series of Indian wars.

At the Atlantic frontier one can study the germs of processes repeated at each successive frontier. We have the complex European life sharply precipitated by the wilderness into the simplicity of primitive conditions. The first frontier had to meet its Indian question, its question of the disposition of the public domain, of the means of intercourse with older settlements, of the extension of political organization, of religious and educational activity. And the settlement of these and similar questions for one frontier served as a guide for the next. The American student needs not to go to the "prim little townships of Sleswick" for illustrations of the law of continuity and development. For example, he may study the origin of our land policies in the colonial land policy; he may see how the system grew by adapting the statutes to the customs of the successive frontiers.[19] He may see how the mining experience in the lead regions of Wisconsin, Illinois, and Iowa was applied to the mining laws of the Sierras,[20] and how our Indian policy has been a series of experimentations on successive frontiers. Each tier of new States has found in the older ones material for its constitutions.[21] Each frontier has made similar contributions to American character, as will be discussed farther on.

But with all these similarities there are essential differences, due to the place element and the time element. It is evident that the farming frontier of the Mississippi Valley presents different conditions from the mining frontier of the Rocky Mountains. The frontier reached by the Pacific Railroad, surveyed into rectangles, guarded by the United States Army, and recruited by the daily immigrant ship, moves forward at a swifter pace and in a different way than the frontier reached by the birch canoe or the pack horse. The geologist traces patiently the shores of ancient seas, maps their areas, and compares the older and the newer. It would be a work worth the historian's labors to mark these various frontiers and in detail compare one with another. Not only would there result a more adequate conception of American development and characteristics, but invaluable additions would be made to the history of society.

Loria,[22] the Italian economist, has urged the study of colonial life as an aid in understanding the stages of European development, affirming that colonial settlement is for economic science what the mountain is for geology, bringing to light primitive stratifications. "America," he says, "has the key to the historical enigma which Europe has sought for centuries in vain, and the land which has no history reveals luminously the course of universal history." There is much truth in this. The United States lies like a huge page in the history of society. Line by line as we read this continental page from West to East we find the record of social evolution. It begins with the Indian and the hunter; it goes on to tell of the disintegration of savagery by the entrance of the trader, the pathfinder of civilization; we read the annals of the pastoral stage in ranch life; the exploitation of the soil by the raising of unrotated crops of corn and wheat in sparsely settled farming communities; the intensive culture of the denser farm settlement; and finally the manufacturing organization with city and factory system.[23] This page is familiar to the student of census statistics, but how little of it has been used by our historians. Particularly in eastern States this page is a palimpsest. What is now a manufacturing State was in an earlier decade an area of intensive farming. Earlier yet it had been a wheat area, and still earlier the "range" had attracted the cattle-herder. Thus Wisconsin, now developing manufacture, is a State with varied agricultural interests. But earlier it was given over to almost exclusive grain-raising, like North Dakota at the present time.

Each of these areas has had an influence in our economic and political history; the evolution of each into a higher stage has worked political transformations. But what constitutional historian has made any adequate attempt to interpret political facts by the light of these social areas and changes?[24]

The Atlantic frontier was compounded of fisherman, fur-trader, miner, cattle-raiser, and farmer. Excepting the fisherman, each type of industry was on the march toward the West, impelled by an irresistible attraction. Each passed in successive waves across the continent. Stand at Cumberland Gap and watch the procession of civilization, marching single file—the buffalo following the trail to the salt springs, the Indian, the fur-trader and hunter, the cattle-raiser, the pioneer farmer— and the frontier has passed by. Stand at South Pass in the Rockies a century later and see the same procession with wider intervals between. The unequal rate of advance compels us to distinguish the frontier into the trader's frontier, the rancher's frontier, or the miner's frontier, and the farmer's frontier. When the mines and the cow pens were still near the fall line the traders' pack trains were tinkling across the Alleghanies, and the French on the Great Lakes were fortifying their posts, alarmed by the British trader's birch canoe. When the trappers scaled the Rockies, the farmer was still near the mouth of the Missouri.

Why was it that the Indian trader passed so rapidly across the continent? What effects followed from the trader's frontier? The trade was coeval with American discovery. The Norsemen, Vespuccius, Verrazani, Hudson, John Smith, all trafficked for furs. The Plymouth pilgrims settled in Indian cornfields, and their first return cargo was of beaver and lumber. The records of the various New England colonies show how steadily exploration was carried into the wilderness by this trade. What is true for New England is, as would be expected, even plainer for the rest of the colonies. All along the coast from Maine to Georgia the Indian trade opened up the river courses. Steadily the trader passed westward, utilizing the older lines of French trade. The Ohio, the Great Lakes, the Mississippi, the Missouri, and the Platte, the lines of western advance, were ascended by traders. They found the passes in the Rocky Mountains and guided Lewis and Clark,[25] Frémont, and Bidwell. The explanation of the rapidity of this advance is connected with the effects of the trader on the Indian. The trading post left the unarmed tribes at the mercy of those that had purchased firearms—a truth which the Iroquois Indians wrote in blood, and so the remote and unvisited tribes gave eager welcome to the trader. "The savages," wrote La Salle, "take better care of us French than of their own children; from us only can they get guns and goods." This accounts for the trader's power and the rapidity of his advance. Thus the disintegrating forces of civilization entered the wilderness. Every river valley and Indian trail became a fissure in Indian society, and so that society became honeycombed. Long before the pioneer farmer appeared on the scene, primitive Indian life had passed away. The farmers met Indians armed with guns. The trading frontier, while steadily undermining Indian power by making the tribes ultimately dependent on the whites, yet, through its sale of guns, gave to the Indian increased power of resistance to the farming frontier. French colonization was dominated by its trading frontier; English colonization by its farming frontier. There was an antagonism between the two frontiers as between the two nations. Said Duquesne to the Iroquois, "Are you ignorant of the difference between the king of England and the king of France? Go see the forts that our king has established, and you will see that you can still hunt under their very walls. They have been placed for your advantage in places which you frequent. The English, on the contrary, are no sooner in possession of a place than the game is driven away. The forest falls before them as they advance, and the soil is laid bare so that you can scarce find the wherewithal to erect a shelter for the night."

And yet, in spite of this opposition of the interests of the trader and the farmer, the Indian trade pioneered the way for civilization. The buffalo trail became the Indian trail, and this became the trader's "trace;" the trails widened into roads, and the roads into turnpikes, and these in turn were transformed into railroads. The same origin can be shown for the railroads of the South, the Far West, and the Dominion of Canada.[26] The trading posts reached by these trails were on the sites of Indian villages which had been placed in positions suggested by nature; and these trading posts, situated so as to command the water systems of the country, have grown into such cities as Albany, Pittsburgh, Detroit, Chicago, St. Louis, Council Bluffs, and Kansas City. Thus civilization in America has followed the arteries made by geology, pouring an ever richer tide through them, until at last the slender paths of aboriginal intercourse have been broadened and interwoven into the complex mazes of modern commercial lines; the wilderness has been interpenetrated by lines of civilization growing ever more numerous. It is like the steady growth of a complex nervous system for the originally simple, inert continent. If one would understand why we are to-day one nation, rather than a collection of isolated states, he must study this economic and social consolidation of the country. In this progress from savage conditions lie topics for the evolutionist.[27]

The effect of the Indian frontier as a consolidating agent in our history is important. From the close of the seventeenth century various intercolonial congresses have been called to treat with Indians and establish common measures of defense. Particularism was strongest in colonies with no Indian frontier. This frontier stretched along the western border like a cord of union. The Indian was a common danger, demanding united action. Most celebrated of these conferences was the Albany congress of 1754, called to treat with the Six Nations, and to consider plans of union. Even a cursory reading of the plan proposed by the congress reveals the importance of the frontier. The powers of the general council and the officers were, chiefly, the determination of peace and war with the Indians, the regulation of Indian trade, the purchase of Indian lands, and the creation and government of new settlements as a security against the Indians. It is evident that the unifying tendencies of the Revolutionary period were facilitated by the previous coöperation in the regulation of the frontier. In this connection may be mentioned the importance of the frontier, from that day to this, as a military training school, keeping alive the power of resistance to aggression, and developing the stalwart and rugged qualities of the frontiersman.

It would not be possible in the limits of this paper to trace the other frontiers across the continent. Travelers of the eighteenth century found the "cowpens" among the canebrakes and peavine pastures of the South, and the "cow drivers" took their droves to Charleston, Philadelphia, and New York.[28] Travelers at the close of the War of 1812 met droves of more than a thousand cattle and swine from the interior of Ohio going to Pennsylvania to fatten for the Philadelphia market.[29] The ranges of the Great Plains, with ranch and cowboy and nomadic life, are things of yesterday and of to-day. The experience of the Carolina cowpens guided the ranchers of Texas. One element favoring the rapid extension of the rancher's frontier is the fact that in a remote country lacking transportation facilities the product must be in small bulk, or must be able to transport itself, and the cattle raiser could easily drive his product to market. The effect of these great ranches on the subsequent agrarian history of the localities in which they existed should be studied.

The maps of the census reports show an uneven advance of the farmer's frontier, with tongues of settlement pushed forward and with indentations of wilderness. In part this is due to Indian resistance, in part to the location of river valleys and passes, in part to the unequal force of the centers of frontier attraction. Among the important centers of attraction may be mentioned the following: fertile and favorably situated soils, salt springs, mines, and army posts.

The frontier army post, serving to protect the settlers from the Indians, has also acted as a wedge to open the Indian country, and has been a nucleus for settlement.[30] In this connection mention should also be made of the government, military, and exploring expeditions in determining the lines of settlement. But all the more important expeditions were greatly indebted to the earliest pathmakers, the Indian guides, the traders and trappers, and the French voyageurs, who were inevitable parts of governmental expeditions from the days of Lewis and Clark.[31] Each expedition was an epitome of the previous factors in western advance.

In an interesting monograph, Victor Hehn[32] has traced the effect of salt upon early European development, and has pointed out how it affected the lines of settlement and the form of administration. A similar study might be made for the salt springs of the United States. The early settlers were tied to the coast by the need of salt, without which they could not preserve their meats or live in comfort. Writing in 1752, Bishop Spangenburg says of a colony for which he was seeking lands in North Carolina. "They will require salt & other necessaries which they can neither manufacture nor raise. Either they must go to Charleston, which is 300 miles distant . . . Or else they must go to Boling's Point in V$^a$ on a branch of the James & is also 300 miles from here . . . Or else they must go down the Roanoke—I know not how many miles—where salt is brought up from the Cape Fear."[33] This may serve as a typical illustration. An annual pilgrimage to the coast for salt thus became essential. Taking flocks or furs and ginseng root, the early settlers sent their pack trains after seeding time each year to the coast.[34] This proved to be an important educational influence, since it was almost the only way in which the pioneer learned what was going on in the East. But when discovery was made of the salt springs of the Kanawha, and the Holston, and Kentucky, and central New York, the West began to be freed from dependence on the coast. It was in part the effect of finding these salt springs that enabled settlement to cross the mountains.

From the time the mountains rose between the pioneer and the seaboard, a new order of Americanism arose. The West and the East began to get out of touch of each other. The settlements from the sea to the mountains kept connection with the rear and had a certain solidarity. But the over-mountain men grew more and more independent. The East took a narrow view of American advance, and nearly lost these men. Kentucky and Tennessee history bears abundant witness to the truth of this statement. The East began to try to hedge and limit westward expansion. Though Webster could declare that there were no

Alleghanies in his politics, yet in politics in general they were a very solid factor.

The exploitation of the beasts took hunter and trader to the west, the exploitation of the grasses took the rancher west, and the exploitation of the virgin soil of the river valleys and prairies attracted the farmer. Good soils have been the most continuous attraction to the farmer's frontier. The land hunger of the Virginians drew them down the rivers into Carolina, in early colonial days; the search for soils took the Massachusetts men to Pennsylvania and to New York. As the eastern lands were taken up migration flowed across them to the west. Daniel Boone, the great backwoodsman, who combined the occupations of hunter, trader, cattle-raiser, farmer, and surveyor—learning, probably from the traders, of the fertility of the lands of the upper Yadkin, where the traders were wont to rest as they took their way to the Indians, left his Pennsylvania home with his father, and passed down the Great Valley road to that stream. Learning from a trader of the game and rich pastures of Kentucky, he pioneered the way for the farmers to that region. Thence he passed to the frontier of Missouri, where his settlement was long a landmark on the frontier. Here again he helped to open the way for civilization, finding salt licks, and trails, and land. His son was among the earliest trappers in the passes of the Rocky Mountains, and his party are said to have been the first to camp on the present site of Denver. His grandson, Col. A. J. Boone, of Colorado, was a power among the Indians of the Rocky Mountains, and was appointed an agent by the government. Kit Carson's mother was a Boone.[35] Thus this family epitomizes the backwoodsman's advance across the continent.

The farmer's advance came in a distinct series of waves. In Peck's New Guide to the West, published in Boston in 1837, occurs this suggestive passage:

> Generally, in all the western settlements, three classes, like the waves of the ocean, have rolled one after the other. First comes the pioneer, who depends for the subsistence of his family chiefly upon the natural growth of vegetation, called the "range," and the proceeds of hunting. His implements of agriculture are rude, chiefly of his own make, and his efforts directed mainly to a crop of corn and a "truck patch." The last is a rude garden for growing cabbage, beans, corn for roasting ears, cucumbers, and potatoes. A log cabin, and, occasionally, a stable and corn-crib, and a field of a dozen acres, the timber girdled or "deadened," and fenced, are enough for his occupancy. It is quite immaterial whether he ever becomes the owner of the soil. He is the occupant for the time being, pays no rent, and feels as independent as the "lord of the manor." With a horse, cow,

203

and one or two breeders of swine, he strikes into the woods with his family, and becomes the founder of a new county, or perhaps state. He builds his cabin, gathers around him a few other families of similar tastes and habits, and occupies till the range is somewhat subdued, and hunting a little precarious, or, which is more frequently the case, till the neighbors crowd around, roads, bridges, and fields annoy him, and he lacks elbow room. The preëmption law enables him to dispose of his cabin and cornfield to the next class of emigrants; and, to employ his own figures, he "breaks for the high timber," "clears out for the New Purchase," or migrates to Arkansas or Texas, to work the same process over.

The next class of emigrants purchase the lands, add field to field, clear out the roads, throw rough bridges over the streams, put up hewn log houses with glass windows and brick or stone chimneys, occasionally plant orchards, build mills, schoolhouses, court-houses, etc., and exhibit the picture and forms of plain, frugal, civilized life.

Another wave rolls on. The men of capital and enterprise come. The settler is ready to sell out and take the advantage of the rise in property, push farther into the interior and become, himself, a man of capital and enterprise in turn. The small village rises to a spacious town or city; substantial edifices of brick, extensive fields, orchards, gardens, colleges, and churches are seen. Broadcloths, silks, leghorns, crapes, and all the refinements, luxuries, elegancies, frivolities, and fashions are in vogue. Thus wave after wave is rolling westward; the real Eldorado is still farther on.

A portion of the two first classes remain stationary amidst the general movement, improve their habits and conditions, and rise in the scale of society.

The writer has traveled much amongst the first class, the real pioneers. He has lived many years in connection with the second grade; and now the third wave is sweeping over large districts of Indiana, Illinois, and Missouri. Migration has become almost a habit in the West. Hundreds of men can be found, not over 50 years of age, who have settled for the fourth, fifth, or sixth time on a new spot. To sell out and remove only a few hundred miles makes up a portion of the variety of backwoods life and manners.[36]

Omitting those of the pioneer farmers who move from the love of adventure, the advance of the more steady farmer is easy to understand. Obviously the immigrant was attracted by the cheap lands of the frontier, and even the native farmer felt their influence strongly. Year by year the farmers who lived on soil whose returns were diminished by unrotated crops were offered the virgin soil of the frontier at nominal prices. Their growing families demanded more lands, and these were dear. The competition of the unexhausted, cheap, and easily tilled prairie lands compelled the farmer either to go west and continue the exhaustion of the soil on a new frontier, or to adopt intensive culture. Thus the census of 1890 shows, in the Northwest, many counties in which there is an absolute or a relative decrease of population. These States have been sending farmers to advance the frontier on the plains, and have themselves begun to turn to intensive farming and to manufacture. A decade before this, Ohio had shown the same transition stage. Thus the demand for land and the love of wilderness freedom drew the frontier ever onward.

Having now roughly outlined the various kinds of frontiers, and their modes of advance, chiefly from the point of view of the frontier itself, we may next inquire what were the influences on the East and on the Old World. A rapid enumeration of some of the more noteworthy effects is all that I have time for.

First, we note that the frontier promoted the formation of a composite nationality for the American people. The coast was preponderantly English, but the later tides of continental immigration flowed across to the free lands. This was the case from the early colonial days. The Scotch-Irish and the Palatine Germans, or "Pennsylvania Dutch," furnished the dominant element in the stock of the colonial frontier. With these peoples were also the freed indented servants, or redemptioners, who at the expiration of their time of service passed to the frontier. Governor Spotswood of Virginia writes in 1717, "The inhabitants of our frontiers are composed generally of such as have been transported hither as servants, and, being out of their time, settle themselves where land is to be taken up and that will produce the necessarys of life with little labour."[37] Very generally these redemptioners were of non-English stock. In the crucible of the frontier the immigrants were Americanized, liberated, and fused into a mixed race, English in neither nationality nor characteristics. The process has gone on from the early days to our own. Burke and other writers in the middle of the eighteenth century believed that Pennsylvania[38] was "threatened with the danger of being wholly foreign in language, manners, and perhaps even inclinations." The German and Scotch-Irish elements in the frontier of the South were only less great. In the middle of the present century the German element in Wisconsin was already so considerable that leading publicists looked to the creation of a German state out of the commonwealth by concentrating their colonization.[39] Such examples teach us to beware of misinterpreting the fact that there is a common English speech in America into a belief that the stock is also English.

In another way the advance of the frontier decreased our dependence on England. The coast, particularly of the South, lacked diversified industries, and was dependent on England for the bulk of its supplies. In the South there was even a dependence on the Northern colonies for articles of food. Governor Glenn, of South Carolina, writes in the middle of the eighteenth century: "Our trade with New York and Philadelphia was of this sort, draining us of all the little money and bills we could gather from other places for their bread, flour, beer, hams, bacon, and other things of their produce, all which, except beer, our new townships begin to supply us with, which are settled with very industrious and thriving Germans. This no doubt diminishes the number of shipping and the appearance of our trade, but it is far from being a detriment to us."[40] Before long the frontier created a demand for merchants. As it retreated from the coast it became less and less possible for England to bring her supplies directly to the consumer's wharfs, and carry away staple crops, and staple crops began to give way to diversified agriculture for a time. The effect of this phase of the frontier action upon the northern section is perceived when we realize how the advance of the frontier aroused seaboard cities like Boston, New York, and Baltimore, to engage in rivalry for what Washington called "the extensive and valuable trade of a rising empire."

The legislation which most developed the powers of the national government, and played the largest part in its activity, was conditioned on the frontier. Writers have discussed the subjects of tariff, land, and internal improvement, as subsidiary to the slavery question. But when American history comes to be rightly viewed it will be seen that the slavery question is an incident. In the period from the end of the first half of the present century to the close of the Civil War slavery rose to primary, but far from exclusive, importance. But this does not justify Dr. von Holst (to take an example) in treating our constitutional history in its formative period down to 1828 in a single volume, giving six volumes chiefly to the history of slavery from 1828 to 1861, under the title "Constitutional History of the United States." The growth of nationalism and the evolution of American political institutions were dependent on the advance of the frontier. Even so recent a writer as Rhodes, in his "History of the United States since the Compromise of 1850," has treated the legislation called out by the western advance as incidental to the slavery struggle.

This is a wrong perspective. The pioneer needed the goods of the coast, and so the grand series of internal improvement and railroad legislation began, with potent nationalizing effects. Over internal improvements occurred great debates, in which grave constitutional questions were discussed. Sectional groupings appear in the votes, profoundly significant for the historian. Loose construction increased as the nation marched westward.[41] But the West was not content with bringing the farm to the factory. Under the lead of Clay—"Harry of the West"— protective tariffs were passed, with the cry of bringing the factory to the farm. The disposition of the public lands was a third important subject of national legislation influenced by the frontier.

The public domain has been a force of profound importance in the nationalization and development of the government. The effects of the struggle of the landed and the landless States, and of the Ordinance of 1787, need no discussion.[42] Administratively the frontier called out some of the highest and most vitalizing activities of the general government. The purchase of Louisiana was perhaps the constitutional turning point in the history of the Republic, inasmuch as it afforded both a new area for national legislation and the occasion of the downfall of the policy of strict construction. But the purchase of Louisiana was called out by frontier needs and demands. As frontier States accrued to the Union the national power grew. In a speech on the dedication of the Calhoun monument Mr. Lamar explained: "In 1789 the States were the creators of the Federal Government; in 1861 the Federal Government was the creator of a large majority of the States."

When we consider the public domain from the point of view of the sale and disposal of the public lands we are again brought face to face with the frontier. The policy of the United States in dealing with its lands is in sharp contrast with the European system of scientific administration. Efforts to make this domain a source of revenue, and to withhold it from emigrants in order that settlement might be compact, were in vain. The jealousy and the fears of the East were powerless in the face of the demands of the frontiersmen. John Quincy Adams was obliged to confess: "My own system of administration, which was to make the national domain the inexhaustible fund for progressive and unceasing internal improvement, has failed." The reason is obvious; a system of administration was not what the West demanded; it wanted land. Adams states the situation as follows: "The slaveholders of the South have bought the coöperation of the western country by the bribe of the western lands, abandoning to the new Western States their own proportion of the public property and aiding them in the design of grasping all the lands into their own hands. Thomas H. Benton was the author of this system, which he brought forward as a substitute for the American system of Mr. Clay, and to supplant him as the leading statesman of the West. Mr. Clay, by his tariff compromise with Mr. Calhoun, abandoned his own American system. At the same time he brought forward a plan for distributing among all the States of the Union the proceeds of the sales of the public lands. His bill for that purpose passed both Houses of Congress, but was vetoed by President Jackson, who, in his annual message of December, 1832, formally recommended that all public lands should be gratuitously given away to individual adventurers and to the States in which the lands are situated."[43]

"No subject," said Henry Clay, "which has presented itself to the present, or perhaps any preceding, Congress, is of greater magnitude than that of the public lands." When we consider the far-reaching effects of the government's land policy upon political, economic, and social aspects of American life, we are disposed to agree with him. But this legislation was framed under frontier influences, and under the lead of Western statesmen like Benton and Jackson. Said Senator Scott of Indiana in 1841: "I consider the preëmption law merely declaratory of the custom or common law of the settlers."

It is safe to say that the legislation with regard to land, tariff, and internal improvements—the American system of the nationalizing Whig party—was conditioned on frontier ideas and needs. But it was not merely in legislative action that the frontier worked against the sectionalism of the coast. The economic and social characteristics of the frontier worked against sectionalism. The men of the frontier had closer resemblances to the Middle region than to either of the other sections. Pennsylvania had been the seed-plot of frontier emigration, and, although she passed on her settlers along the Great Valley into the west of Virginia and the Carolinas, yet the industrial society of these Southern frontiersmen was always more like that of the Middle region than like that of the tide-water portion of the South, which later came to spread its industrial type throughout the South.

The Middle region, entered by New York harbor, was an open door to all Europe. The tide-water part of the South represented typical Englishmen, modified by a warm climate and servile labor, and living in baronial fashion on great plantations; New England stood for a special English movement—Puritanism. The Middle region was less English than the other sections. It had a wide mixture of nationalities, a varied society, the mixed town and county system of local government, a varied economic life, many religious sects. In short, it was a region mediating between New England and the South, and the East and the West. It represented that composite nationality which the contemporary United States exhibits, that juxtaposition of non-English groups, occupying a valley or a little settlement, and presenting reflections of the map of Europe in their variety. It was democratic and nonsectional, if not national; "easy, tolerant, and contented;" rooted strongly in material prosperity. It was typical of the modern United States. It was least sectional, not only because it lay between North and South, but also because with no barriers to shut out its frontiers from its settled region, and with a system of connecting waterways, the Middle region mediated between East and West as well as between North and South. Thus it became the typically American region. Even the New Englander, who was shut out from the frontier by the Middle region, tarrying in New York or Pennsylvania on his westward march, lost the acuteness of his sectionalism on the way.[44]

The spread of cotton culture into the interior of the South finally broke down the contrast between the "tide-water" region and the rest of the State, and based Southern interests on slavery. Before this process revealed its results the western portion of the South, which was akin to Pennsylvania in stock, society, and industry, showed tendencies to fall away from the faith of the fathers into internal improvement legislation and nationalism. In the Virginia convention of 1829-30, called to revise the constitution, Mr. Leigh, of Chesterfield, one of the tide-water counties, declared:

> One of the main causes of discontent which led to this convention, that which had the strongest influence in overcoming our veneration for the work of our fathers, which taught us to contemn the sentiments of Henry and Mason and Pendleton, which weaned us from our reverence for the constituted authorities of the State, was an overweening passion for internal improvement. I say this with perfect knowledge, for it has been avowed to me by gentlemen from the West over and over again. And let me tell the gentleman from Albemarle (Mr. Gordon) that it has been another principal object of those who set this ball of revolution in motion, to overturn the doctrine of State rights, of which Virginia has been the very pillar, and to remove the barrier she has interposed to the interference of the Federal Government in that same work of internal improvement, by so reorganizing the legislature that Virginia, too, may be hitched to the Federal car.

It was this nationalizing tendency of the West that transformed the democracy of Jefferson into the national republicanism of Monroe and the democracy of Andrew Jackson. The West of the War of 1812, the West of Clay, and Benton and Harrison, and Andrew Jackson, shut off by the Middle States and the mountains from the coast sections, had a solidarity of its own with national tendencies.[45] On the tide of the Father of Waters, North and South met and mingled into a nation. Interstate migration went steadily on—a process of cross-fertilization of ideas and institutions. The fierce struggle of the sections over slavery on the western frontier does not diminish the truth of this statement; it proves the truth of it. Slavery was a sectional trait that would not down, but in the West it could not remain sectional. It was the greatest of frontiersmen who declared: "I believe this Government can not endure permanently half slave and half free. It will become all of one thing or all of the other." Nothing works for nationalism like intercourse within the nation. Mobility of population is death to localism, and the western frontier worked irresistibly in unsettling population. The effect reached back from the frontier and affected profoundly the Atlantic coast and even the Old World.

But the most important effect of the frontier has been in the promotion of democracy here and in Europe. As has been indicated, the frontier is productive of individualism. Complex society is precipitated by the wilderness into a kind of primitive organization based on the family. The tendency is anti-social. It produces antipathy to control, and particularly to any direct control. The tax-gatherer is viewed as a representative of oppression. Prof. Osgood, in an able article,[46] has pointed out that the frontier conditions prevalent in the colonies are important factors in the explanation of the American Revolution, where individual liberty was sometimes confused with absence of all effective government. The same conditions aid in explaining the difficulty of instituting a strong government in the period of the confederacy. The frontier individualism has from the beginning promoted democracy.

The frontier States that came into the Union in the first quarter of a century of its existence came in with democratic suffrage provisions, and had reactive effects of the highest importance upon the older States whose peoples were being attracted there. An extension of the franchise became essential. It was *western* New York that forced an extension of suffrage in the constitutional convention of that State in 1821; and it was *western* Virginia that compelled the tide-water region to put a more liberal suffrage provision in the constitution framed in 1830, and to give to the frontier region a more nearly proportionate representation with the tide-water aristocracy. The rise of democracy as an effective force in the nation came in with western preponderance under Jackson and William Henry Harrison, and it meant the triumph of the frontier—with all of its good and with all of its evil elements.[47] An interesting illustration of the tone of frontier democracy in 1830 comes from the same debates in the Virginia convention already referred to. A representative from western Virginia declared:

> But sir, it is not the increase of population in the West which this gen-

tleman ought to fear. It is the energy which the mountain breeze and western habits impart to those emigrants. They are regenerated, politically I mean, sir. They soon become *working politicians;* and the difference, sir, between a *talking* and a *working* politician is immense. The Old Dominion has long been celebrated for producing great orators; the ablest metaphysicians in policy; men that can split hairs in all abstruse questions of political economy. But at home, or when they return from Congress, they have negroes to fan them asleep. But a Pennsylvania, a New York, an Ohio, or a western Virginia statesman, though far inferior in logic, metaphysics, and rhetoric to an old Virginia statesman, has this advantage, that when he returns home he takes off his coat and takes hold of the plow. This gives him bone and muscle, sir, and preserves his republican principles pure and uncontaminated.

So long as free land exists, the opportunity for a competency exists, and economic power secures political power. But the democracy born of free land, strong in selfishness and individualism, intolerant of administrative experience and education, and pressing individual liberty beyond its proper bounds, has its dangers as well as its benefits. Individualism in America has allowed a laxity in regard to governmental affairs which has rendered possible the spoils system and all the manifest evils that follow from the lack of a highly developed civic spirit. In this connection may be noted also the influence of frontier conditions in permitting lax business honor, inflated paper currency and wild-cat banking. The colonial and revolutionary frontier was the region whence emanated many of the worst forms of an evil currency.[48] The West in the War of 1812 repeated the phenomenon on the frontier of that day, while the speculation and wild-cat banking of the period of the crisis of 1837 occurred on the new frontier belt of the next tier of States. Thus each one of the periods of lax financial integrity coincides with periods when a new set of frontier communities had arisen, and coincides in area with these successive frontiers, for the most part. The recent Populist agitation is a case in point. Many a State that now declines any connection with the tenets of the Populists, itself adhered to such ideas in an earlier stage of the development of the State. A primitive society can hardly be expected to show the intelligent appreciation of the complexity of business interests in a developed society. The continual recurrence of these areas of paper-money agitation is another evidence that the frontier can be isolated and studied as a factor in American history of the highest importance.[49]

The East has always feared the result of an unregulated advance of the frontier, and has tried to check and guide it. The English authorities would have checked settlement at the headwaters of the Atlantic tributaries and allowed the "savages to enjoy their deserts in quiet lest the peltry trade should decrease." This called out Burke's splendid protest:

> If you stopped your grants, what would be the consequence? The people would occupy without grants. They have already so occupied in many places. You can not station garrisons in every part of these deserts. If you drive the people from one place, they will carry on their annual tillage and remove with their flocks and herds to another. Many of the people in the back settlements are already little attached to particular situations. Already they have topped the Appalachian Mountains. From thence they behold before them an immense plain, one vast, rich, level meadow; a square of five hundred miles. Over this they would wander without a possibility of restraint; they would change their manners with their habits of life; would soon forget a government by which they were disowned; would become hordes of English Tartars; and, pouring down upon your unfortified frontiers a fierce and irresistible cavalry, become masters of your governors and your counselers, your collectors and comptrollers, and of all the slaves that adhered to them. Such would, and in no long time must, be the effect of attempting to forbid as a crime and to suppress as an evil the command and blessing of Providence, "Increase and multiply." Such would be the happy result of an endeavor to keep as a lair of wild beasts that earth which God, by an express charter, has given to the children of men.

But the English Government was not alone in its desire to limit the advance of the frontier and guide its destinies. Tidewater Virginia[50] and South Carolina[51] gerrymandered those colonies to insure the dominance of the coast in their legislatures. Washington desired to settle a State at a time in the Northwest; Jefferson would reserve from settlement the territory of his Louisiana Purchase north of the thirty-second parallel, in order to offer it to the Indians in exchange for their settlements east of the Mississippi. "When we shall be full on this side," he writes, "we may lay off a range of States on the western bank from the head to the mouth, and so range after range, advancing compactly as we multiply." Madison went so far as to argue to the French minister that the United States had no interest in seeing population extend itself on the right bank of the Mississippi, but should rather fear it. When the Oregon question was under debate, in 1824, Smyth, of Virginia, would draw an unchangeable line for the limits of the United States at the outer limit of two tiers of States beyond the Mississippi, complaining that the seaboard States were being drained of the flower of their population by the bringing of too much land into market. Even Thomas Benton, the man of widest views of the destiny of the West, at this stage of his career declared that along the ridge of the Rocky Mountains "the western limits of the Republic should be drawn, and the statue of the fabled god Terminus should be raised upon its highest peak, never to be thrown down."[52] But the attempts to limit the boundaries, to restrict land sales and settlement, and to deprive the West of its share of political power were all in vain. Steadily the frontier of settlement advanced and carried with it individualism, democracy, and nationalism, and powerfully affected the East and the Old World.

The most effective efforts of the East to regulate the frontier came through its educational and religious activity, exerted by interstate migration and by organized societies. Speaking in 1835, Dr. Lyman Beecher declared: "It is equally plain that the religious and political destiny of our nation is to be decided in the West," and he pointed out that the population of the West "is assembled from all the States of the Union and from all the nations of Europe, and is rushing in like the waters of the flood, demanding for its moral preservation the immediate and universal action of those institutions which discipline the mind and arm the conscience and the heart. And so various are the opinions and habits, and so recent and imperfect is the acquaintance, and so sparse are the settlements of the West, that no homogeneous public sentiment can be formed to legislate immediately into being the requisite institutions. And yet they are all needed immediately in their utmost perfection and power. A nation is being 'born in a day.' . . . But what will become of the West if her prosperity rushes up to such a majesty of power, while those great institutions linger which are necessary to form the mind and the conscience and the heart of that vast world. It must not be permitted. . . . Let no man at the East quiet himself and dream of liberty, whatever may become of the West. . . . Her destiny is our destiny."[53]

With the appeal to the conscience of New England, he adds appeals to her fears lest other religious sects anticipate her own. The New England preacher and school-teacher left their mark on the West. The dread of Western emancipation from New England's political and economic control was paralleled by her fears lest the West cut loose from her religion. Commenting in 1850 on reports that settlement was rapidly extending northward in Wisconsin, the editor of the *Home Missionary* writes: "We scarcely know whether to rejoice or mourn over this extension of our settlements. While we sympathize in whatever tends to increase the physical resources and prosperity of our country, we can not forget that with all these dispersions into remote and still remoter corners of the land the supply of the means of grace is becoming relatively less and less." Acting in accordance with such ideas, home missions were established and Western colleges were erected. As seaboard cities like Philadelphia, New York, and Baltimore strove for the mastery of Western trade, so the various denominations strove for the possession of the West. Thus an intellectual stream from New England sources fertilized the West. Other sections sent their missionaries; but the real struggle was between sects. The contest for power and the expansive tendency furnished to the various sects by the existence of a moving frontier must have had important results on the character of religious organization in the United States. The multiplication of rival churches in the little frontier towns had deep and lasting social effects. The religious aspects of the frontier make a chapter in our history which needs study.

From the conditions of frontier life came intellectual traits of profound importance. The works of travelers along each frontier from colonial days onward describe certain common traits, and these traits have, while softening down, still persisted as survivals in the place of their origin, even when a higher social organization succeeded. The result is that to the frontier the American intellect owes its striking characteristics. That coarseness and strength combined with acuteness and inquisitiveness; that practical, inventive turn of mind, quick to find expedients; that masterful grasp of material things, lacking in the artistic but powerful to effect great ends; that restless, nervous energy;[54] that dominant individualism, working for good and for evil, and withal that buoyancy and exuberance which comes with freedom—these are traits of the frontier, or traits called out elsewhere because of the existence of the frontier. Since the days when the fleet of Columbus sailed into the waters of the New World, America has been another name for opportunity, and the people of the United States have taken their tone from the incessant expansion which has not only been open but has even been forced upon them. He would be a rash prophet who should assert that the expansive character of American life has now entirely ceased. Movement has been its dominant fact, and, unless this training has no effect upon a people, the American energy will continually demand a wider field for its exercise. But never again will such gifts of free land offer themselves. For a moment, at the frontier, the bonds of custom are broken and unrestraint is triumphant. There is not *tabula rasa*. The stubborn American environment is there with its imperious summons to accept its conditions; the inherited ways of doing things are also there; and yet, in spite of environment, and in spite of custom, each frontier did indeed furnish a new field of opportunity, a gate of escape from the bondage of the past; and freshness, and confidence, and scorn

214

of older society, impatience of its restraints and its ideas, and indifference to its lessons, have accompanied the frontier. What the Mediterranean Sea was to the Greeks, breaking the bond of custom, offering new experiences, calling out new institutions and activities, that, and more, the ever retreating frontier has been to the United States directly, and to the nations of Europe more remotely. And now, four centuries from the discovery of America, at the end of a hundred years of life under the Constitution, the frontier has gone, and with its going has closed the first period of American history.

From *The Frontier in American History* (New York: Holt, Rinehart, and Winston, 1920).

## NOTES

[1] A paper read at the meeting of the American Historical Association in Chicago, July 12, 1893. It first appeared in the Proceedings of the State Historical Society of Wisconsin, December 14, 1893, with the following note: "The foundation of this paper is my article entitled 'Problems in American History,' which appeared in *The Ægis*, a publication of the students of the University of Wisconsin, November 4, 1892. . . . It is gratifying to find that Professor Woodrow Wilson—whose volume on 'Division and Reunion' in the Epochs of American History Series, has an appreciative estimate of the importance of the West as a factor in American history—accepts some of the views set forth in the papers above mentioned, and enhances their value by his lucid and suggestive treatment of them in his article in *The Forum*, December, 1893, reviewing Goldwin Smith's 'History of the United States.'" The present text is that of the *Report of the American Historical Association* for 1893, 199-227. It was printed with additions in the *Fifth Year Book of the National Herbart Society*, and in various other publications.

[2] "Abridgment of Debates of Congress," v, p. 706.

[3] Bancroft (1860 ed.), iii, pp. 344, 345, citing Logan MSS.; [Mitchell] "Contest in America," etc. (1752), p. 237.

[4] Kercheval, "History of the Valley"; Bernheim, "German Settlements in the Carolinas"; Winsor, "Narrative and Critical History of America," v, p. 304; Colonial Records of North Carolina, iv, p. xx; Weston, "Documents Connected with the History of South Carolina," p. 82; Ellis and Evans, "History of Lancaster County, Pa.," chaps. iii, xxvi.

[5] Parkman, "Pontiac," ii; Griffis, "Sir William Johnson," p. 6; Simms's "Frontiersmen of New York."

[6] Monette, "Mississippi Valley," i, p. 311.

[7] Wis. Hist. Cols., xi, p. 50; Hinsdale, "Old Northwest," p. 121; Burke, "Oration on Conciliation," Works (1872 ed.), i, p. 473.

[8] Roosevelt, "Winning of the West," and citations there given; Cutler's "Life of Cutler."

[9] Scribner's Statistical Atlas, xxxviii, pl., 13; McMaster, "Hist. of People of U.S.," i, pp. 4, 60, 61; Imlay and Filson, "Western Territory of America" (London, 1793); Rochefoucault-Liancourt, "Travels Through the United States of North America" (London, 1799); Michaux's "Journal," in *Proceedings American Philosophical Society*, xxvi, no. 129; Forman, "Narrative of a Journey Down the Ohio and Mississippi in 1780-'90" (Cincinnati, 1888); Bartram, "Travels Through North Carolina," etc. (London, 1792); Pope, "Tour Through the Southern and Western Territories," etc. (Richmond, 1792); Weld, "Travels Through the States of North America" (London, 1799); Baily, "Journal of a Tour in the Unsettled States of North America, 1796-'97" (London, 1856); Pennsylvania Magazine of History, July, 1886; Winsor, "Narrative and Critical History of America," vii, pp. 491, 492, citations.

[10] Scribner's Statistical Atlas, xxxix.

[11] Turner, "Character and Influence of the Indian Trade in Wisconsin" (Johns Hopkins University Studies, Series ix), pp. 61 ff.

[12] Monette, "History of the Mississippi Valley," ii; Flint, "Travels and Residence in Mississippi," Flint, "Geography and History of the Western States," "Abridgment of Debates of Congress," vii, pp. 397, 398, 404; Holmes, "Account of the U.S."; Kingdom, "America and the British Colonies" (London, 1820); Grund, "Americans," ii, chaps. i, iii, vi (although writing in 1836, he treats of conditions that grew out of western advance from the era of 1820 to that time); Peck, "Guide for Emigrants" (Boston, 1831); Darby, "Emigrants' Guide to Western and Southwestern States and Territories"; Dana, "Geographical Sketches in the Western Country"; Kinzie, "Waubun"; Keating, "Narrative of Long's Expedition"; Schoolcraft, "Discovery of the Sources of the Mississippi River," "Travels in the Central Portions of the Mississippi Valley," and "Lead Mines of the Missouri"; Andreas, "History of Illinois," i, 86-99; Hurlbut, "Chicago Antiquities"; McKenney, "Tour to the Lakes"; Thomas, "Travels Through the Western Country," etc. (Auburn, N.Y., 1819).

[13] Darby, "Emigrants' Guide," pp. 272 ff; Benton, "Abridgment of Debates," vii, p. 397.

[14] De Bow's *Review*, iv, p. 254; xvii, p. 428.

[15] Grund, "Americans," ii, p. 8.

[16] Peck, "New Guide to the West" (Cincinnati, 1848), chap. iv; Parkman, "Oregon Trail"; Hall, "The West" (Cincinnati, 1848); Pierce, "Incidents of Western Travel"; Murray, "Travels in North America"; Lloyd, "Steamboat Directory" (Cincinnati, 1856); "Forty Days in a Western Hotel" (Chicago), in *Putnam's Magazine*, December, 1894; Mackay, "The Western World," ii, chap. ii, iii; Meeker, "Life in the West"; Bogen, "German in America" (Boston, 1851); Olmstead, "Texas Journey"; Greeley, "Recollections of a Busy Life"; Schouler, "History of the United States," v. 261-267; Peyton, "Over the Alleghanies and Across the Prairies" (London, 1870); Loughborough, "The Pacific Telegraph and Railway" (St. Louis, 1849); Whitney, "Project for a Railroad to the Pacific" (New York, 1849); Peyton, "Suggestions on Railroad Communication with the Pacific, and the Trade of China and the Indian Islands"; Benton, "Highway to

the Pacific" (a speech delivered in the U.S. Senate, December 16, 1850).

[17] A writer in *The Home Missionary* (1850), p. 239, reporting Wisconsin conditions, exclaims: "Think of this, people of the enlightened East. What an example, to come from the very frontier of civilization!" But one of the missionaries writes: "In a few years Wisconsin will no longer be considered as the West, or as an outpost of civilization, any more than Western New York, or the Western Reserve."

[18] Bancroft (H. H.), "History of California," "History of Oregon," and "Popular Tribunals"; Shinn, "Mining Camps."

[19] See the suggestive paper by Prof. Jesse Macy, "The Institutional Beginnings of a Western State."

[20] Shinn, "Mining Camps."

[21] Compare Thorpe, in *Annals American Academy of Political and Social Science*, September, 1891; Bryce, "American Commonwealth" (1888), ii, p. 689.

[22] Loria, Analisi della Proprieta Capitalista, ii, p. 15.

[23] Compare "Observations on the North American Land Company," London, 1796, pp. xv, 144; Logan, "History of Upper South Carolina," i, pp. 149-151; Turner, "Character and Influence of Indian Trade in Wisconsin," p. 18; Peck, "New Guide for Emigrants" (Boston, 1837), chap. iv; "Compendium Eleventh Census," i, p. x1.

[24] See *post*, for illustrations of the political accompaniments of changed industrial conditions.

[25] But Lewis and Clark were the first to explore the route from the Missouri to the Columbia.

[26] "Narrative and Critical History of America," viii, p. 10; Sparks' "Washington Works," ix, pp. 303, 327; Logan, "History of Upper South Carolina," i; McDonald, "Life of Kenton," p. 72; Cong. Record, xxiii, p. 57.

[27] On the effect of the fur trade in opening the routes of migration, see the author's "Character and Influence of the Indian Trade in Wisconsin."

[28] Lodge, "English Colonies," p. 152 and citations; Logan, "History of Upper South Carolina," i, p. 151.

[29] Flint, "Recollections," p. 9.

[30] See Monette, "Mississippi Valley," i, p. 344.

[31] Coues', "Lewis and Clark's Expedition," i, pp. 2, 253-259; Benton, in Cong. Record, xxiii, p. 57.

[32] Hehn, *Das Salz* (Berlin, 1873).

[33] Col. Records of N. C., v, p. 3.

[34] Findley, "History of the Insurrection in the Four Western Counties of Pennsylvania in the Year 1794" (Philadelphia, 1796), p. 35.

[35] Hale, "Daniel Boone" (pamphlet).

[36] Compare Baily, "Tour in the Unsettled Parts of North America" (London, 1856), pp. 217-219, where a similar analysis is made for 1796. See also Collot, "Journey in North America" (Paris, 1826), p. 109; "Observations on the North

American Land Company" (London, 1796), pp. xv, 144; Logan, "History of Upper South Carolina."

[37] "Spotswood Papers," in Collections of Virginia Historical Society, i, ii.

[38] [Burke], "European Settlements" (1765 ed.), ii, p. 200.

[39] Everest, in "Wisconsin Historical Collections," xii, pp. 7 ff.

[40] Weston, "Documents connected with History of South Carolina," p. 61.

[41] See, for example, the speech of Clay, in the House of Representatives, January 30, 1824.

[42] See the admirable monograph by Prof. H. B. Adams, "Maryland's Influence on the Land Cessions"; and also President Welling, in Papers American Historical Association, iii, p. 411.

[43] Adams' Memoirs, ix, pp. 247, 248.

[44] Author's article in *The Ægis* (Madison, Wis.), November 4, 1892.

[45] Compare Roosevelt, "Thomas Benton," chap. 1.

[46] *Political Science Quarterly*, ii, p. 457. Compare Sumner, "Alexander Hamilton," chaps. ii-vii.

[47] Compare Wilson, "Division and Reunion," pp. 15, 24.

[48] On the relation of frontier conditions to Revolutionary taxation, see Sumner, "Alexander Hamilton," chap. iii.

[49] I have refrained from dwelling on the lawless characteristics of the frontier, because they are sufficiently well known. The gambler and desperado, the regulators of the Carolinas and the vigilantes of California, are types of that line of scum that the waves of advancing civilization bore before them, and of the growth of spontaneous organs of authority where legal authority was absent. Compare Barrows, "United States of Yesterday and To-morrow"; Shinn, "Mining Camps"; and Bancroft, "Popular Tribunals." The humor, bravery, and rude strength, as well as the vices of the frontier in its worst aspect, have left traces on American character, language, and literature, not soon to be effaced.

[50] Debates in the Constitutional Convention, 1829-1830.

[51] [McCrady] Eminent and Representative Men of the Carolinas, i, p. 43; Calhoun's Works, i, pp. 401-406.

[52] Speech in the Senate, March 1, 1825; Register of Debates, i, 721.

[53] Plea for the West (Cincinnati, 1835), pp. 11 ff.

[54] Colonial travelers agree in remarking on the phlegmatic characteristics of the colonists. It has frequently been asked how such a people could have developed that strained nervous energy now characteristic of them. Compare Sumner, "Alexander Hamilton," p. 98, and Adams, "History of the United States," i, p. 60; ix, pp. 240, 241. The transition appears to become marked at the close of the War of 1812, a period when interest centered upon the development of the West, and the West was noted for restless energy. Grund, "Americans," ii, chap. i.

# APPENDIX
## *Robert M. La Follette and "Iago"*

As a University of Wisconsin freshman, young Turner was caught up in the fervor over the oratorical successes of a senior, Robert M. La Follette. An event early in May 1879, as reported by Turner himself, epitomizes the admiration of "A Portage University Student Enthusiastic Over The Oratorical Contest." In his story of that title, the impressionable freshman described the evening in Madison that started at 7:30 P.M. In a group, he went first to the Athenian Society (of which La Follette was a member). The society members were eagerly awaiting the outcome of the oratorical championship of the state, in which La Follette was competing that evening in Beloit. About 10:15, Turner went downtown with the Athenians and squeezed into the telegraph office. The news of La Follette's victory was received joyously. The group of sixty went back to campus, got into the gymnasium, and danced for two hours! They then left to meet the 2:25 A.M. train bringing La Follette back to Madison.

The following newspaper text of "Iago" is as it appears in Turner's scrapbook. The stylized editing is retained, with the summary of the argument as well as the internal headnotes.

# IAGO
## Abstract of Argument.

1. Mental analysis.
   Has but two of the three constituents of mind.
   Loss of emotional nature has cost him his moral parts.
   What he lacks in feeling, he has gained in knowing—he knows everything; he feels nothing.
2. Originality of his methods of meanness, as shown in his relations to the other characters of the tragedy.
   Display of his intellectual acuteness—his power of dissimulation, his *manner* and his *means*.

219

3. He is a being without conscience, but his acute mind redeems him to us as a subject.
   His questioning, his "reasons," the result of his mental mechanism, not the protest of conscience.
4. Contrasted with Richard III., Iago is more perfect as a devil, Richard more perfect as a villain. Richard's conscience finally asserts itself; Iago has none—hence, is his superior in pure hellish consistency.
5. Iago, Shakespeare's conception of the Evil Principle: hence, the vagueness of his fate, which can be explained in no other way. It is consistent with a devil—not with the villain of a tragedy.

Shakespeare's Iago personifies two constituents of mind—*intellect* and *will*. These alone are the springs of his action, the source of his power. What he lacks in emotion, he has gained in intellectual acuteness, but the result is deformity. The character is not *un*natural; it is fiendishly natural. His reasoning power is abnormally developed; but he has no feeling, no sympathy, no affection, no fear. His, is

## COLD PASSION OF INTELLECT,

whose icy touch chills the warm life in all it reaches. He is an intellectual athlete, and is unceasing in his mental gymnastics. His contempt for all good is supreme; his greatest crime is his greatest pleasure; and his own hypocrisy gladdens and intoxicates him. Whatever is most mean, whatever is most hard, whatever is vilely atrocious and dangerously difficult, he seizes with greedy glee. Skeptical of all virtue, to him love is lechery, truth-telling stupid goodness, and lying, daring to be ingenious.

The emotions are the native soil of moral life. From the feelings are grown great ethical truths, one by one, forming at last the grand body of the moral law. But Iago is emotionally a cipher, and his poverty of sentiment and wealth of intellect render him doubly dangerous. Here we have

## THE KEY TO HIS CHARACTER

—he is possessed of an inflexible will, of an intellect, pungent, subtle, super-sensual. He not only knows more than he feels; he knows everything, feels nothing.

The other characters of the tragedy of Othello—a tragedy which Macaulay pronounced Shakespeare's greatest—are but puppets, moving at the will of this master. He reads them at a glance, by a flash of instinct. He wastes no words on Roderigo, other than to make the "fool his purse." But upon Othello he plays with more subtlety, and infinitely greater zest. Upon him, he exercises his crafty ingenuity; and the "double knavery," the "How? how?" whets him keen. Now flashes forth the invisible lightning of his malignant mind, and woe to all virtue within its reach. Now we see his character in all its artful cunning, all its devilish cruelty. With what marvellous skill he makes his first attack! He does nothing in the common way.

## HIS METHODS

have the merit of originality. He does not assail Desdemona's virtue with a well conned story, but is seemingly surprised into an exclamation, appearing to utter his suspicions by the merest accident. And, when he has engaged Othello's ear, note his matchless cunning; he comes and goes, and comes and goes again, with his ingenious innuendoes; changing like the chameleon, quick to take his cue from the Moor, yet craftily giving direction to the other's thoughts; cursing Cassio with his protestations of love, and damning Desdemona while joining in a benediction to her honesty. The "constant, loving, noble nature" of the Moor changes quickly under the "almost superhuman art" of Iago; but too well he knows the human mind to gorge it with suspicion; and, with every dose of poison, gives just a little antidote. With pious self-accusation, he says "tis my nature's plague to spy into abuses;" and "oft my jealousy shapes faults that are not;" but carefully adds, "it were not for your quiet nor your good to let you know my thoughts;" and is equally careful to tell them; smothering with one hand all suspicion of his perfidy, and kindling with the other the consuming fires of the Moor's jealousy.

Iago's manner of practising on Othello is only matched by the means he employs.

## LIKE THE GENUINE DEVIL,

he destroys the entire household—not through some unguarded vice, but through its very virtues. He sets all goodness by the ears. The strength of the Moor's affection is made a fatal weakness; and, more than this, the very medium of all their misery is she,

> "Of spirit so still and gentle that her motion
> Blushed at herself."

Iago and Desdemona! Strange, unspeakable union of opposites! Weird harmony of discord! Sombre mingling of a smile and a sneer! O the poet whose genius could compound these elements without an explosion! O this "unequal contest between the powers of grossness and purity!" That Desdemona, whose childlike nature is a diving fusion of innocence and chastity, should be played off against a moral outlaw, a being whose livery is "heavenly shows" and whose logic is the "divinity of hell," is a juxtaposition appalling, fascinating! 'Tis Diana in the talons of a Harpy. That virtue should be "turned into pitch," that "out of goodness" should be made "the net to enmesh them all," that innocence should become the instrument of the infernal, is a "moral antithesis" that preludes the oncoming of chaos. And it comes like the quick night and consummates the tragedy; while over all, in sullen silence, gloats the imp of darkness.

Somewhere, THOMAS CARLYLE has said, "there are depths in man that go the length of lowest Hell, as there are heights that reach highest Heaven;" but Iago is a magnet with only one pole which ever points towards the internal. Why is it, then, that this character does not disgust us? Why do we follow his intricate windings with such intense interest? Why do we tolerate him? We find the answer in his great intellect. This is [the]

### CORE OF HIS CHARACTER;

abstract intellectuality united to volitional force, devoid of all morality, divorced from all feeling. He is hardly human, yet he sounds humanity like a philosopher. He is wanting in ethical parts; yet he makes the nicest moral distinctions. He is a fraction, yet greater than a unit; a part, yet more than the whole. He is a paradox. In his deep schemes, we nearly forgot the villain. His triumph over all obstacles pins the attention to his intellectual powers. He is "instinct with thought." This redeems him to us as a subject, and yields another explanation for what has been termed his "little trace of conscience." His self-questionings, his subtle sophisms, his cataclysm of reasons, are not the weak protest of a moral part, but the logical outcome of a sleepless intellect. He is emphatically a being of reasons. He will do nothing except he furnish to himself the "why!" It is not that he requires these reasons as a "whetstone for his revenge," it is not that his "resolution is too much for his conscience," but rather that he revels in reasons, that his hungry mind will have its food. He "suspects the lusty Moor," and fears "Cassio with his night-cap, too," on occasion; not that he dreads to destroy either without some motive, but because his mental constitution demands a reason for all things. SCHLEGEL defines wickedness as "nothing but selfishness designedly unconscientious;" but Iago makes no effort to deceive himself, for he says:

> When devils will their blackest sins put on,
> They do suggest at first with heavenly shows
> As I do now.

He does not care to justify himself, except as an intellectual satisfaction.

222

### HE DESIRES NO MORAL VINDICATION.

In fact, he commits crime merely for crime's sake, and there is no sin that he will not claim as his own. Think of it! a being who clutches at wickedness with all the greed of a miser. Thoroughly passionless, coldly intellectual, he is forced into the self-confession that he is no libertine; yet, fearful lest the admission has cost him one hellish trait, he quickly adds that he "stands accountant for as great a sin." This is a moral defiance sublimely hideous, but hardly reconcilable in a being with even a "little trace of conscience." Were there a single golden thread of moral sense to knit him to the good in humanity, it would shine forth when DESDEMONA—whose only offence against him is that she is pure—sinks under his cursed cunning. But it is a quality he feels not, knows not; and what COLERIDGE calls *"the motive-hunting of a motiveless malignity;"* this constant combing of his wits for reasons, is simply a service performed at the mandate of the craving intellect.

These are the premises from which, as a conclusion, we deduce Iago—a character without a conscience.

Mark the "steep inequality"

### BETWEEN HIM AND RICHARD III.:

The Duke of Gloster, born with teeth, a twisted body and a majestic mind, cuts his way through those of his own flesh, to a throne. Malignant and artful, hypocritical and heartless, he "seems a saint when most he plays the devil." Monster, he stands apart from men; he is "like himself alone," and he stalks along his bloody course, a solitary creation. Brave, he has the tragic audacity to defy destiny, the impudent confidence to enter the lists against the Unknown. But hidden away somewhere in his black soul is a germ of conscience disguised as superstitious fear,—a germ of conscience which starts forth when that towering will is off guard; coming in the thin substance of a dream, yet so terrible that the remorseful "drops hang on his trembling flesh." Here is his humanity, his mortal weakness; and through this the "all-powerful and ever-watchful Nemesis hurls her lance, barbed to the shaft with retribution. Pursued by croaking phantoms, scourged by the invisible lash of violated conscience, he flings himself into the conflict, and with a royal flourish, in perfect keeping with his character, closes the tragedy. His death satisfies the equation of right.

### SOME QUALITIES IN COMMON.

Both have mighty intellects; both are wily, cunning, crafty; both dissimulators; both actors. But farther than this they are profoundly unlike. Richard III. is more humanly terrible; Iago more devilishly perfect. Richard loves nothing human; Iago hates everything good. Rich-

223

ard is arrogant, passionate, powerful, violent; Iago, egotistical, cold, cynical, sly. Richard is fire; Iago, ice. Richard III. is more objective; Iago more subjective. Richard would pulverize the universe; Iago would like to reverse the order of things. In point of satanical finish, Iago is Richard—and more. Richard III. murders many, and sweats with horror; Iago few, and forgets remorse. Richard III. mounts the throne of England on a score of dead bodies; Iago wins the throne of Hell in three strides. The conscience of Richard wakes from its swoon; Iago has no conscience. Richard III. is a monstrosity; Iago, a psychological contradiction.

We offer Iago then as SHAKESPEARE'S conception of the Evil Principle. And how perfect the creation. In the whole course of his crime, he betrays never a weakness, never a check of conscience—nothing to mar the

## ELEGANT SYMMETRY OF HIS FIENDISHNESS.

From the time he lays down the postulate that "I am not what I am," till he attains his infernal majority, he is the same refined, pitiless, sarcastic devil. He is often surprised but he is never disconcerted. He plans, but it is because he likes the mental exercise. It has been said that "deep rogues take all their villainy *a priori;* that they do not construct plans in anticipation." Iago's carefully perfected schemes would seem to rebuke this philosophy were it not that they appear, rather, meat for his mind, than directions for his diabolisms. Indeed it is in those unpremised scenes where the occasion fails to fit his plans, where all the odds are arrayed against him, that he achieves the greatest triumph. This is nothing short of Stygian sill; and it is just here that he attains the dignity of a devil. That dignity would have been sacrificed in his death. By all the principles of dramatic tragedy, Othello is his fit executioner. Significant fact! we are only promised that his "punishment shall tormet him much and hold him long." This is to appease the moral demand, and in its vagueness the poet seeks to avoid a decline in tragic intensity. This we offer as the ethical and aesthetical reason for the indefiniteness thrown about Iago's fate by the dramatist. He had pushed his creation to the verge of the finite, punishment was demanded, none could be devised which would requite him.

The full course of tragedy, the might evolution of its events, must yield an apt sequence.

## A SUBLIME COMPLETENESS,

else it falls in its aim. SCHILLER says: "Life is great only as a means of accomplishing the moral law; and nothing is sublimer than a criminal yielding his life because of the morality he has violated." With the single

224

exception of Iago, SHAKESPEARE has availed himself of his principle. The Thane of Cawdor tops all his murders with his own head; Lady Macbeth bleaches in death the "damned spot" from her unclean hand; Richard III. seals with his own blood on Bosworth field the sublime in his career; but Iago is just beyond the reach of death, and we can fancy him disappearing in the darkness of which he is a part.

There are two fitnesses in a villain's death—the moral fitness and the tragic fitness. The one, the ethical satisfaction at the inevitable recoil of the broken moral law; the other, the grandeur of a *finale*. To condense into one moment the whole of life, to put a flat on existence, to engulf a soul in the awful immensity of its own acts—this is sublime. But to have conceived and brought forth a being so super-physical, so positively devilish, so intensely infernal, that his death would be bathos— this is genius.

### AND THIS IS IAGO,

The polished, affable, attendant; the wit, the reveler, the boon companion; the supple sophist, the nimble logician; the philosopher, the moralist—the scoffing demon; the goblin whose smile is a stab and whose laugh is an infernal sneer; who never exhausts his resources, his snares, his perfidies; who has sworn eternal vengeance on virtue everywhere; who would turn cosmos into chaos. This compound of wickedness and reason, this incarnation of intellect, this tartarian basilisk stands the logical conclusion in a syllogism whose premises are "Hell and Night." He is a criminal climax: endow him with a single supernatural quality and he is the supreme devil of fiction.

This is the text of "Iago" as delivered by La Follette on 2 May 1879. The copy is pasted in Turner's scrapbook, the cover of which is dated 1876. In Box 62.

225

# Index

Adams, Herbert Baxter: requests study, 25; invites Turner to speak, 42.

"Address to the Romans": reactions to, 10.

Adelphia: Turner's literary society, 23, 99n39.

*Aegis, The:* publishes "Problems in American History," 41.

Allen, William F.: directs Turner's work, 25; receives letter from Turner, 27.

Alliteration: early use by Turner, 8; use by La Follette, 16; in "The Poet of the Future," 23; in "American Colonization," 34; in frontier thesis, 48.

"American Colonization": preparation, 32-34; stylistic characteristics, 34-36; relation to frontier thesis, 39-41.

American Historical Association: 1893 meeting, 3; 1888 meeting, 27; Turner invited to 1893 meeting, 42; and "germ" theory of American history, 43-44; reactions to Turner's 1893 paper, 45-46; influence of Turner's paper, 46-48.

*Anaphora:* early use by Turner, 8; use by Robert Ingersoll, 12; use by La Follette, 16; in Turner's Commonplace Book, 17; in Turner's "The Poet of the Future," 23; in "American Colonization," 34; in frontier thesis, 48-49, 54; influences attention, 57.

*Anastrophe:* use by Turner, 17.

Antithesis: early use by Turner, 8; use by Macauley, 9; use by Ingersoll, 13; use by La Follette, 16; in "Imaginativeness of the Present," 18; as style, 19; use by Turner, 21; in "The Poet of the Future," 23; in "Architecture Through Oppression," 24; in American Colonization," 34, 36; in the frontier thesis, 49-50, 54.

"Architecture Through Oppression": wins prize, 24.

Aristotle: style, 54-55; *ethos* or source credibility, 71.

Armstrong, Neil: style and memorability, 56.

Attention: influenced by style, 55-58; in communication and persuasion, 59.

*Auxesis:* as source of style, 58; in frontier thesis, 73-74.

Beckoning archetype: in persuasion, 62; for model behavior, 63; in economic endeavors, 64-65; Daniel Boone, 65; in political issues, 66; in World War I, 66-68; international issues, 68; long-term persuasiveness, 69-70, 81-82; persistent appeal of pioneer, 88; frontier thesis and rhetorical vision, 93-94.

Buffon, George: concept of style, 33.

Burrows Prize: Turner wins, 22.

Carter, Jimmy: presidential campaign, 86.

Chaining out of messages: frontier thesis, 79-80; other discourse, 81; frontier thesis and rhetorical vision, 92.

Characterization: in La Follette's "Iago," 16; in Woodrow Wilson's *Division and Reunion*, 29; in Reuben Gold Thwaites' writing, 29; by students, 29; source of persuasiveness, 29-31; in Dante and Kipling, 28; in frontier thesis, 53-54, 60-61; by Turner, 78; in Turner's undergraduate training, 94.

Churchill, Winston: style and memorability, 57.

Cicero: style, 10.

Commonplace Book: lists speakers, 11; imitates La Follette, 17.

Communication Mosaic: defined, 93; frontier thesis in, 94.

Competence: as dimension of *ethos*, 71; image in frontier thesis, 73, 75; in opinion leadership, 77.

Credibility: see *ethos.*

Dante's *Inferno:* influence of, 28.

Declamation: as rhetorical exercise, 7, 10.

Demosthenes: style 10.

Dynamism: as dimension of *ethos,* 71; in frontier thesis, 73-74; John Kennedy, 84-85.

Eloquence: in Adams Sherman Hill, *Principles of Rhetoric,* 31-32.

Emerson, Ralph Waldo: style, 6.

Emphasis: in communication and persuasion, 59.

*Epanaphora:* see *anaphora.*

*Ethos:* Aristotle on, 71; defined in persuasion theory, 71; Turner's, 72-75, 81; credibility of history as a mode of discourse, 75-76; in frontier thesis, 94.

Figure and Ground: in communication, 94.

Frankenburger, David B., 26.

*Franklin in France:* reviewed by Turner, 26.

*Frequentatio:* use by Ingersoll, 12, 13; in frontier thesis, 53.

Frontier Thesis: antecedents in "American Colonization," 32-41; antecedents in "Problems in American History," 41; late preparation, 42; as rhetorical discourse, 43-44; reactions in Chicago, 45-46; first publications, 46; reprints, 46, 47; as an oration, 47, 62; style, 48-50; reactions from historians, 50-52.

Frontiersmen as models: see pioneer and beckoning archetype.

"Germ" theory of American history: in "American Colonization," 35-38; and American Historical Association, 43, 44.

Gibbon, Edward: in Hill's *Principles of Rhetoric,* 20.

"Golden Mean" of style: Turner's early efforts, 21; final appraisal, 95.

Good will: dimension of *ethos,* 71; Josiah Strong lacking, 73; Turner's image in frontier thesis, 73.

Harvard History Club: honors Turner, 3, 14, 24, 94.

Hill, Adams Sherman, *Principles of Rhetoric:* 17; influence on American rhetorical theory, 19-20; criticism of Macaulay, 20-21; discusses vivacity in style, 31-32.

Hortatory discourse: displays persuasive intent of author, 47; characterizes frontier thesis, 50-52, 62.

Identification: as technique in persuasion, 30-31.

Ideology: in persuasion, 62.

"Imaginativeness of the Present": drafts in the 1881-82 Commonplace Book, 17; reworked from "The Power of the Press," 22; basis of Burrows Prize oration, 22.

*Incrementum:* see *auxesis.*

Influence: of frontier thesis, 81-82.

Ingersoll, Robert: as model for Turner, 11-12; style, 13.

Kennedy, John F.: style and memorability, 56; news of death, 80; political success, 84-85.

Kipling, Rudyard: effect on Turner, 28.

La Follette, Robert M.: influence on Turner, 3, 14; "Iago" oration, 14-17, 24-25, 94-95; Turner's identification with, 17; as model for Turner, 94-95.

Lewis Prize in oratory: 24.

Lincoln, Abraham: characterized by Turner, 27; style and memorability, 57.

Lysias: as model for Turner, 10.

Macaulay, Thomas Babington: *History of England,* 7; style, 9; use of antitheses, 9; in Hill's *Principles of Rhetoric,* 20-21.

Merk, Frederick: Turner's student, 89; style, 90-91; *History of the Westward Movement,* 89-91; contemporary reception, 91.

Mobility: in American life, 87-88.

Motion pictures: portrayals of pioneers, 83-84; war films, 84; *Deliverance,* 89.

Motivation: influence on style, 43.

Myth: in persuasion, 60; in rhetorical vision, 63; in frontier thesis, 68-69; long-term influence of Turner, 92-93.

National Board for Historical Service, 66-67.

"New Frontier" slogan: John Kennedy's use, 70; impact, 84-85.

Novelty: Aristotelian concept of style, 55; influence on attention, 55-56.

Opinion leader: defined, 78; Turner as, 78.

Oratorical contests: as experience, 8-9; importance in American universities, 9; at the University of Wisconsin, 22-24.

"Pencils and Scissors" column: style, 6-7, 17; treatment of Robert Ingersoll, 12.

Persuasion: in frontier thesis, 43, 47, 50-52; in history, 52-53; as process, 59-60; characterization as source of role model, 62; importance of *ethos*, 71; credibility of history as mode of discourse, 75-76; two-step flow of communication, 77-78; rhetorical vision, 92.

Pioneer: as example of model behavior, 63; imitate in economic endeavors, 64-65; Daniel Boone, 65; in political issues, 66; in World War I, 66-68; international issues, 68; long-term persuasiveness, 69-70; in popular culture, 76; long-term appeal, 84-85.

"Poet of the Future": wins Burrows Prize, 22; style, 23.

Popular culture: portrayals of pioneers, 76; World War II films, 83-84; *The Green Berets*, 84.

Portage, Wisconsin: boyhood environment, 4; cultural and literary environment, 5-6; oratorical activities for Turner, 5-7.

"Power of the Press": 7; style, 8; relation to "The Imaginativeness of the Present," 22.

"Problems in American History":

early version of frontier thesis, 41; precursor of style in frontier thesis, 49; and rhetorical purpose of frontier thesis, 52, 70.

Reactions to Turner's orations: "The Power of the Press," 8; "Address to the Romans," 10; "The Poet of the Future," 23.

Reinforcement: Turner corroborates popular culture, 76-77; Turner as opinion leader, 78.

Rhetorical "Second Persona" in Discourse: use in persuasion, 62; Turner's pioneer portrayal, 62-70.

Rhetorical training: University of Wisconsin curriculum, 9-10; grades earned in rhetoric 9-10, 24; Turner teaches, 25.

Rhetorical vision: defined, 63; "chaining out" of messages, 80-81; role in persuasion, 92.

Roosevelt, Franklin: style and memorability, 57.

Roosevelt, Theodore: "The Hunter Type," 27; *The Winning of the West*, 27-28; reaction to frontier thesis, 63-64; on Turner's *ethos*, 72.

"Significance of History": style in historical writing, 31.

Similarity: dimension of *ethos*, 71; role in opinion leadership, 77; Turner as opinion leader, 78.

*Sinathrismus:* see *frequentatio*.

Small, Albion: response to "Problems in American History," 42.

Spencer, Herbert: "Philosophy of Style," 17.

Strong, Josiah: *ethos*, 72-73.

Style: Turner's early concept, 7-8; classical practices and definitions, 10; La Follette's, 16 ; Turner's in Commonplace Book, 17-18, 21-22; as taught in nineteenth-century America, 19-21; Turner's in college orations, 23-24; Turner on style in history; 27, 31; in Hill's *Principles of Rhetoric*, 31-32; as index of Turner's historical creativity, 32-34; motivation and effects on style, 42-43;

defined, 48; in frontier thesis, 50, 54; stylistic "foregrounding," 54; by Aristotle, 54-55; effects on attention, 55-58.

*Symphoresis:* see *frequentatio.*

*Synonimia:* see *frequentatio.*

Thwaites, Reuben Gold, 29.

*Traductio,* 57.

Trucks: appeal of off-the-road vehicles, 88.

Trustworthiness: dimension of *ethos,* 71.

Turner, Andrew Jackson: influence on young Turner, 6.

Turner, Frederick Jackson: in Portage, 5-6; early concepts of style, 7-8; high school oration, 7-8; University of Wisconsin student, 9-10; interest in Robert Ingersoll, 11-14; influence of Robert M. La Follette's "Iago," 3, 14-17, 94; practices style, 17-19, 21; studies rhetoric, 17-20, 31-32; has a "golden mean" for style, 21, 95; wins prize for "The Poet of the Future," 22-23; wins prize for "Architecture Through Oppression," 24; imitates style of La Follette, 22-25; writes and publishes on the Grignon Tract, 25; teaches at the University of Wisconsin, 25-26; begins appreciating characterization in discourse, 26-29; praises characterization in historical writing, 29, 31; prepares "American Colonization" and isolates frontier thesis concept, 33-41; writes and publishes "Problems in American History," 41; invited to present paper in Chicago, 42; procrastinates about writing, 42-43; his purpose in relation to "germ" theory, 43-44, 52; immediate reactions to address, 45-46; publications on frontier thesis, 46-47; negative reactions to hortatory tone, 47-48, 50-51; style in frontier thesis, 48-50; reactions to style and characterization in frontier thesis, 53-54, 57-58; persuasive influence on American attitudes, 60-70; *ethos* and credibility for Americans, 71-75; as opinion leader in two-step flow of communication, 77-78, 81-82; long-term influence, 82, 84-94.

Two-step flow of communication: defined, 77-78; Turner as an opinion leader therein, 78.

Type-Token-Ratio: influence on style and memorability, 57.

Vivacity: as quality of style for history, 31; discussed in *Principles of Rhetoric,* 31-32.

Wayne, John: portrayals, 84.

Wilson Woodrow: *Division and Reunion,* 29; and Turner's procrastination about AHA paper, 42.

*Wisconsin State Register:* Andrew Turner as publisher, 6; reviews "The Power of the Press," 7; publishes Turner's monograph on the Grignon Tract, 25; coverage of "savages," 48.

Wisdom of the rustic: defined as contemporary rhetorical technique, 85.